HAND BOOK OF FIBRE GLASS MOULDING

HAND BOOK OF FIBRE GLASS MOULDING

Written By :

EIRI Consultants and Engineers

ENGINEERS INDIA RESEARCH INSTITUTE

4449, Nai Sarak, Main Road, Delhi-110 006 (India)

Ph. : 91-11-23918117, 23916431, 23840361

Fax : 91-11-23916431, 23918117

* **E-Mail :** eirisidi@bol.net.in

* **Website :** www.eiriindia.org

Sole Distributor :

INDIAN INSTITUTE OF CONSULTANTS,

4/27, Roop Nagar, Delhi-110007

Printed and Published by :

ENGINEERS INDIA RESEARCH INSTITUTE

4449, Nai Sarak, Main Road, Delhi-110 006 (India)
Ph. : 91-11-23918117, 23916431, 23840361
Fax : 91-11-23916431, 23918117
✶ **E-Mail :** eirisidi@bol.net.in
✶ **Website :** www.eiriindia.org

Distributed by :

SMALL INDUSTRY RESEARCH INSTITUTE
INDIAN INSTITUTE OF CONSULTANTS

ISBN : 81-86732-94-2
Printed in New Delhi (India)

Rs. 450

Printed and Published by Sudhir Gupta for
"Engineers India Research Institute", 4449, Nai Sarak, Main Road,
New Delhi-110 006 and Printed at Swastik Offset, Delhi

Preface

Fibre reinforced plastics offer almost unlimited possibilities for shape, size and colour mid can be produced with a variety of surface fmishes. Sandwich construction can be used for lightweight mouldings. Unidirectional carbon fibre is used as reinforcement, exceptional strength to weight ratios can be achieved. However, before any object can be made it has to be designed.

Factors which influence design are

1. resin selection

2. reinforcement selection and moulding process.

The choice of moulding process will be affected by

1. the number of mouldings to be produced,

2. production rate,

3. moulding complexity and .

4. size of moulding.

Another factor which may need to be considered is the means by which the finished moulding will be transported to its final destination. In the case of very large objects this may mean that several moulded parts have to be produced for assembly on site.

In many cases the final design will be a compromise between the requirements of the designer and the moulder. In this respect there should be considerable liaison between designer and moulder to ensure that the final moulding meets as many of the original design requirements as is possible, taking into account production rate and moulding cost. Often all requirements may be met with no difficulty.

*The book '**Hand Book of Fibre Glass Moulding**' covers various methods including Reinforced Plastics and Composites, Product Introduction, Designing in Fibre Reinforced Plastics, Details of Moulds, Processes of Mouldings, Polyester Resins, Catalysts, Accelerators and Inhibitors for Unsaturated Polyester Resins, Epoxy Resins, Curing Agents for Epoxide Resins, Reinforcement Agents in Polymers, Fibre Glass Reinforced Plastics Pipe, Acrylic Sheet and Moulded Products, Bath Tub (Acrylic), Dough Molding Compound (DMC), Bulk Moulding Compound (BMC), Sheet Moulding Compound (SMC), FRP Products, Fibre Glass Sheet, Fibre Reinforced Plastics, Fibre Glass, Fibre Glass Wire.*

The book has been written for the benefit and to prove an asset and a handy reference guide in the hands of new entrepreneurs and well established industrialists.

Director

ENGINEERS INDIA RESEARCH INSTITUTE

Nai Sarak, Main Road,
Delhi-110 006 (India)
E-mail : eirisidi@bol.net.in

CONTENTS AND SUBJECT INDEX

1

Reinforced Plastics and Composites

INTRODUCTION

A reinforced plastic, or composite, is a polymer resin matrix combined with a reinforcing agent or agents. The reinforcement improves strength and stiffness properties compared to the neat resin. Almost every type of thermoplastic or thermosetting resin can be reinforced. "Hybrid", composites combine more than one type of reinforcement, such as carbon and glass fibres. At the same time, enhancement are continually engineered into existing materials. In addition, most resin types can be formulated or processed with a variety of fillers, additives, extenders, and chemicals. By selecting ingredients and setting process conditions, as designer or an engineer specifies a custom "material system". The composite is engineered to meet specific application, performance, and/or processing needs. Probably no other branch of plastics is more complex and diverse than the field of reinforced plastics and composites.

For many applications it is possible to increase the strength of plastics by means of reinforcement. A reinforced plastic consists of two main components: a matrix, or resin used as the base binding material which usually takes the form of fibres. On an above the other additives used are catalyst accelarators colorants of pigments and hardening agents. In general the matrix has a low strength in comparison to the reinforcement, which is also much stiffer, but brittle. To gain maximum benefits from the reinforcement the fibres should bear as much as possible of the applied stress. The function of the matrix is simply to support the fibres and transmit the external loading to them by shear at the fibre matrix interface. Plastics are very suitable in this context since they are easily formed into shape and provided that a good interfacial bond is achieved, the improvements in strength and stiffness can be significant. A wide variety of combinations of fibres and matrix are used in practice. The major materials as matrix or resin used for reinforced plastics are unsaturated polyester resin, epoxy, silicon, furnace, fridel-crast polymer, phenol formaldehyde, urea formaldehyde, melamine formaldehyde. etc.

TERMINOLOGY

"Reinforced plastics" and "composites" are just wo of the many terms used to describe these materials. A glossary of designations includes the following :

1. *Advanced composites* : Reinforced plastics with properties higher than "conventional" performance; usually have a reinforcing fibre with a higher modulus than E-glass fibres and a resin matrix with higher properties than polyesters.
2. *Composites* : Used interchangeably with "reinforced plastics": because the dictionary definition of composites is broader in meaning, the reinforced industry often uses "composites" and "composite" with a modifier, as in " advanced composites" or "fibre glass composite".
3. *Fibre glass*: Technically, glass in fibrous form; however, the term is often used to describe fibre glass-reinforced plastics and applications, as in "fibre glass" boat or " fibre glass" door.
4. *FRP* : Used specifically for fibre glass-reinforced plastics.
5. *GFRP* : Glass fibre-reinforced plastic.
6. *GRP* : Widely used in Europe to mean glass-reinforced plastics, or more specifically, glass reinforced polyester.
7. *Laminate* : Originally reserved formaterial system with layers, such as lay-up, but often used to generically describe reinforced plastics, as in pounds of "laminate" per part.
8. *Reinforced plastics* " Polymer-based matrices that incorporate fibrous reinforcements, flakes, and other mechanical (as opposed to chemical) additives to enhance properties.
9. *RP*: Reinforced plastics.
10. *RTP* : Sometimes used to distinguish "reinforced thermoplastics" from reinforced thermosetting plastics.

THERMOSETTING PLASTICS

Reinforced plastics traditionally have been associated with thermosetting resins. Thermoset resins "cure" into a hardened, irreversible state, in which the molecular structure of the polymer is cross-linked. Cure can be accelerated, enhanced, or controlled by heat, radiation, or light. Many reinforced plastics moulding, processes use the application of pressure to improve surface finish and meet requirements for close dimensional tolerances.

Unsaturated polyesters are by far the most widely reinforced resin matrix. Thermoset polyesters provide a good combination for performance, handleability, and resonable costs. The three major categories of thermoset polyesters are orthophthalics, isophthalics and vinyl esters—listed in ascending order of cost of resistance to moisture, weathering, and chemicals. This family of materials also is extremely versatile. Because of their widespread and long-term use, thermoset polyesters often are relegated to merely a "conventional" status. However, a deeper understanding of polymerisation has been accompanied by a growing number of ways to precisely manipulate, and replicate, chemical reactions. As a result, resin manufacturers are producing thermoset polyester systems that are engineered to address specific process and end-performance needs.

Polyester cure, or molecular cross-linking starts when the resin and a monomer, such as styrene, are mixed with a catalyst. The catalyst for thermoset polyesters usually is an organic peroxide. Accelerators can be used to speed curing; inhibitors slow the cure rate for better control of the moulding process and tog ive the resin a longer shelf life. Thixotropics and viscosity suppressants are used to control the flow of liquid resin to suit the moulding process.

Epoxies bridge the cost and performance gap between polyesters and high performance polymers. Because of an inherently adhesive nature, epoxies generally are more difficult to handle than polyesters. Epoxies perform well at elevated temperatures and in corrosive environments. This resin family exhibits the shrinkage when cured. Epoxy resins, co-relate with a hardener to achieve cross-linking and cure. The major hardeners for reinforced epoxies are amines and anhydrides.

Phenolics typically are used for application calling for heat resistance, good dielectrics, retardancy, and low-smoke characteristics, phenolic resin cure through the catalysed action of phenol and formaldehyde. Phenols are available in either liquid or powder form. Elastomers, fluoropolyemers, and graphites are used in phenolic compounds for improved impact strength and lubricity.

Polyurethanes are premominant among the reactive thermosetting polymers. These resins cure when isocyanate and polyol compounds are brought together in an exothermic reaction. Other reactive resins include polydicyclopentadiene and thermoset acrylics, based on methacrylates. These resins are used in the reaction injection moulding processes.

Other thermoset resins that are reinforced include terephthalic, alkyd and diallyl phthalate polyesters, silicones, melamines, bismaleimides and thermoset polyimides.

THERMOPLASTICS

Thermoplastics polymers have a linear macromolecular structure that will repeatedly soften when they are heated to their melt temperature and harden, or cure, when they are cooled. It would be impractical to list all the thermoplastic resins availabel for reinforcing. Within each thermoplastic family, there are often scores of different varieties. For example, a nylon (or polyamide) can be semicrystalline or amorphous, depending on how it is manufactured. There also are several commercially available constructions of polyethylenes, polypropylenes, styrenic resins, thermoplastic polyesters, fluoroploymers, liquid crystal polymers, and thermoplatic elastomers, to name a few. Other thermoplastic families are based on polyphenylenes, ketones, and sulphones. Also widely used are acetals, acrylics, polycarbonates, polyvinyl chloride, and polyarylates. In addition, new thermoplastic materials are continually being developed through copolymerisation, in blending, and alloying. Some blends and alloys are made to differ simply to varying the percentages of the different resins used. Most thermoplastic polymers and alloys can be effectively reinforced to enhance performance and/or lower costs.

FILLERS AND ADDITIVES

Fillers and additives are used in both thermosets and thermoplastics to change a resin system's performance, process, or cost parameters. A filler can be a simple resin extender— low cost bulk that does not have a debilitating effect on the properties needed for the application. Some phenolic compounds, for instance, include wood "flour" ground from hardwoods and crushed nut shells. Other fillers provide a measured improvement in the performance of the compound and/or finished part. For example, calcium carbonate improves the surface gloss of rigid PVCs, and talc improves the heat deflection temperature of polypropylenes. Both these fillers see widespread use because of their low cost and their ability to be used at high filler loadings. Adding alumina trihydrate is one approach to achieving flame-retardant characteristics. Another class of additives inhibits degradation from ultraviolet light. Conductive additives are used in reinforced plastics applications that require shielding from eleactromagnetic or radio frequency interference. Colorants provide integral colour that will not chip or face.

Metallic stearates are mixed into moulding compounds to help finished parts release from the mould surface. Thermoplastic additives are used in thermoset formulations to control the shrinkage that occurs during cure. Very low shrinkage permits intricate moulding to close tolerances and results in exceptionally smooth, Class A, surface finishes.

REINFORCEMENTS

The mechanical strength of a reinforced plastic component is largely dependent on the amount, arrangement and type(s) of reinforcing fibre (s) in the resin matrix. Typically, the higher the fibre content is, the greater the strength. The arrangement has to do with the way that fibres are positioned.

The general arrangements for reinforcing fibres are :

1. *Unidirectional*: the greatest strength is in the direction of the fibres.
2. *Bidirectional* : two arrangements of fibres are at an angle to each other; strength is in each direction of fibre orientation.
3. *Multidirectional or isotropic*: strength can be uniformly distributed with chopped fibres arranged in all directions or with various orientations of continuous fibres in a fabric.

The most common reinforcement type for plastics is glass in fibrous form. Numerous compositions and fibre orientations are available to meet specific cost, process, and performance needs. New technology continually enhances existing fibre glass forms and introduces new glass fibres to meet the changing needs to industry. Glass fibre reinforcements are made by drawing molten glass from a furnace through small, tubelike bushings. As a drawn filament cools, it is gathered together with other filaments to form a strand that is pulled by a winder. A surface treatment, or sizing, is applied to the fibres for two major reasons : first like starch on textiles, the sizing protects fibre integrity during further handling steps; second the sizing contains a chemical that helps the fibre bond on the resin matrix for which is it intended. Strands are processed into shippable fibre glass reinforcement types, described below.

Continuous roving is bundled, untwisted strands that are supplied as cylindrical packages, called doffs, or balls. For some moulding processes, continuous roving is chopped into specified lengths to provide isotropic strength properties within the resin matrix. For other processes, the fibre is used continuously within the matrix for exceptional strength in the fibre's longitudinal direction. "Bulked" continuous roving has inherent loops in both axial and transverse directions. The result is multiaxial reinforced with uniaxial imput.

Reinforcing *roll goods* include mats made with randomly dispersed chopped fibres or continuous fibre strands, laid down in a swirl pattern. In either case, the fibres are held together with resin-compatible binder. Woven roving is a heavy, drapable, fabric like product that is woven from continous rovings. Mats and woven rovings are sold in various densities, or weights per unit square. Reinforcement fabrics are woven from textured glass fibre yarns in a variety of weaves and weights per unit square. Non woven fabrics ar made by knitting layers of fibre glass yarn together in unidirectional patterns. Combination products are made by stitching, needling, or bonding two or more different types of roll goods together. A typical combination is Bi-Ply(R) chopped strand mat/woven roving product. The benefit is the ability to lay up two different layers of reinforcing materials in a single step.

Chopped strands are available in various lengths for compounding with resins and additives. The fibre length varies by compound but is usually in the 1/8 inch (3.2 mm) to 2 inch (50 mm) range. Chopped strands are availabe with several different surface treatments, each designed for a specific thermosetting or thermoplastic resin.

Continous filament yarns are used in woven and non-woven reinforcing fabrics. These yarns are made by twisting and /or playing a number of fibre glass stands together. A proprietary yarn is engineered for the braiding of three dimensional reinforcement structures. This special yarn does not require the user to burn off the sizing for handleability before adding a second sizing for resin compatibility. A single dual-purpose sizing protects the fibre during braiding and still provides compatibility with polyester and epoxy resins.

As the name suggests, *milled fibres* are made by hammer milling fibre glass. The fibre are supplied in length categories by running them through different screen sizes. Milled fibres do not provide as good stiffness and strength properties as chopped strands, which are longer. Instead, the function of milled fibres is to control heat distortion of the resin and to improve the surface finish of moulded parts.

Glass flakes are used in resinous coatings to increase resistance to permeability from moisutre, vapours and solvents. Glass flakes also have been used in urethanes to enhance the surface finish of reaction injection moulded parts.

Conventional fibres are called E-glass. S-2 Glass fibres provide higher tensile strength and modulus than E-glass, S-2 Glass reinforcements are lower in cost than other high modulus fibres such as aramid and carbon.

Aramid fibres combine low density with high tensile properties. The fibres are made by extruding a solution of a liquid crystal thermoplastic polymer through a spinneret. Major forms available for reinforcing plastics are continuous filament yarns, rovings, and chopped fibres.

Carbon fibres are fine filaments made up mostly of elemental carbon. Fibre types range from amorphous carbon to crystalline graphite. Depending on its raw material input, a carbon fibre can have a stiffness or Young's modulus less than that of a glass fibre or three times that of steel. The most widely used carbon fibres for reinforcement have a modulus in the 30 to 40 million psi (207 to 268 GPa) range. Carbon reinforcement are available as short-length fibres, textles, twisted and non-twisted yarns, continous filament, and tows.

Other fibre reinforcements are made of high molecular weight polyethylene, nylon, thermopastic polyester, and ceramic.

When two or more reinforcing fibres, such as glass and carbon, are used in a common resin matrix, the resulting composite is called a hybrid. These reinforcing arrangements are used to combine the higher performance of one fibre system with the lower cost of another.

Reinforcing fillers include mica platelets, fibrous and dinely divided wallastonite and hollow and solid glass microspheres.

PREFORMS, COMPOUNDS AND PREPREGS

For some processes, reinforcing fibers are specially prepared prior to moulding. Preforms are preshaped reinforcements that are combined with resin during moulding. Compounds and prepregs are fibre-resin combinations that are prepared prior to moulding.

A *preform* is an arrangement of fibres configured to replicate the shape of the finished part. The fibres are held together with a resinous binder. Preforms are placed in the mould cavity between male and female dies used in compression, resin transfer, or reaction injection moulding. In the directed fibre approach to making preforms, fibres are chopped onto a rotating screen that is configured to simulate the shape of the finished part. The chopped fibres enter enter a sprayed stream of resinous binder that is directed toward the screen. The fibres are held in place as the preform is removed from the screen.

Preforms also can be made in a plenum chamber, where fibre roving is chopped over the preforming screen as air is drawn from behind the screen to hold the fibres in place. The fibres are oversprayed with the resinous binder. Both directed fibre and plenum chamber preforms are placed in an oven where the binder cures, and the preform shape takes a set.

A more automated approach to making preforms is to use thermoformable continuous strand mat, which incorporates a binder system that allows the mat to take a shape when heated. For load-bearing applications, this mat ensures consistent, precise placement of reinforcement, especially for resin transfer and reaction injection moulding.

Another way to make preforms is to braid the fibres into a replicate shape. Braids provide high, three-dimensional strength properties. Braided reinforcing structures can incorporate more than one fibre type, such as glass and aramid.

Sheet moulding compound (SMC) is an integrated, ready-to-mould composition of glass fibres, resin and filler. SMC is made by metering a resin paste onto a thin plastic carrier film. The resin typically is thermoset polyester. SMCs also made with vinyl easter, epoxy, phenolic, and polyimide resins. The compound is made by chopping continous fibres onto the resin paste as it is conveyed on the film, and the glass and resin mixture is covered with an additional layer of resin on a second carrier film. Compaction rollers knead the fibres into the resin for uniform fibre distribution and wetting Fig. (1.1).

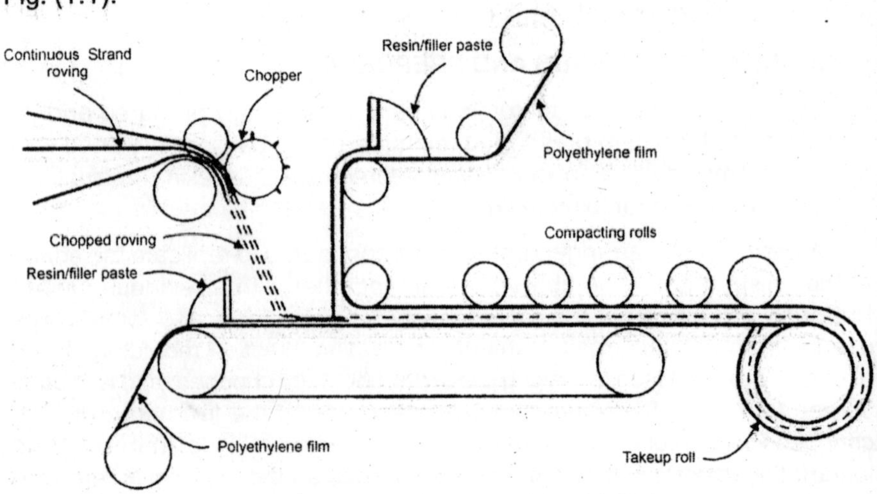

Fig. 1.1 Typical sheet moulding compound (SMC) machine.

The compound sandwiched between the carrier films is gathered into rolls or layered into containers and stored until it matures. Upon maturation, SMC is tackfree and has a leather like feel; the carrier sheets ae removed, and the sheet is prepared into a charge of predetermined weight and shape. The charge is placed on the bottom of two mould halves in a compression press.

SMC typically has 20 to 25% glass fibres by weight. Typical fibre length is 1 inch (25 mm), and fibres are deposited in a random pattern that provides isotropic orientation. However, strength properties can be enhanced by increasing the fibre content, increasing the fibre length, and/or introducing directionally oriented fibres.

Bulk moulding compound (BMC) is mixed of chopped glass fibres and resins with necessary fillers and additives. The premixed material has a doughlike consistency and is supplied in bulk form or as an extruded rope for ease of handling. BMC is compression-, transfer-, or injection-moulded.

Thermoset prepregs are made by combining liquid resin with woven and/or continuous fibre reinforcement. Through controlled chemical reaction, the resin is brought to its B-stage, which is a take-free condition that meets particular handling and processing conditions. Prepregs are cured with heat and often are refrigerated to prevent premature cure. A prepreg also can be a three-dimensional braided structure of preimpregnated fibres. Prepreg tapes automated and precise placement of reinforcement in the finished part.

Several different techniques are used to produce thermoplastic prepregs. Because no chemical catalyst is needed to initiate thermoplastic cure, B-staging is not needed. Heat and pressure are applied to consolidate the reinforcing fibre and thermoplastic resin. Fibres can be preimpregnated or encapsulated in a resin solution, resin melt, or resin in powder form. Other thermoplastic prepregs are fabrics of commingled reinforcement and resin yarns. Thermoplastic prepregs also can be reinforced thermoplastic shapes that are re-formed under heat and pressure in a post-fabrication step. For example, filament winding and pultruding fibres with thermoplastics create composites that can be-re formed. Another thermoplastic prepreg, stampable sheet, is made by extruding thermoplastic polymer with reinforcement, generally continous strand mat.

Pelletised compounds are made by extruding resin compound, usually thermoplastics, with chopped strands. the extrudate is cut to specific lengths to form pellets, and the pelletised compound is metered into injection moulding machines or extruders and processed into an end-use component or profile. The pellet ensures good control of fibre glass content through out the finished part. Compounds also can contain a variety of fillers and additives, depending on the cost/performance needs of the finished part. Each extruded pellet contains a near-equal amount of additive for good distribution throughout the moulded part. Examples of additives are colorants, lubricants, flame retardants, and impact modifiers.

Long fibre compounds are used in applications needing additional strength and stiffness properties. These compounds can be blended wth conventionally reinforced and unreinforced compounds. One technique for making long fibre compounds is to pull continuous reinforcement through the resin as it is being extruded. The resin-encapsulated strand then is coold and chopped to length, typically more than one inch. Long fibre compounds also are made by pultruding continuous fibre through a thermoplastic resin bath. The cooled pultrudate then is chopped into a compound with specific length fibres.

PROCESSES

Many molding and fabrication processes are available to those who want to benefit from reinforced plastics and composites. Each process has characteristics, advantages and limitations relating to: (i) part size, complexity and volume; (ii) cost, performance and appearance specifications; (iii) cost, durability and nature of the tooling or forming mould; and (iv) compatibility with various resins, reinfrocements and additives. This section lists processes in six general moulding categories; open, compression, injection, reactive and resin transfer, continuous, and other processes.

Open (or Contact) Moulding

Lay-up is the most basic and one of the longest used reinforced plastics moulding process. The mould typcially is a female cavity, and the mould surface is treated with a release agent, usually wax, that will facilitate removal of the finished part. A liquid gel coat of polyester, polyurethane, or other resin usually is applied to the mould surface; when the part is moulded and removed, this gel coat will form the exterior surface of the part. In some cases, a vacuum- formed or thermoformed thermoplastic sheet can be used instead of a gel coat; then liquid resin, normally thermoset polyester, is combined with layers of reinforcement in roll form—mat, woven roving, fabric, or combination product. In practice, this is much like pouring concrete over steel reinforcing bars. To prevent voids in the finished part, air entrapped in the resinated reinforcement is worked out by using rollers or squeegees. Layers of reinforcement and resin are added to build the laminate to desired thickness. Usually, laid-up parts cure at ambient temperatures, but heat, catalysts, and accelerators, can help speed resin cure.

Lay-up is suited to making large structures requiring high strengths. Traditionally, this process is called hand lay-up because layers of fibre glass mat or woven roving are manually placed in the mould cavity; but lay up can be automated by running fibre glass woven roving through an impregnation machine, and then robotically laying the wet reinforcement in place. This automated technique is used to fabricate large yachts, commercial fishing vessels, and naval minehunters. However, most lay-up is accomplished manually (Fig. 1.2). In fact the labour intesnsive nature of the process is a major limitation, especially for annual volumes above 1000 parts. Another disadvantage is that the process produces only one finished surface.

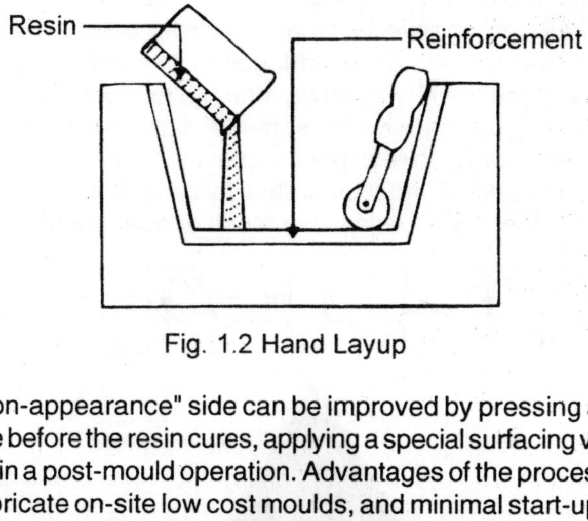

Fig. 1.2 Hand Layup

The "non-appearance" side can be improved by pressing a film against the laminate before the resin cures, applying a special surfacing veil, or coating the surface in a post-mould operation. Advantages of the process include the ability to fabricate on-site low cost moulds, and minimal start-up costs. Also, there is virtually no limit to the size of a laid-up part because, properly applied, succeding layers of resin and reinforcement build into an integral laminate.

Bagging and autoclaving techniques can be used to improve a laid-up laminate. In vacuum bagging, a mould release film is placed over the reinforcement/resin composition. The film edges are sealed, and vacuum is drawn from within. Atmospheric pressure works the film toward the laminate to create a smoother surface, eliminate voids, and force out entrapped air and rexcess resin. In pressure bag moulding, a deflated bag is placed on top of the film. An airtight seal is placed over the bag, and the bag is inflated. The resultant pressure against the laminte provide the same surface and removal benefits as vacuum bagging. An advanced modification of bagging is to place the laminate and mould inside an autoclave. Pressures inside the airtight autoclave build to about 80 psi (0.55 MPa) as the mould release film is drawn to the laminate. The result is enhanced densification. The autoclave often can be heated to accelerate cure and increase productivity. Bag and autoclave assisted lay-up is used extensively to fabricate high-strength aircraft and aerospace components. The resin-fibre composition often is a prepreg, as described above.

Spray-up, is in a sense, a mechanised version of lay-up. A spray up simultaneously sprays resin and chops continous glass strand into specific length fibres. Chopped fibres enter the resin spray stream, and the combined fibre-resin material is applied to the mould. As in lay-up, the reinforced polymer composition usually backs up a gel coat or thermoplastic skin. Also like-lay up, the fibre-resin composition is rolled out to effect complete wetting of fibres and remove voids and bubbles before the resin cures. Spray-up and lay-up often are used together to combine the automated aspects of one process with the higher strength reinforcement of the other. Part volumes can be higher with sprayup, but, because of increased equipment needs, spray-up requires a higher initial investment than lay-up. Unless the spraying action is accomplished by computer-controlled robotics, process control of spray up relies very much or operator skill (Fig. 1.3).

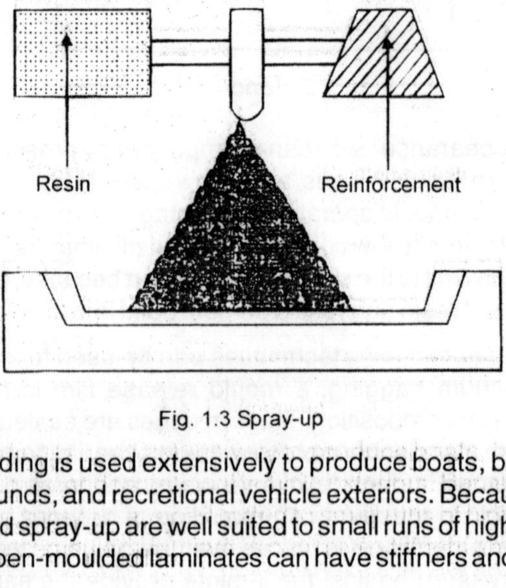

Fig. 1.3 Spray-up

Open moulding is used extensively to produce boats, bathtubs, shower stalls and surrounds, and recretional vehicle exteriors. Because of low tooling costs, lay-up and spray-up are well suited to small runs of highly individualised applications. Open-moulded laminates can have stiffners and cores integrally moulded in. Stiffener and core materials may be cardboard, balsa, resin-compatible foams, reinforced or unreinforced plastics, metal, or one of many honeycomb materials. One type of cored laminate is a sandwich construction—outer skins of reinforced plastics over a central core material. Sandwich laminates combine exceptionally high strength and stiffness with light weight.

Compression Moulding

Compession moulding is accomplished with matched male and female dies, usually machined from tooling grade metals. During moulding, the top mould half closes on the resin and reinforcement charge in the bottom mould half. As the mould halves come together, the charge fills the part cavity between them; the part forms and cures as the mould halves are brought together under heat and pressure. Thus the part cures while he press is closed. Cure cycles vary by material system, process temperature and pressure, and part thickness and complexity. The mould charge can be a sheet moulding compound, bulk moulding compound, resin-impregnated preform, or prepreg. (Fig. 1.4).

The most advanced form of reinforced plastics compression moulding is sheet moulding compound (SMC). The automotive industry makes widespread use of SMC, especially for car and truck body panels. In-mould coatings are applied to produce the smooth Class A surfaces specified by automotive engineers. SMC panels are bonded to each other and to metals. SMC moulding cycles can be 60 seconds or less; battering the one minutes threshold ensures that parts are compatible with the just-in-tie delivery schedules established by automative assembly plants.

Another variation of compression processing, wet moulding, entails applying a liquid resin system to reinforcing materials or a preform. Resin is applied to the reinforcement just before or after it is placed in the bottom mould half. Cold moulding is wet compression moulding accomplished with ambient cure resins. The only heat comes from the exothermic reaction of resin cure, and pressures are low. The moulds themselves often are reinforced plastics.

Transfer moulding is related to compression moulding, In this case, the reinforced thermoset compound first is heated in a chamber or pot separate from the matched dies. Then, a plunger or ram transfers the hated material into the closed mould. The part cures under compressive pressure. This technique facilitates the compression moulding of small, intricate parts in multicavity moulds.

The injection-compression moulding combination starts by injecting the

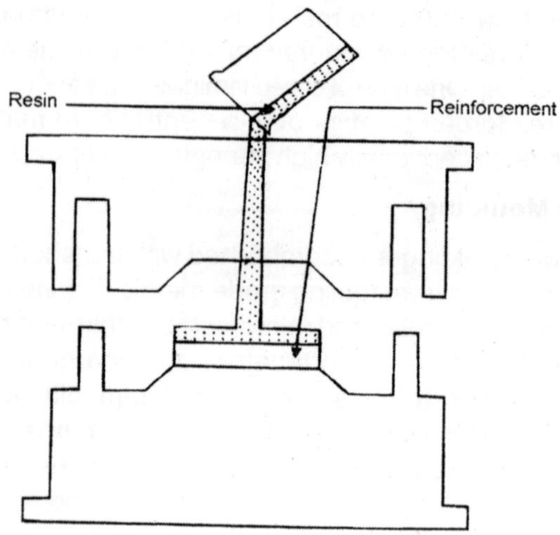

Fig. 1.4 Compression moulding

multicavity moulds.

The injection-compression moulding combination starts by injecting the moulding compound into a slightly open set of matched metal dies; compression of the mould havles is completed after the compound fills the mould cavity. The compound can be based on either thermoset or thermoplastic resins.

For stamping, or flow forming of reinforced thermoplastics, the charge usually is in sheet form. The sheet is prehated into a soft state, then placed between mould havles. Press closure occurs at rates faster than those of other compression moulding variations; hence the term "stamping". However, unlike steel stamping, the press is held shut until the reinforced thermoplastic laminate has cooled. Although the strike time for thermoplastic sheet is longer, a single strike can accomplish complex configurations that require several progressive strkes with sheet metal.

Injection Moulding

When pelletised compound is used, injection moulding of reinforced thermoplastics is very much like injection moulding of unreinforced thermoplastics. The compound is fed from a hopper into a heated cylinder where the resin softens into a flowable polymer melt. During a mould cycle, a rotating screw ram injects the melt into the cavity formed when mould halves are brought together. For injection moulded thermoplastics, mould

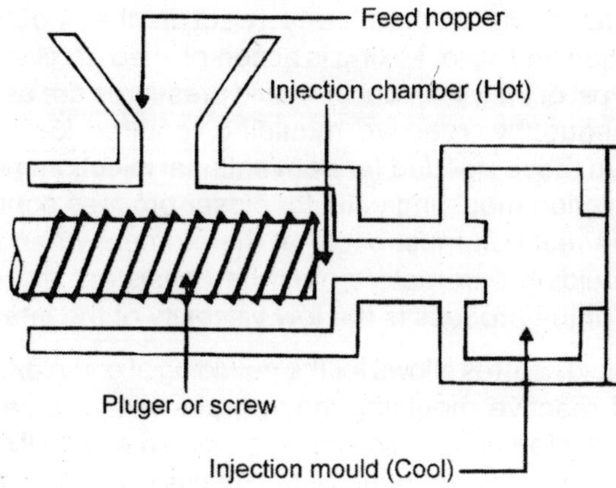

Fig. 1.5 Injection moulding thermoplastics.

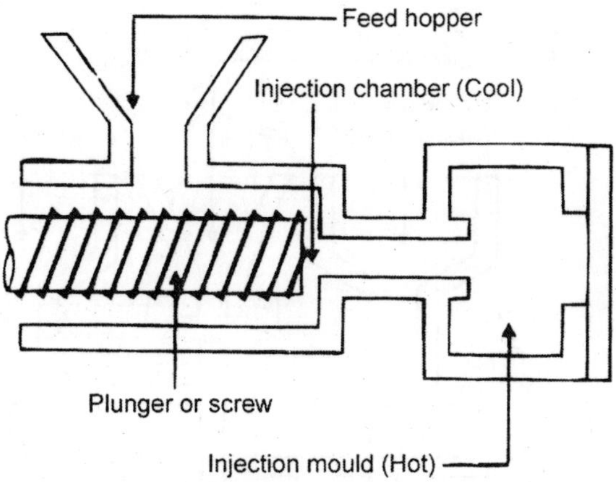

Fig. 1.6 Injection moulding thermosets.

are kept relatively cool so the melt can freeze, or solidify,to form finished part (Fig. 1.5).

For injection-moulded thermosets, the ignition cylinder is cool instead of heated, and moulds are heated instead of cool. A plunger low-shear screw-ram injects the reinforced compound into the mould cavity. The hollow mould activates the thermoset cure chemicals (Fig. 1.6.)

Reactive and Resin Transfer Moulding

Reaction injection moulding (RIM) involves bringing liquid, polymer-

The intermediate chemically react in the mould to effect rapid polymerisation and cure. Mixing is accomplished at relatively high prssures (up to 3500 psi or 24 MPa), but in-mould pressures are as low as 50 psi (345 kPa). consequently, reacitve moulding requires lower-cost tooling and presses than those needed for conventional injection moulding. However, reaction injection moulding calls for closer process controls. Because the timing of the reaction must occur at the moment when the cavity is filled, reactive moulding parameters must be consistent for every shot. A key advantage of the process is the low viscosity of the intermediates.

Their liquid natures allows for the moulding of complex parts. Two different versions of reactive moulding incorporate reinforcements. One of these processes, reinforced reaction injection moulding (RRIM), incorporates the reinforcing agent in the mterial system that is injeced from the mixing head.

The reinforcement— usually milled glass fibre or glass flakes— is added to one or both resin intermediates before resin components are mixed. It

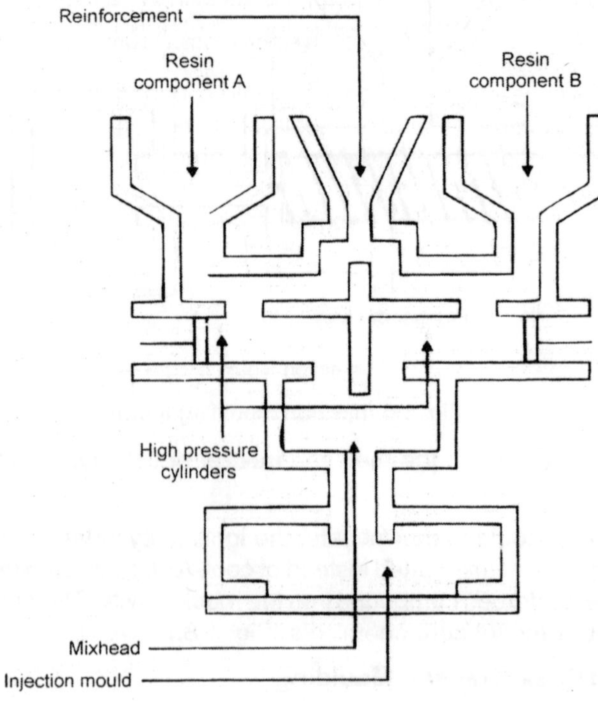

Fig. 1.7. Reinforced reaction injection moulding

increases flexural modulus, improves thermal resistance and, for some applications, enhances the surface finish (Fig. 1.7).

In structural reaction injection moulding (SRIM), the reinforcing medium is placed in the mould before the mould halves are closed, and the mixed resin becomes the matrix for the reinforcement that is already in the part cavity.

The reinforcement typically is a thermoformed mat or fibre-directed preform. These forms withstand fibre "wash" or movement of reinforcement caused by the pressure of injected resin. SRIM can be used to produce large structural parts for automobiles and trucks; for example, SRIM prototypes of pickup truck beds have been made with thermoformable continuous fibre glass strand mat. Highly automated equipment produces mat preforms at a rate fast enough to keep pace with the rapid reaction moulding process.

Resin transfer moulding (RTM) is similar to SRIM in that resin is introduced into a closed mould that already contains the reinforcing agent. In both processes, no press is needed, however, the resin chemistry for RTM is quite different from that of SRIM. Catalysed resin is pumped into the mould to form the part; and the resin can be formulated to cure without heat, orheating coils can be incorporated into the mould to speed cure of an elevated-temperature resin formulation.

The advantages of resin transfer moulding are the relatively low investments needed for equipment and tooling and the ability to mould large, highly reinforced structures. RTM parts can incorporate cores, inserts, and encapsulates (Fig. 1.8).

Continuous Processes

Pultrusion uses one or several different forms of continuous reinforcement, such as rovings, mats, woven rovings, fabrics, and/or cloths, with the type and the amount of reinforcement depending on the desired properties. Surfacing veils are used to give the moulded part a smooth, resin-rich finish. Typically the reinforcement or reinforcement combination is drawn through a resin bath where the fibres are impregnated. After excess resin is stripped off, the fibres are sent through a forming station where fibres are oriented for proper entry into a heated steel die, inside which the fibre-resin laminate takes on its final cross-sectional shape. Heat completes the cure. Downstream from the die, pulling devices move the rigid profile forward to an area where profiles are cut to length.

fibres are oriented for proper entry into a heated steel die, inside which the fibre-resin laminate takes on its final cross-sectional shape. Heat completes the cure. Downstream from the die, pulling devices move the rigid profile forward to an area where profiles are cut to length.

This same pulling action is used to continously draw the fibres through the resin bath, forming station, and die. Pultrusion is use to produce a wide variety of profiles with a continous cross section. It is possible to pultrude fibre and resin encapsulate over wood, foam, metal and other cores (Fig. 1.9).

Reinforcing fibres for pultrusion are predminantly glass. Graphite tow and aramid fibres also are used. Resins are usually thermoset, especially polyester and vinyl ester. Epoxy is used in pultrusion but is difficult to process. Advances in resin chemistry and adjustments in the process are expanding the possibilities of pultrusion beyond traditional resins. For example, acid-free phenolics have been developed to resist sticking. Fibres enter the die in a dry state, are preformed and are pulled through a special chamber. There, fibre wetout is accomplished by injecting the phenolic resin into the chamber. Other variations of the pultrusion process also eliminate the traditional resin bath impregnation. For instance, either reactive or thermoplastic resins can be polymerised in the die as the fibres are being pulled through. Thermoplastic pultrusion also in accomplished by pulling multiples of preheated thermostatic prepregs through a heated die. Profiles pultruded with thermoplastic resins can be heated and re-formed. The result combines the high cross-sectional strength of pultrusion with the design flexibility of compression moulding.

Parts typically made by the pultrusion process include electrical safety

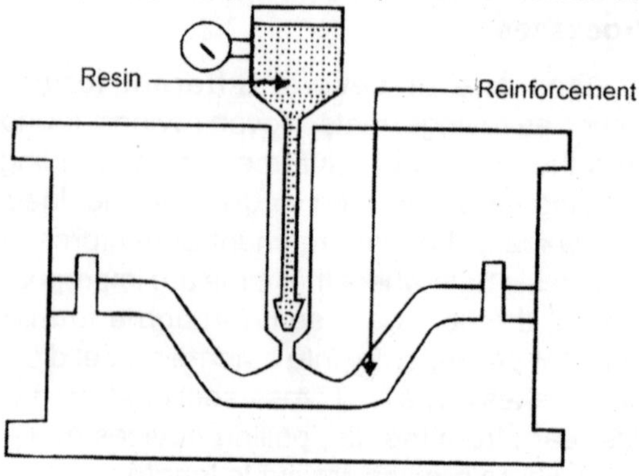

Fig. 1.8. Resin transfer moulding

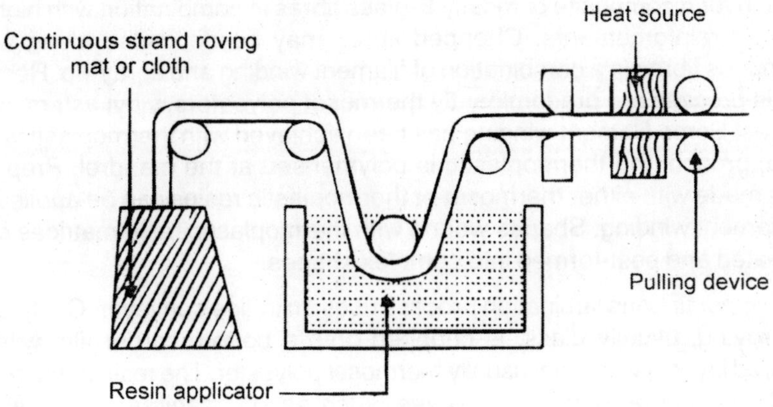

Fig. 1.9. Pultrusion

ladder rails and rungs, grating profiles, nonconductive cable supports, and structural beams for corrosive environments. The process is also used tomake automotive driveshafts, siding for buses and buildings and structural framing for orbiting space satellites.

Pulforming is an offshoot of pultrusion. Resin wet reinforcement is pulled through female mould cavities. The moulds rotate on a turntable. The female cavities are enclosed by co-rotating male mould havles placed over them or the female moulds are covered by a rotating contact plate or belt. Each part cures as the closed mould rotates toward a cutoff station. Applications made this way include automotive leaf springs and hammer handles.

Filament winding is another continuous process. continuous reinforcement is drawn through a resin-impregnation bath and wound wet under tension on a rotating mandrel. The angle of the fibres on the mandrel varies by application, and fibre lay-down patterns are controlled through a fibre delivery device. Fibre patterns typically criss-cross and overlap to produce good multidirectional strength properties. Possible fibre patterns include helical, circumferential, polar and non-linear. When the parts is wound to the desired thickness, it is removed from the mandrel. Ambient and oven cure resins are used (Fig. 1.10).

The traditional filament winding mandrel is cylindrical; and typical applications are storage tanks, piping and chimney liners. However, spheres, "eggs", and non symmetrical shapes are possible as long as the shape can be formed by a continuous fibre path. The wind pattern can be computer-controlled over six different axes. In the pin winding variation, continuous fibre is wound around end pins, with winding accomplished inside a cavity wind a hybrid composite of mostly E-glass fibres in combination with higher modulus reinforcements. Chopped fibres may be deposited along with continuous fibres in a combination of filament winding and spray-up. Resins for this process are predominantly thermoset polyesters, vinyl esters, and epoxies. Some filament winding has been achieved with thermoplastics. In one approach, the thermoplastic is polymerised at the mandrel. Prepreg tapes made with either thermoset or thermoplastic resins can be applied in dry filament winding. Shapes wound with thermoplastic resin matrices can be heated and post-formed into complex shapes.

The continuous lamination process uses an in-line conveyor. Continous fibre roving, usually glass, is chopped onto a bottom carrier film with a doctored layer of wet resin, usually thermoset polyester. The resin formulation usually incorporates many additives, such as UV stabilisers, colorants, flame retardands, and fillers.

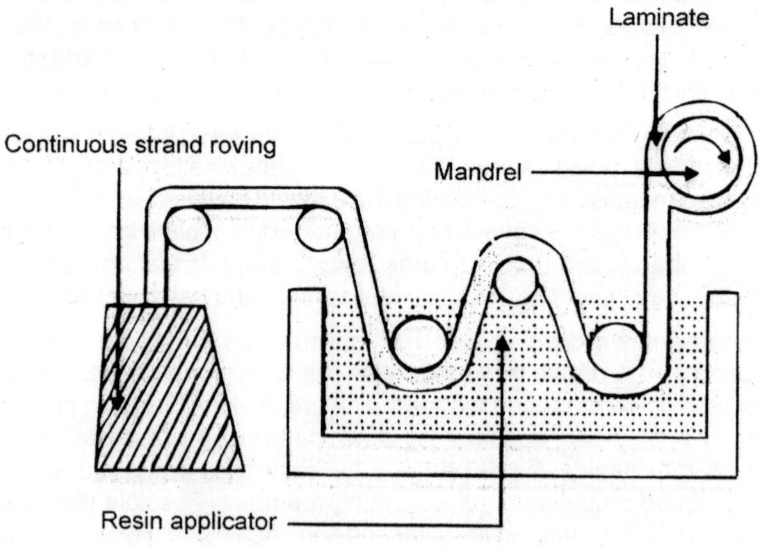

Fig. 1.10 Filament winding

The film, with fibres and resin, is conveyed downstream, where a pressure roller works the fibres into the resin before a top film is applied. The film/composite/film sandwich is pulled through compression rollers to remove air and establish thickness. Finally, the laminate enters a forming / curing area. Most sheet is either made flat by special shoes or corrugated by shaping rollers. After cure, outer carrier films are stripped off, and the laminate is trimmed and cut to length. The light transmittance of reinforced plastic panels made this way is design-engineered for the application, and can range from 95% to complete opaqueness. Typical applications are skylights, greenhouse panels, building sidewalls and truck-trailer linears.

Other moulding Processes

The inflatable pressure bag technique results in hollow reinforced plastics shapes, such as seamless tanks. The bag is placed inside a preformed fibre glass shape, and the bag-in-glass assembly then is placed inside an unheted, hollow mould. The mould is either open-ended or a two part clamshell. After the fibres are resin-impregnated , the bag is inflated to push the reinforced composite against the mould walls. After resin cure. The bag is deflated and removed from the interior of the part.

Cylindrical piping, tubing, tanks and other containers can be formed by using the centrifugal casting process. Chopped strand mat is placed inside a hollow, cylindrical mould, and resin is sprayed on the mat as the mandrel rotates slowly. One variation is to chop fibres inside the mandrel instead of using mat. When desired resin and glass contents are reached, the rotational speed is increased. Centrifugal force effect resin wet-out and fibre compactation, and heat accelerates the cure.

In encapsulation, chopped strands or milled fibres are mixed with catalysed polyesters, epoxies, or silicones. The composition is poured into open cavities containing electrical or electronic components, such as terminal blocks, and these components are encapsulated in the composition of protection and electrical insulation. Rotational moulding, also called rotomoulding, is done with chopped strands or milled fibres and thermoplastic resin powder. Reinforcements can be added at any stage of the moulding cycle but usually are part of a premould blend. Materials are charged into a hollow heated mould that is rotated in one or two planes. Heat-fused resin encapuslates the fibres, and the composite takes shape against the inner mould walls. When ready the mould and/or the part is chilled to "freeze" the part for removal. A water mist often is sprayed internally.

Other reinforced thermoplastics composites are made by extrusion, extrusion-blow moulding, and thermoforming. These processes are covered in more detail in other chapters of this book. Originally developed for unreinforced thermoplastics, the processes are also run with fibre-reinforced compounds. Fibres bring about specific property enhancements, such as higher thermal resistance or impact strength. Extrusion and extrusion-blow moulding materials typically are pelletised compounds. Premixed blends and direct feeding also are possible. Thermoforming is accomplished on extruded sheetstock.

FEATURES AND BENEFITS

Reinforced plastics and composites present a matrix of performance and cost options. This family of materials should be considered when application of market needs include one or more of the attributes discussed in the following paragraphs. With so many moulding and fabrication techniques available, the design flexibility obtainable with reinforced plstics exceeds that of virtually all other material systems. Parts can be as large and structural as a military mine-hunter vessel or as small and intricate as an electronic connector. Also, reinforced plastics and composites offer an almost limitless range of resins and reinforcement types, forms, and orientations.

Reinforced plastics provide an excellent combination of high strength with light weight. Because of excellent strength-to-weight ratios, tensile strengths by weight typically exceed those of many grades of iron and steel. In addition, flexural, and impact strengths are equal to or better than those of many metals. Being lighter than alternatives, composites lower energy consumption needs for transportation uses, such as automotive body penels; and lighter-weight piping or structurals cost less to transport and are easier to install. Light weight also can reduce load-bearing stresses for better performance and lower costs.

Reinforced plastics offer very good dimensional stability. It often is this property that dictates the use of reinforced plastics when unreinforced thermoplastics meet other design requirements. The inclusion of reinforcing fibres elevates the resin's ability to maintain critial tolerances over a wide range of temperatures and physical stresses. Fibres also improve the material's thermal coefficient of expansion. In addition, a reinforced plastic enclosures or car panel will not take a "set" when impacted by a force that normally would dent sheet metal.

Through parts consolidation, a single moulded reinforced plastic component replaces several parts that would require numerous assembly steps. This ability to combine parts ideally suits reinforced plastics to quality philosphies that emphasise just-in-time deliveries. Using reinforced plastics, fabricators delivery a "black box" modular subassembly that is easily integrated into the production line.

Reinforced plastics are well know for their corrosion resistance. The resistance to acids, alkalis, hydrocarbons, and solvents varies by resin matrix; thus the resin is selected to meet an application's need to resist specific levels of corrosion, pressure, and temperature (Table 1.1). Even the most basic composite using an orthophthalic polyester resin will not rust or corrode. However, for more demanding environments, resin options include isophthalic polyesters, vinyl esters, and epoxies. Composites engineered for corrosion resistance typically use a surfacing veil or mat. These surface treatments create a resin rich surface that resists corrosive media. Reinforced plastics are excellent dielectrics. Like corrosion resistance, electrical resistance can be application-specific. Glass in any form including fibrous, is a very low conductor of electricity. In fact, the designation of conventional glass fibres as E-glass is derived from the fibres' early use in electrical applications. Generally, thermoset resins offer better dielectric properties than thermoplastics. Reinforcement polyesters are widely used in applications designed to provide protection from electric shocks.

Table 1.1 Chemical resistance notations by materials family.

Thermosets

Epoxies are highly resistant to water, alkalies and organic solvents. Although standard epoxies have only a fair resistance to acids and oxidising agents, they can be formulated for better resistance to these agents. They should be tested before used.

Polyester thermosets are available in many formulations. They can be formulated for good to excellent resistance to acids, weak alkalies and organic solvents. However, they are not recommended for use with strong alkalies.

Polyurethane is normally used for its structural properties when moulded. It is highly resistant to most organic solvents. It is not recommended for use with strong acids and alkalies, steam fuels, and ketones.

Thermoplastics

ABS is highly resistant to weak acids and alkalies and provides good resistance to most organic solvents. It is attacked by sulphuric and nitric acids, and is soluble in esters, ketones and ethylene dichloride.

Acetal is highly resistant to strong alkalies. Most organic solvents do not seriously alter its properties (test before use). It is not recommended for use in strong acids.

Nylons, as a group, are inert to most organic solvents. They resist alkalies and salt solutions and they are attacked by strong mineral acids and oxidising agents.

Polyphenylene Oxide provides excellent resistance to aqueous media. It is softened by aromatic hydrocarbons.

Polycarbonates resist weak acids and alkalies, oil and grease. They are attacked by strong acids, alkalies, organic solvents, and fuels (test before use).

Thermoplastic polyesters are resistant to most organic solvents, weak acids and alkalies. They are not recommended with strong acids and alkalis or for prolonged use in hot water.

Polypropylene provides good resistance to acids, alkalies and organic solvents even at higher temperatures. It is, however, soluble in chlorinated hydrocarbons.

Polyphenylene sulphide provides excellent resistance to organic solvents (below 375°F). It is unaffected by strong alkalies or aqueous organic salt solutions.

Polystyrene provides good resistance to alkalies, most organic solvents, weak acids, and household chemicals, it is not recommended for use with strong acids, ketones, esters, and some chlorinated hydrocarbons (test before use)

Metals

Cold rolled Steels are rusted by water, oxygen and salt solutions. Not recommended for use with acids. They do, however, have good resistance to alkalies.

Stainless steels have poor acids resistivity (especially hydrochloride and sulphuric) as well as poor chloride solution resistivity. They do offer good resistance to alkalies and organic solvents.

Aluminium has poor acid resistance (especially hydrochloride and sulphuric) and also poor chloride salt resistance (must be chemically treated for appearance when exposed to weather).

Megnesium poorly resists acids except hydrofluoric, however, it has good resistance to alkalies. It corrodes in the presence of salt, salt spray or industrial atmospheres.

Zinc offers good atmospheric resistance but is not recommended for use with strong acids, bases, and steam.

Integral finishes and surfaces are possible with reinforced plastics and composites. Colorants can be added to the resin formulation to produce a part that needs no painting; moreover, the colour will not chip or scratch. Surfaces can incorporate textures, ridges, grids, and similar treatments replicated from the surface of the mould; and they can be mirror like to meet automotive body panel requirements for a Class A finish.

A key economic benefit of turning to reinforced plastics and composites is moderate tooling costs. Amortization of the tooling investment does not require production volumes in the hundreds of thousands. For lower pressures and volumes, the moulds themselves often incorporate reinforced plastics. For high-volume moulding, such as fibre glass/polyester automotive body panels, tooling costs are subtantially lower than for the tooling needed for sheet metal. In addition, reproducing complex shapes in sheet metal requires several progressive stamping tools.

By offering shorter lead times, reinforced plastics are helping marketers to become more competitive. Short lead times man that the product is becoming profitable sooner. Also, the compressed time frame from idea to finished part can make an important contribution toward simultaneous engineering. This strategy computer-integrates all essential product development programmes to occur during the same, compressed time sequence. Decisions related to engineering, materials analysis, design of tooling, fixtures, and process control are made concurrently instead of successively. For one moulder-assembler, this technique took a heavy-duty truck hood and fender assembly from concept to finished part in12 months. The standard development cycle for this process of 24 to 36 months can prove costly to competitors in global markets.

MARKETS AND APPLICATIONS

The automotive market has been, is, and is projected to be the largest consumer of reinforced plastics and composites. The most visible applications are exterior body panels. In addition to their use on cars with plastics-intensive bodies, reinforced plastis body panels are assembled on vehicle alongside steel body panels. For example, fibre glass composite doors and liftgates offer light weight anc corrosion resistance. Outer panels often are bonded to fibre glass composite inner panels that combine several parts into a single unit with moulded-in assembly guides. Other reinforced plastic exterior panels on cars include grille opening panels, rear and/licence plate panels, and spoilers.

A huge opportunity for reinforced plastics is emerging in structural automotive applications. Examples are composite drives shafts, wheels and leaf springs. Developmental work with structural cross members may be the precursor to major chasis components moulded of composites. In addition, each of the big automakers has a programme for making pickup truck beds of rienfored plastics. Processes under evaluation for this application are compression moulding, structural RIM and resin transfer moulding.

Another area where reinforced plastics use is growing is underhood. Initially used in trucks, vinyl ester SMC oil pans, crankcases, and rocker covers are under study for automobiles.

Other automotive applications of reinforced plastics include headlamp housings, spare tyre covers, and bumber beams. In addition to cars and light trucks, reinforced plastics are widely used for other ground transportation vehicles. Examples include hood/fender assemblies and engine components for heavy duty trucks, body panels and engine components for recreational vehicles, and pultruded body panels and air ducts for buses.

The marine maket has been a large user of reinfored plastics for years. The use of fibre glass reinforced polyester in pleasure boats is a mature application. However, some high-performance boats are made with enhanced-performance materials, such as glass fibres and vinyl esters. In addition to pleasure boats and sailboards, fibre glass-reinforced plastics are specified for the hulls and decks of commercial fishing boats and military minehunters.

Corrosion-resistant materials are a class of reinforced plastics often referred to as a market. However, these materials are engineered to resist corrosive environments in a variety of different markets. Major user-industries that benefit from special reinforced plastics are chemical processing oil and gas, pulp and paper, waste-water, air pollusion control, and electroplating. Probably the best-known corrosion resistant-material application is the underground gasoline stroage tank.

Major *construction market* applications are paneling and skylights, bathtubs and shower stalls, and doors and windows. Reinforced plastics also are used in industrial and commercial buildings that need specific characteristics. For instance, radar installations or computer test sites benefit from good dielectric properties, and light weight is preferred for architectural assemblies that are crane-lifted. As noted above, there also are many corrosion-resistant applications in the construction market.

For reinforced plastics and composites, the aircraft/aerospace/military market is low in volume but high in value. Both commercial and military aircraft make extensive use of reinforced plastics materials that are referred to as "advanced composites". This designation is given to composites that consist of fibres with a higher modulus than conventional E-glass fibres and a resin matrix with higher properties than polyestrs. One of the more impressive applications of advanced composites for aircraft is the fuselage for Beech Aircraft's Starship business turboprop. The pressurised fuselage is graphite fibre-reinfroced epoxy prepreg over a honeycomb core. More than 70% of the aircraft's structural weight is advanced composites.

Advanced composites also are used for helicopter rotor blades, aircraft wing and tail components, and engine ducts. Also, because of their radar transparency, advanced composites play a key role in radar-evading "stealth" technologies. In general, the composite aircraft components have performed better than comparable metallic omponents. In another military use, properly engineered composites work well as protective armour against ballistics attack. Reinforced plastics also are used for temporary runway pads for military aircraft and portable bridges for troops and artillery.

Electrical/electronic market applications vary widely. Composite ladder rails and rungs, stand-off poles, and conduit for power cables provide protection against electrical shock. One of the more unusual electrical uses is an all composites building in which artificial lightning is generated to test the effect of lightning on aircraft and aerospace vehicles. Glass fabrics impregnated epoxy laminates are used to insulate printed circuitry. Lighting poles, electrical connections, and antennae also are moulded of reinforced plastics.

New assembly techniques create opportunities for increased use of reinforced plastics in the appliance market. The base of a large appliance, such as a refrigerator, now must act as an assembly pallet with moulded-in snap-fit and alignment features. The refrigerator motor and compressor components are robotically assembled from the base up; so the base not only must be moulded to close tolerances but must be strong and rigid. Reinforced plastics are well suited to these design parameters. Reinforced plastics also are an alternative to porcelainised metals for dishwashers, washers, drayers, ranges, and refrigerators. Other appliance applciations are panels for toasters and toaster ovens, storage trays for refrigerators, housings for microwavble waffle irons, and skirts for steam irons.

The *business equipment market* chooses reinforced composites for parts consolidation, close moulding tolerances, and heat resistance. For example, in fibre glass/thermoset polyester, a computer printer mainframe is injection -moulded as a unit. Previously, the part was an assembly of 15 machined, cast aluminium and sheet metal parts. The heat shield on a photocopier is glass reinforced, RIM polyacrylamate. Another equipment example is a reinforced phenolic computer planer board with moulded-in slots for adding computer cards.

Most composite applications in the consumer goods market are related to sports and recreation. Composite bicycle frames are lightweight and stiff; the increased stiffness reduces side motions that waste pedal power. Carbon fibre-reinforced arrow shafts resul in higher arrow speeds and more accuracy compared to aluminium shafts. Also graphite fibre reinforced epoxy baseball and softball bats can be find-tuned to sound like wood or metal when the bat meets the ball. Reinforced plastic skis made with braided preforms have exceptional torsional stiffness. Other consumer applications for composites include dual-ovenable cookware, planters, and furniture.

In addition to their uses for the markets mentioned above,reinforced plastics are made into stadium are institutional seaitng, power saw tables, road repair plates, and decking for platform tennis. Medical applications include artificial joints and bones, casts and equipment housings. Materials handling and industrial machinary also are potential markets for the growth of reinforced plastics because of their light weight, durability, and vibration dampening.

Thus, reinforced plastics and composites are proven engineering materials uniquely capable of meeting a wide range of cost and performance requirements. Reinforced plastics and composites offer a combination of properties not found in other materials. The versatility of this family of materials is evident in its tens of thousands of different applications— from intericate electronic connectors to oceangoing vessels. With so many variables in reinforcing materials, resin matrices and processes, it is possible to design-engineer a composite to be market-and application-specific.

2

Product Introduction

Designing with glass fibres, as with any other material, is a combination of art and science. The creative element of the design process is often associated with shape, geometry, colour and surface texture, that is with the visual and tactile attributes of the structure or component. Beneath the surface are the technical aspects of the design; the choice of materials, their properties, loads, failure criteria, fabrication and processing methods.

Good design needs to integrate a number of elements which, all too often, are considered separately; size, geometry, loads and displacements, suitable materials, and so on. Lack of integration makes for an inferior and inefficient product. With traditional engineering materials, such as metals, it is possible to produce a working design, even if it is not an efficient one. This arises because, essentially, the properties of most of the material are known to a high degree of accuracy, with relatively little ambiguity, and this information is available in reference books and is backed up by suitable design codes. The costs of traditional materials are also generally low, so that there may be no great benefit in excessive optimization.

Another important' consideration is that traditional materials are isotropic and essentially homogeneous; their mechanical and physical properties do not depend upon the direction in which they are measured and do not vary from point to point in a given volume, unless one considers a very small scale of structure. The only common materials which are different in these aspects are wood and concrete.

Fibrous composite materials are different, and it is essential to consider all the aspects of the design together if an efficient, safe and cost-effective structure or artefact is to be produced. There are several reasons for this of which the designer must be aware:

- the fibre glass material and structure are usually fabricated at the same time, and little or no modification to the final product is possible after manufacture;
- the materials are highly anisotropic and heterogeneous. This is a consequence of théir fibrous structure and of the comparatively large size of the fibres (typically 10μm diameter). The strength and stiffness properties of polymer composites reflect the properties of the fibres only in the direction parallel to them; in any other direction they are, at best, a poor compromise of fibre and matrix properties and, at worst, the properties of the matrix alone, which is by definition the more compliant and weaker component of the system;
- for any given combination of polymers and fibres there is a large number of possible materials which can be made, depending on the relative proportions of the components and. the orientation of the fibres. Further variability is due to the effect of fibre length in short fibre com posites, the mixing of fibres (hybrid materials) and the use of core materials to produce sandwich structures.

There are various design implications due to these differences :

- property data are relatively scarce and it is not always apparent how to use the information available to estimate the properties of other fibre / resin combinations;
- there is a need to understand how composite properties relate to those of the components;
- it is necessary to understand how composite properties change With fibre volume fraction and fibre orientation;
- care must be exercised to allow for the very low transverse and shear properties of the materials.

However, the very variety of raw materials and methods of combining them in the final product, plus the excellent specific properties give the designer a new freedom to tailor the material to the function required.

In order to take full advantage of the potential of the fibre-reinforced polymer matrix composites in engineering applications, the (often additional) cost of materials and fabrication methods must be offset by design solutions which are directed to specific applications. Effective design with composites means exploiting all the advantages that they can offer to provide either competitive alternatives to existing materials, or specific, unique, benefits such as mass reduction or a smaller number of parts. To achieve this it is important to think in terms of the com posite from the beginning of the design process.

One-for-one substitution of a metal component already integrated into a structure with a composite equivalent is unlikely to be satisfactory. The composite unit must not only be judged in terms of the cost of materials and fabrication but also in terms of, possibly, reduced weight or simpler assembly.

3

Designing in Fibre Reinforced Plastics

Fibre reinforced plastics offer almost unlimited possibilities for shape, size and colour mid can be produced with a variety of surface fmishes. Sandwich construction can be used for lightweight mouldings. Unidirectional carbon fibre is used as reinforcement, exceptional strength to weight ratios can be achieved. However, before any object can be made it has to be designed.

Factors which influence design are

1. resin selection
2. reinforcement selection and moulding process.

The choice of moulding process will be affected by

1. the number of mouldings to be produced,
2. production rate,
3. moulding complexity and .
4. size of moulding.

Another factor which may need to be considered is the means by which the finished moulding will be transported to its final destination. In the case of very large objects this may mean that several moulded parts have to be produced for assembly on site.

In many cases the final design will be a compromise between the requirements of the designer and the moulder. In this respect there should be considerable liaison between designer and moulder to ensure that the final moulding meets as many of the original design requirements as is possible, taking into account production rate and moulding cost. Often all requirements may be met with no difficulty.

Selection of Material

Some of the factors which need to be considered are listed below.

1. Mechanical/physical properties:
   Strength/weight ratio.
   Specific gravity.
   Is Strength, stiffness or impact resistance of prime importance?
   Is fatigue life important?
   Is the component structural or non-structural?

2. Thermal properties/fire resistance:
   Heat deflection temperature.
   Operating temperature.
   Coefficient of expansion.
   Humidity conditions.
   Fire resistance.

3. Chemical resistance:
   Will contact be with liquids or gases, aqueous or solvent solutions?
   Is it a mixture or single component?
   Is contact continuous or intermittent?
   Will the composition change from one period to the next?
   What are the operating temperatures and temperature fluctuations?
   Is the material acidic, alkaline, oxidising or reducing?

4. Biological:

   Is food contact involved?
   Are bacteria, microbes or termites likely to cause a problem?

5. Electrical properties:

   Breakdown voltage, tracking resistance.
   Surface and volume resistivity.
   Dielectric constant, dissipation factor (tan □).

6. Outdoor weathering:

   UV exposure.
   Will the moulding be subjected to tropical, marine, European or arctic climate and for how long?

7. Clarity and colour:

   Transparent, translucent or opaque.
   Colour.
   Surface finish. Resistance to yellowing.

8. Which performance specifications have to be met:

9. Performance testing and guarantees:

   Who carries out testing and to which specifications and under which conditions if a choice exists?

Process Selection

Once the above factors have been considered. Other factors have to considered, some of which may well be influenced by material choice and operating temperature. Some of these points are:

Moulding size—is the moulding small, medium or large?

Unit cost—this includes material and production costs.

Is a gelcoat required ?— not possible with SMC/DMC.

Number of mouldings and production rate. Is it a one-off moulding or are 10,000 mouldings required? This affects not only choice of moulding process but also the type of mould to be used.

Is one smooth surface acceptable?— if so, an open mould process can be used, or must both surfaces be smooth?—in which case a closed mould process is necessary.

How does section thickness vary?

What is the overall shape?

Can the moulding be produced by filament winding, pultrusion, continuous sheet production or some other automated process?

Are there any undercuts? If there are, then a split mould will be needed.

Are the major surfaces flat, of single curvature or double curvature?

With large flat surfaces, must these be free from shrink marks? If so, then a hot cured low profile resin system will be needed.

Are there any sharp edges or small radii to be accommodated? If so, then a press moulding process may be needed.

Is sandwich construction required?

Are ribs or buoyancy panels to be included in the moulding?

Is precise fibre alignment required to obtain design strength in any particular direction?

Is heat cure required to achieve maximum chemical or thermal resistance?

If themoulding is large, is there a suitable press or post curing oven available or must a heated mould be used?

Once these questions and perhaps others have been answered it is probable that the choice of manufacturing process will have been narrowed down to just one or two processes, in which case design can then proceed. Alternatively the production process may have been selected at an early stage and design and material selection geared to this.

Section thickness

Section thickness can affect a number of factors, including mechanical strength, material costs, production. costs, cycle times and peak curing temperature.

By increasing the reinforcement to resin ratio, mechanical strength can be increased for any given laminate thickness. This can also be affected by the type of reinforcement used. Typical reinforcements, which may be used, listed in order of increasing strength, include chopped strands woven rovings and unidirectional rovings.

Care must be taken during the production of thick section to ensure that there is not excessive heat build-up from exothermic heat of reaction. This can result in discoloration of the moulding and can also produce distortion and shrinkage marks. Thick sections may have to be built up in stages, allowing the exothermic heat to dissipate at each stage. Since FRP laminates are generally poor thermal conductors, this may be a relatively slow process and will clearly slow down production rate. Care must also be taken to ensure that no delamination occurs when the fmal moulding is put into service.

Flanges and corners

Flanges can provide adequate stiffening on small mouldings without the need to incorporate ribs. Their design will depend to some extent on the moulding process, particularly with regard to the radius of the corner. Some typical recommended minimum radii are given below.

Hand/spray lay-up	6 mm
Pressure / vaccum bag	12 mm
Preform / matched die Moulding	3 mm
SMC/DMC	0.5 mm

Inserts

Inserts for the subsequent assembly of panels can be incorporated with little difficulty, particularly with hand or spray lay-up techniques. Generally the laminate will be increased in thickness around the insert to hold it in place and to provide adequate stress distribution. Many different threaded inserts are available with large perforated heads to ensure adequate bonding and to prevent them from being pulled out during use.

Flat Sheets

These can be produced by continuous laminating by machine in a similar manner to corrugated sheets. Other methods used include hot press moulding with sheet moulding compounds and hand/ spray lay-up. With hand/ spray lay-up a slow curing resin system will generally give a better distortion - free laminate than a fast curing system.

It is only since the introduction of low profile sheet moulding compounds that it has 'been possible to product large flat mouldings, free from shrink marks, by hot press moulding techniques. Hot press moulding offers considerable production advantages for such items as vehicle bodies where high production rates are necessary.

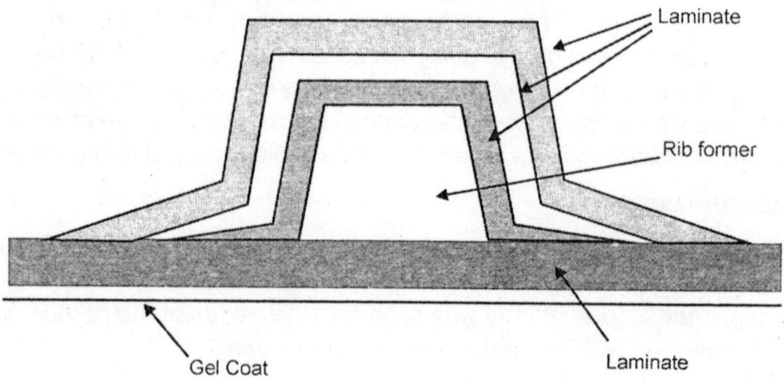

Laminate lay-up over preformed rib.

Where ribs have to be added to flat sheets for stiffening, these should be applied after the laminate has cured, otherwise shrinkage will occur resulting in sink marks appearing on the opposite side of the laminate. Ribs are frequently made from performed profiles applied to the laminate and then over laminated, each successive layer of mat placed over the rib being slightly larger than the preceding one to ensure adequate load distribution. These profiles, which may be hollow or solid, may consist of rigid foam, paper rope, cardboard, preformed laminates or a variety of other materials. A typical lay-up is shown in figure.

Building and Cladding Panels

These can be produced in a variety of ways, as flat or contoured sheets, or by sandwich construction. Great care should be taken in the design of joints to withstand thermal movements and in the case of cladding panels, to resist weathering and rain penetration. Further information on design and specification of G RP cladding can be found in a conference report on this topic.

Hollow Structures

These may consist of structures open on one side only, such as tanks, troughs and boats, all of which can be produced by conventional technigues. Alternatively they may consist of structures open on two sides, such as pipes. Here, filament winding or centrifugal casting can be used for production. With filament winding or centrifugal casting can be used for production. With filament winding, pipes of up to about 400 mm diameter can be made on a solid mandrel; above the size a split or collapsible mandrel should be used. The mandrel predetermines the inside diameter of the pipe. With centrifugal casting the mould determines the external diameter.

With filament winding, where greater chemical resistance is required than can be obtained with the resin system alone, a liner may be applied to the mandrel surface before winding commences. This liner ay be a thermoplastic such as PVC or a synthetic rubber, depending on end use.

Closed hollow structures can be made by filament winding on a water soluble or low melting wax or alloy mandrel. In this case the mandrel can only be used once and is removed after winding and cure is completed. Such structures find application as pressure vessels for storage and particularly as pressure vessels for rockets and other space activities. Such vessels are frequently made with epoxide resin systems.

4

Details of Moulds

Before any moulding process can be undertaken a suitable mould must be made. This is one of the most important steps since it affects the quality of the moulding and ease of production. A poor quality mould can result in many scrap mouldillgs.

With the wide range of possible moulding processes available, many different types of mould are required. These can be made from a similarly wide variety of materials including wood, plaster, concrete, epoxide and polyester resins, non-ferrous metals, steel or a combination of these. However, the most commonly used material is glass fibre reinforced polyester (GRP).

Factors which affect choice of mould material include the number and size of the mouldings to be produced, the type and finish required and the moulding process. For long runs, matched metal moulds are invariably used but, where only a few mouldings are to be produced, wooden or plaster moulds will often suffice. Intermediate quantities of mouldings, ranging from a few hundreds to a thousand or so, are generally produced using GRP moulds, which epoxy moulds becoming more common as the number of mouldings increases above this. Typical mould life for a number of different mould materials is shown in table.

Whichever mould material chosen, the finished moulding will reproduce an exact replica of the mould surface in reverse, and moulding accuracy and tolerance will be governed by the accuracy and rigidity with which the mould is made.

Mould Material	Number of releases	Process suitability: Hand/ spray lay-up	Press Moulding: cold	Press Moulding: hot
Plaster	1–5	feasible		
Wood	1–100	feasible		
GRP—stiffened	100-200	common		
GRP—filled with concrete	100-3000		common	
Steel	upto 1 million			common

Plaster Moulds

These can be divided into two broad categories: those made as master patterns for GRP mould production or those used directly of moulding. an example of the latter type can be found in the filament winding of cylinders and spheres where the mould is used once and then has to be broken up to extract it from the moulding.

In general, it is unlikely that a solid block of plaster will be used as a pattern; more probably a wooden frame will be prepared which will than be covered with plaster. A typical plaster pattern is shown in figure. This consists of a wooden frame suitably prepared with braces and stringers to keep it rigid. It must be solid enough to support the weight of plaster to be used and must not distort during preparation of the GRP mould. Wire netting is fixed to the frame to act as support for the plaster. Next several layers of plaster reinforced with hessian are applied, followed by a layer of plaster roughly shaped to the final pattern. The pattern is finished with a thin layer of plaster carefully applied to bring it to the correct dimensions for the mould. This final layer must be accurately finished and well polished to ensure a smooth surface. It is preferable to use a low expansion type of plaster for this application. Once the pattern has been completed it should be allowed to dry for at least 24 h before hardening at between 60 and 80°C for an hour or two. after the plaster pattern has been hardened its dimensions should be checked to ensure that no changes have taken place. Any oversize areas can be very lightly rubbed down.

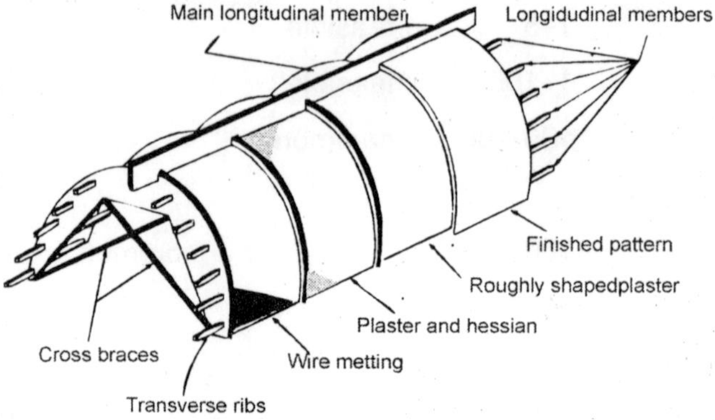

Construction of a plaster pattern

Construction of a plaster pattern.

Since plaster moulds are porous the surface must be scaled with a solution of shellac, cellulose acetate, nitrocellulose or polyvinyl alcohol before waxing and polishing. More than one coat of sealer may be necessary depending on the porosity of the surface. It is this surface which will be reproduced on the GRP mould and hence on the final mouldings and so extreme care at this stage will be well rewarded.

Whilst a pattern of this type is generally used to prepare a GRP mould it can also be used to make a prototype moulding. Clearly, if this is the case, it will have to be made. in the shape of the mould rather than as a prototype of the finished moulding.

With the filament winding of spheres and cylinders some form of disposable mandrel has to be used, since these are continuous structures with only a small hole at either end. One procedure is to use a plaster or clay mandrel which is strong enough to withstand the winding process but which can be washed out with water after use. Such mandrels can be hollow cast in two sections and then assembled and coated with a further layer of plaster to give a smooth continuous finish.

Wooden Moulds

These may be carved from solid blocks of wood or constructed from several pieces stuck together. Plywood or block board can be used for flat surfaces. Whichever procedure is adopted the quality of the mould affects the quality of the moulding. The skills required for mould making are those needed in coach building or cabinet making.

GRP Moulds

These are made from glass reinforced polyester resin systems by hand or spray lay-up techniques, on patterns which may be made from wood, plaster or any other suitable material. One of the main reason for the prevalence of such moulds is that moulders haveall the necessary materials readily to hand.

In preparing a pattern for a GRP mould, due account should be taken of the shrinkage of the resin during cure. Once the pattern has been completed, it must be sealed to make it nonporous and then polished to a high gloss finish using silicone-free wax polish. This should be applied in several layers polishing each as it is applied. As many as six coats of polish may be necessary. Next the pattern should be coated with a release film of polyvinyl alcohol by cloth, sponge or spray, making sure that this film is completely uniform with no imperfections and so dust, hairs or other foreign particles present. This film must be allowed to dry thoroughly before any resin is applied to it, otherwise the laminate may stick to the pattern and cause irreparable damage.

During the design of a mould, consideration should be given as to how the edge of the mould will be finished. In many cases, if suitably reinforced, the edge can act as a guide for trimming 'green' mouldings.

Single one-part moulds

The gelcoat should be applied to the suitably released pattern by brush, roller or spray, to a thickness of about 0.6 mm. This is roughly double the thickness recommended for mouldings, to allow for rubbing down during the life of the mould. To assist in this rubbing down process, the gelcoat can be applied in three layers to alternate colours, for example, black, green, black. In this way rubbing down can be controlled with no fear of going down to the glass reinfrocement. The colours should preferably contrast with that to be used for the final moulding. If mouldings are to be produced which do not require a high gloss finish, a self-releasing gelcoat can be used for the mould surface.

When the gelcoat has cured sufficient to give a tacky surface, a coat of laminating resin system is applied, into which is placed a layer of surfacing tissue followed by a layer of 300 g/m^2 chopped stand mat. This should be thoroughly consolidated with a laminating roller to eliminating all voids.

Further resin and reinforcement are applied by either hand or spray layup techniques, allowing the resin to gel between the application of each two layers of reinforcement. This is to prevent any exotherm from occuring and to prevent any stresses from being built into the laminate which may distort the mould during use.

To prolong the life of a mould a heat resistant resin system may be used. Once the final coat of resin system has been applied, the mould should be allowed to cure for at least two weeks at room temperature. In addition a post cure of several cure of several hours at 65-70°C can be given to prevent distortion during use.

Large moulds should be stiffened with ribs on the reverse side. These can be constructed from plastic of metal tubing, foamed plastic or paper rope. Wooden ribs may also be used but these may cause distortion of the mould after prolonged use. The formers should be shaped to the contours of the mould and covered with two or three layers of resin impregnated glass reinforcement. It is essential that the main laminate is cured and is of adequate thickness before application of the ribs, to prevent contractions of the resin around the ribs causing sink marks in the laminate surface.

The mould should, not be removed from the pattern until it is fully curved. Any modification or fixing which need to be applied to the mould are best carried out whilst the mould is still on the pattern, providing this does not impede removal from the pattern.

Most moulds will require mounting on a frame so that they stand flat on the floor or can be rotated or titled. Such frames may be of wooden or tubular metal construction and should be sufficiently rigid to prevent distortion of the mould during use. They can also be used to support the mould during post cure.

Where greater rigidity of the mould is needed, the back can be filled with a rigid polyurethane foam composition, foamed in place.

Epoxide Resin Moulds

Epoxide resin moulds can be some ways be considered as intermediate between GRP and steel moulds. They have long service lives with many thousands of mouldings being produced from one mould. Since epoxy moulds generally have a specific gravity of around 1.8, there is a considerable weight saving over steel moulds. Also, unlike steel, epoxy moulds will not corrode and therefore do not require protecting with grease during storage. If damaged, they can be frequently be repaired with no long term detrimental effect. Steel moulds on the other hand are in most cases impossible to repair if damaged.

Epoxide resins also offer several advantages over polyester resins for mould making. They exhibit negligible shrinkage during cure, remain dimensionally stable once cured and can be cast in thick cross-sections with low exotherm, providing that the correct system has been selected. In the main, the properties of epoxide resin systems are governed by the choice of curing agent or hardener rather than the resin, although the final cured properties depend on both the resin and curing agent used.

Steel Moulds

These are required for hot press, centrifugal, transfer and injection moulding pultrusion. They may also be used with other moulding processes. The fabrication of steel moulds is a highly skilled operation best left to experienced tool makers and so will only be considered briefly here. Tool steel and meehanite, flame hardened and hard chrome plated are undoubtedly the best materials although other metals such as zinc and aluminium may also be used. In designing the mould, an adequate taper must be incorporated to permit easy removal of the moulding.

Centrifugal moulding

Most moulds used for centrifugal moulding are cylindrical and made from tool steel with a hard chrome finish. Tapered moulds may be used for rods and tubes according to one patented process. Whichever mould design is used, the mould must be evenly balanced about its central axis to prevent any asymmetrical thrust on the bearings during rotation.

Transfer and injection moulding

Moulds used for transfer and injection moulding can be of single- or multi -cavity design and are broadly similar to those used for the injection moulding of thermoplastic materials. However, thermosets are generally harder, more rigid and less easily deformed than thermoplastics and so moulds must be designed for the particular material to be processed. They are usually made from hardened tool steel and chrome plated to about 0.07 mm thickness.

Pultrusion

With pultrusion, heated dies rather than moulds are used. These should be made from hard chrome plated, hardened tool steel for preference. Two types of die are used, those through which fibres impregnated with resin from a resin bath are drawn and those which incorporate injection nozzles to impregnate the fibres within the die. These need to be designed to suit the particular equipment being used. As with matched metal moulds an experienced die maker should be employed.

Aluminium Alloy moulds

These are light in weight with high rigidity and provide a good quality finish. They are not as hard wearing as steel moulds and can therefore be more easily damaged. They are, however easier to machine.

Nickel Shell Moulds

A nickel shell backed by a resin core can give a life similar to that achieved with steel but at reduced mould cost. Such moulds can be used for the resin injection moulding process.

Other moulds

Example of these include wax, water soluble hot melt thermoplastics and inflatable balloons used for the manufacture of cylinders and spheres by filament winding. The reason for using these materials in ease of removal once the winding has been completed and the resin cured. Hollow plaster and wax mandrels can be used. These are made in two halves which are then joined together to form the finished mandrel.

5

Processes of Moulding

Contact Moulding -Wet Lay up

Contact moulding is the most commonly used method for the manufacture of both small and large reinforced polyester products such as boat hulls, vehicle bodies, GRP building panels and cladding, ducts and tanks and many other mouldings where small production runs are required. A single mould is used, with the laminate applied to the suitably released mould surface. The result is a moulding with only one smooth surface, that is contact with the mould. Moulding thickness is generally in the range 2-10 mm although there is no basic upper limit.

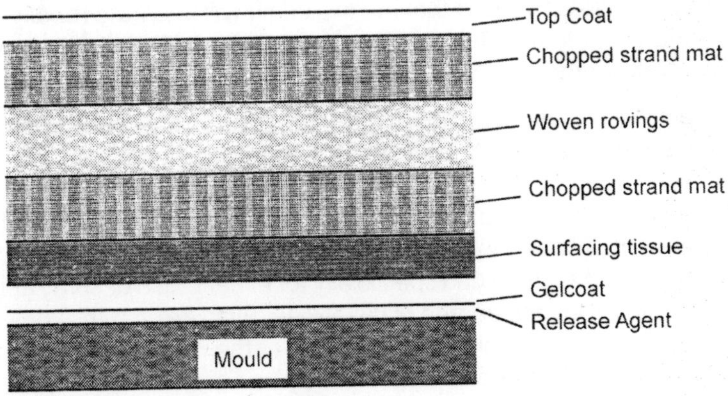

Typical laminate construction.

Since the resins most widely used with this process are the polyester resins, moulding procedure has been described with these in mind. Epoxide and other resin systems are discussed later on.

The mould is frequently made form GRP using one of the specially developed tooling grade polyester resins. Such moulds generally have a life of between 500 and 1000 releases. Other mould materials used include tooling rade epoxide resin systems, wood plaster of paris and metal supported on a suitable framework. A metal mould will give the greatest number of releases and provide the longest working life but will be the most expensive to produce.

Two fabrication techniques are used :

a. hand lay-up;
b. spray lay-up.

Mould preparation and gelcoat application, is the same for both techniques.

Before use, the mould surface must be coated with a good quality silicone-free wax and thoroughly polished to give a smooth glossy finish. For a new mould severl applications of wax may be necessary to build up sufficient thickness. A mould release agent such as polyvinyl alcohol is then generally applied using spray or spong rather than brush, since brushing can result in a streaky finish. For the best results two coats should be applied, allowing the first to dry before application of the second coat. It is essential that the mould is completely covered, leaving no bare patches, since the gelcoat will reproduce any defects in this release film. Care at this stage is well rewarded by the quality of the moulding produced. The advantage of using polyvinyl alcohol as the release film is that the moulding will separate readily from the mould and the release film can then the washed off both the mould and moulding with water.

When the release agent is completely dry, the gelcoat is applied by brush or spray. With brush application a wide brush with long soft hairs is preferred and two coats and generally necessary to prevent brush marks from showing, the second coat being applied once the first has sufficiently cured (2—4 h). With srpay application, the full thickness can be applied in one coat. Gelcoat are supplied specifically for either brush or spray application and usually differ in their degree of thixotropy. Final gelcoat thickness should be between 0.3 and 0.6 mm and uniform over the whole mould surface. Gel time of the gelcoat is bulk should preferably be about 15 min. Styrene fumes should be extracted from the mould using a suitable extraction system to ensure even gelation of the gelcoat.

The conditio of the gelcoat can be determined by touching it. If it feels tacky but is not easily removed by the finger, then it is ready for application of the next coat of resin system.

In some cases a surfacing tissue may be used to reinforce the gelcoat. This is applied immediately after the gelcoat while the resin is still wet and lightly rolled to displace all air bubbles outwards. This procedure does, however, result in a lower quality surface finish. Also, since the durability of the moulding depends on the quality of the exposed surface, this procedure is not recommended where the moulding is to be subjected to wet or chemical environments. A surface tissue may, however, be applied with the first coat of laminating resin where it is beneficial is protecting the reinforcement, particularly when the moulding is used in wet or chemical environments. In this way the resin-rich surface provided by the gelcoat is preserved.

Most moulding faults can be traced back to insufficient care during application of the gelcoat. Insufficient film thickness can result in excessive evaporation of styrene monomer from the gelcoat so that is dries instead of cures. Too rapid an application of the second layer of gelcoat or the laminating resin, before the first layer has cured, can result in the wrinkled finish. Too thick a gelcoat can, even several months after demoulding, crack and craze and is also more sensitive to impact on the reverse side of the moulding, when cracks and other damage may occur.

Hand lay-up

Once the gelcoat has sufficient cured, a coat of laminating resin system is applied by brush, paint roller or spray followed by the first layer of chopped strand mat (preferably 300 g/m^2 or less) or if desired a surface tissue. Since surface tissues are relatively expensive they are generally only used where a very high quality finish is needed or where the mouldings are to be subjected to chemical environments and therefore good durability is essential. Sufficient resin should be applied to wet out completely this first layer of reinforcement so that all trapped air can be forced out by rolling with a split washer or similar type of laminating roller. At the corners of the mould the glass mat should be cut and butted together to ensure that bridging does not occur. Rolling her may be best accomplished by the use of a single washer roller or a stippling brush. The resin to glass ratio at this stage should be about 2:1. Once all the air has been displaced and the mat thoroughly impregnated with resin it can be advantageous to allow this layer to gel before laminating is continued.

With large moulds, where more than one sheet of chopped strand mat has to be applied to cover the surface, these sheets may either be butted together and the joint compacted using a stippling brush with a rotating motion to spread the strands across the joint or applied with about 30 mm overlap.

It is essential that joints in different layers are staggered to prevent either excessive laminate thickness or laminate weakness at the join.

Advantages and disadvantages of hand lay-up

Advantages

1. Simple technique
2. Low capital costs– cheap moulds.
3. Large complex shapes can be produced.
4. No process limitation on moulding size.

Disadvantages

1. High labour content.
2. Low production speed.
3. Moulding quality is dependent on operator skill.
4. Mouldings have only one smooth glossy surface.

Spray lay-up

Once the gelcoat has sufficiently cured the laminate can be applied. If a surface tissue is to be used a layer of laminating resin is applied to the gelcoat either by brush, roller or spray and the surface tissue, previously cut to shape, laid in the wet resin and rolled carefully to displace all trapped air outwards. The laminate is then built up from chopped fibre rovings and polyester resin sprayed simultaneously onto the mould. Continuous rovings are red to an air driven chopper unit attached to the spray gun, where they are cut into suitable lengths (12-62mm) and conveyed to the mould surface by the stream of polyester resin from the spray gun. Three types of spray equipment are available.

1. The catalyst injection system where pre-accelerated polyester resin is fed to the spray gun and mixed with a pre-determined proportion of peroxide catalyst in the gun head.

2. The catalyst spray system where pre-accelerated polyester resin and peroxide catalyst are both fed to the spray gun and sprayed separately so that the two streams of material mix outside the gun but before reaching the mould surface.

3. The twin pot system where pre-accelerated and pre-catalysed polyester resin are fed separately to the spray gun and sprayed so that the two streams of material mix outside the gun head but before reaching the mould surface.

All spray guns and ancillary equipment contaminated withcatalysed resin must be thoroughly cleaned immediately after use to prevent clogging from gelled resin particles and to prevent such particles from contaminating the laminate.

Before spray lay-up is commenced the gel time of the resin system should be checked by spraying a small quantity of resin system without glass, into a can. Also, the resin/glass ratio should be checked to ensure that the spray gun and chopper unit the functioning correctly. Generally the resin to glass ratio will be between 2:5: 1 and 3.5:1.

The flrst layer of polyester resin and glass flbre should be thinly applied (approx. lmm) and rolled carefully, first with a short-nap mohair roller and then with a metal laniinating roller to ensure that the catalysed and accelerated resins are thoroughly mixed and the glass completely wetted out. Care should be taken to ensure that no air bubbles are trapped in this layer and that the resin glass mixture completely wets the gelcoat with no bridging in the corners. This layer of laminate should preferably be allowed to gel before further application of resin or glass.

Subsequent layers of resin/glass can be built up at about 2 mm per time, rolling thoroughly as before between each application to disperse all air inclusions. If thicker layers are applied between rolling, difficulty will be experienced in removing all trapped air and an inferior laminate will result. This procedure is continued until the require laminate thickness has been achieved. A stronger laminate can be produced if alternate layers are sprayed at 90° to each other.

As with hand lay-up, woven rovings can be incorporated into the laminate to increase stiffness and to strengthen it. If these are to be used sufficient resin system must be sprayed into the mould prior to applying the woven rovings so that on rolling the resin system displaces the air outwards as the resin is forced through the reinforcement. Resin sprayed on top of poorly wetted rovings will result in air entrapment. The woven rovings should be cut to size prior to laminating and should always be alternated with sprayed laminate to give a strong com posite structure. Without this layer of sprayed laminate in between each layer of woven rovings, there is a risk that the laminate will fail in shear when flexed in service.

The largest area practicable should be sprayed at anyone time prior to rolling, to minimise overspray. Care should be taken to ensure that each sprayed layer is thoroughly consolidated before the resin begins to gel.

Where very thick laminates are to be made, it may be desirable to build the laminate up in several stages, allowing the resin to gel after each stage. In this way excessive exotherm can be prevented and the laminate remains controllable during application.

Spray rates can generally be varied between 2 and 10 kg of laminate per minute with most spray equipment.

With deep moulds styrene fumes should be removed from the mould using an appropriate extraction system to ensure uniform cure of the laminate.

As with hand lay-up, a surfacing tissue may be applied to the final layer of sprayed laminate to give a relatively smooth resin-rich fmish. This can then be coated with a topcoat to balance up the laminate and seal all the glass reinforcement in.

Cure, trimming, post cure and demoulding are the same as for hand lay-up.

Epoxide resins

A similar spray technique can be employed with epoxide resins. However, due to the different mixing ratios of resin to curing agent, polyester spray equipment is generally unsuitable. The resin and curing agent can either be pre-mixed and sprayed through a single-component spray gun or used separately with a two-component gun fitted with appropriate metering pumps to ensure that the correct resin/ curing agent ratio is maintained. This will generally vary from 4: I up to 5:3. With some resin systems heated two-com ponent spray equipment may have to be used. All other laminating procedures are the same as for polyester resins.

Furane resins

Equipment has recently become available for spray lay-up with furane resin systems. Procedures are similar to those use with polyester resin systems.

Advantages and disadvantages of spray lay-up Advantages

1. Spray equipment is portable.
2. Capital outlay is small compared with other mechanised techniques.
3. Rovings are used, the least expensive form of reinforcement.
4. Production rates can be higher than with hand lay-up since shorter gel times can be tolerated.
5. Reduced labour costs are obtained with high volume production.

Disadvantages

1. Mouldings have only one smooth surface.
2. Uniformity of lay-up depends even more than with hand lay-up on the skill of the operator.
3. Spray lay-up is uneconomical for small volume production.
4. An even spray pattern is difficult to achieve on small moulds.

Vacuum Bag Moulding

Vacuum bag moulding can be used both with wet lay-up systems and prepregs. It is suitable for limited production runs and for the manufacture of complex components which cannot be made practically by compression moulding. Both large and small components can be made and it is frequently used for the production of aircraft parts. One advantage that prepreg systems have over wet lay-up is that unidirectional prepregs can be used and accurate fibre alignment achieved. This can be essential for aerospace applications where strength to weight ratio is of prime importance.

Epoxide and polyster resin systems are equally suitable for processing by vacuum bag moulding as are glass, carbon and. synthetic fibre reinforcements.

Wet lay-up

A single mould is used— either male or female—to which the laminate is applied by either hand or spray lay-up. Before gelation of the resin, pressure is exerted on the moulding by means of a flexible bag, frequently made from neoprene. This is brought about by sucking air out of the bag with a vacuum pump. It is generally necessary to tailor to bag to the shape of the mould to prevent wrinkles from forming in it and the laminate. Heat is frequently applied to speed up cure. The mould is coated with release agent and the wet lay-up applied by either hand or spray techniques and consolidated. A porous release cloth or flim is then placed directly onto the wet resin to permit easy separation from the rest of the bagging material. This release material may consist of a light glass cloth fabric (70 g/m^2) coated with PTFE or a Cellophane, Layers of bleeder cloth are next placed over the release material. The number of layers will depend on the component thickness and amount of resin to be absorbed. These layers ensure efficient removal of air and surplus resin from inside the bag. Glass mat, jute or paper cloths may be used as bleeder cloth. These should extend some 100-200 mm on either side of the component. With flat mouldings a pressure plate may be placed over the laminate to give a smooth top surface and to equalise the pressure. If this is done, a further layer of bleeder cloth is generally placed over the pressure plate to ensure that all air pockets are eliminated. Edge dams of compressible material may be placed around the edge of the layup to prevent excessive sideways movement and tapering of the moulding.

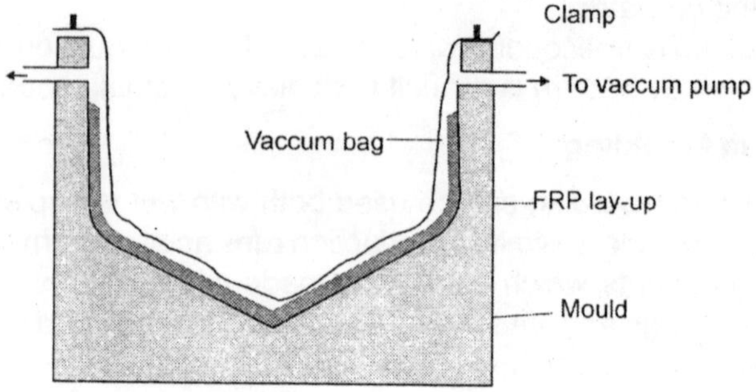

Vaccum bag moulding

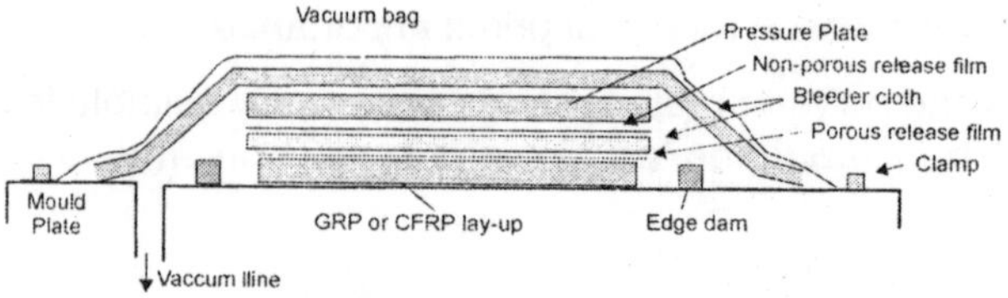

Flat sheet vacuum bag moulding.

Once all the various layers are in position the vacuum bag is placed over the whole assembly and sealed around the edges. Vacuum is then slowly applied. As air is withdrawn from the bag, air pockets and wrinkles can be smoothed out using a roller. Where heat cure is to be used the whole assembly is transferred to an oven or autoclave. The cure cycle will depend on the resin system being used. Vacuum should only be released after the moulding has cooled to room temperature. After cure the moulding is removed from the vacuum bag, the bleeder cloth and release fIlm stripped off and the edges trimmed. Post cure can then be given if necessary.

Prepreg system

Prepreg systems used with vacuum bag moulding include polyester sheet moulding compounds, epoxide resin impregnated cloths, unidirectional glass and carbon fIbre systems.

The prepreg is cut to shape and placed in the mould by hand, taking care to ensure that all trimmings are excluded from the mould. Where unidirectional prepregs are used these are generally cross-plied at some predetermined angle to provide maximum strength, perhaps in one direction, in the cured moulding.

Once the prepreg has been placed in the mould it is covered with an appropriate layer of perforated release film or fabric and bleeder cloth. The procedure thereafter is identical to that used for processing wet lay-up systems, except that with prepreg, heat cure is essential. The application of heat causes the resin to melt and flow together to give a uniform composite.

The vacuum bag technique can be combined with the pressure bag technique, whereby pressure is applied to the outside of the bag once the bag has been evacuated. This has the advantage that a higher pressure can be applied to the laminate than can be achieved by vacuum alone. In practice this is generally accomplished by using an autoclave. The bag is first evacuated then pressure is applied and finally the vacuum lines are vented to the atmosphere. Where pressure is applied by means of an autoclave, normal strength moulds can be used since the pressure is applied to all sides of the mould. If, however, pressure is applied to one side of the mould only, then a stronger mould may be necessary.

Since thin sections are often moulded by the vacuum bag technique, great care needs to be taken to the removal of the laminate from the mould and in stripping off the release film, since damage to the laminate can easily occur.

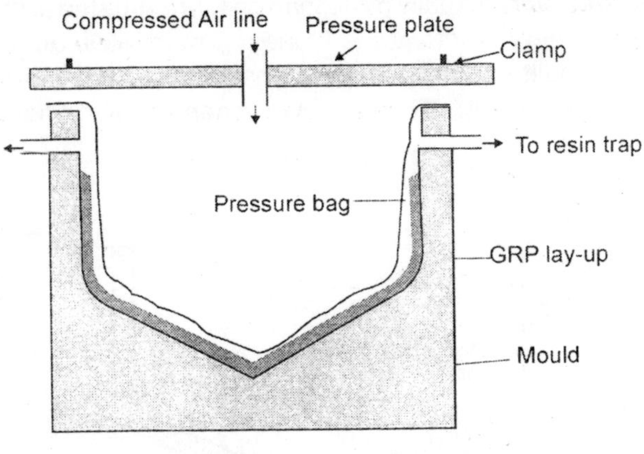

Pressure bag moulding

Pressure Bag Moulding

This is similar to vacuum bag moulding. Both prepreg and wet lay-up systems can be used, with pressure applied to the outside of an inflatable bag placed over the laminate. The advantage of this technique over vacuum bag moulding is that a higher pressure can be applied to the laminate. However, where pressure is applied to one side of the mould only, then a very strong mould be used. the altemative is to use an autoclave, whereby heat and pressure can be applied simultaneously and to all sides of the mould. Higher pressures can be achieved using an autoclave than are possible with a pressure bag alone.

Lay-up is more or less identical to that used for vacuum bag moulding except that the perforated release sheet is replaced by a solid release film and bleeder fabric is unnecessary since excess resin is squeezed to the edge of the mould.

Resin Injection or Resin Transfer Moulding

Resin injection or resin transfer moulding is an intermediate process between contact moulding and cold press moulding, suitable for use with polyester and epoxide resin systems. The process is generally suitable for runs of between 100 and 1000 mouldings.

Mouldings produced by resin injection have two smooth moulded surfaces and can be made in matched GRP or lightweight metal moulds. Although moulds have to be stiffened to withstand injection pressure they do not have to be as heavy as for cold press moulding. Both mould halves are designed to fit tightly together with a rubber gasket seal and are usually fitted with quick release clamps. Injection points, usually more than one, are situated at the lowest part of the mould and vent points at the highest part to allow air to escape. An overspill area is built into the mould to ensure that after trimming, a good quality moulded edge is left. This is shown schematically in figure.

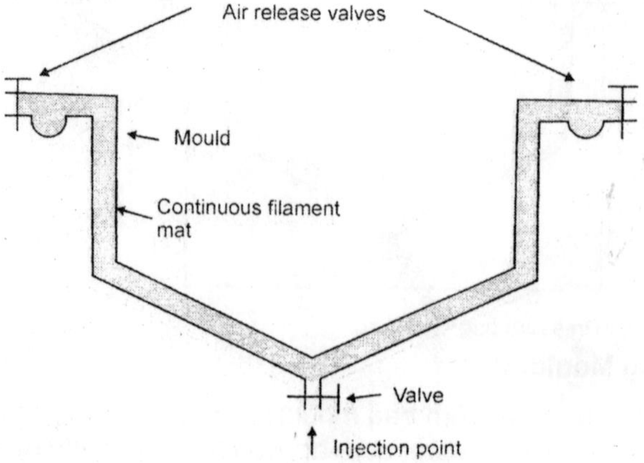

Resin injection

Correct mould design is essential to ensure that mouldings of the correct weight and dimensions are produced. Any excess moulding thickness will only waste expensive materials. Since injection pressures of up to 2 MPa are used the mould must be designed accordingly.

As with other moulding processes both mould halves are cleaned, polished and coated with release agent. A gelcoat is then applied to both halves and allowed to cure. Reinforcement, cut to shape, is placed in one half of the mould and the mould closed. The reinforcement most often used is continuous filament mat although chopped strand mat and woven rovings, with a layer of continuous filament mat or chopped strand mat in contact with the mould surface, may also be used. If chopped strand mat is used it must have a styrene insoluble binder to prevent the fibres from being washed away as the resin is injected. If desired, a surfacing tissue can be used between the gelcoat and the reinforcement. The total weight of reinforcement used is generally of the order of 30% by weight of the finished moulding.

If ribs, stringers, frames or foam buoyancy panels are to be included in the moulding these are placed in appropriate positions within the mould before closure. They are usually wrapped with glass mat prior to insertion.

Resin is injected under pressure, starting with the lowest injection point, making sure first that all vents are open. Injection pressure can be up to 2 MPa, with volume ranging from 0.5 to 10 kg/min, depending on mould size and equipment available. Either twin pot or catalyst injection systems are available, both offering different advantages for different types of operation.

Vent holes are closed once the resin starts to exude from them. Similarly injection points are sealed once they are finished with, the final one being sealed when the mould has been completely filled. The injection nozzle can then be removed and the equipment used on another mould, thus making full use of it.

The moulding is generally allowed to cure at room temperature, although it may be transferred to an oven if required. Minimal trimming is necessary after cure. Demoulding is the same as for contact moulding, except that both halves of the mould have to be removed.

Resin systems should be designed for injection and should have low viscosities to ensure adequate penetration through the reinforcement. A high reactivity low exotherm system is preferred, with a pot-life long enough to permit the mould to be completely filled before gelation of the resin and preferably before any noticeable viscosity increase occurs. The system used should also have low shrinkage on cure to prevent shrinkage marks from marring the surface of the moulding. Care must be taken in selecting the catalyst/accelerator system, taking into account moulding thickness, to ensure that excessive exotherm does not occur. If this happens, distortion of the moulding may occur and certainly mould life will be shortened. Acetylacetone peroxide is often used as catalyst with a cobalt octoate accelerator. Reactivity can be boosted by using dimethylaniline as additional accelerator.

The advantages of the resin injection process over contact moulding are:

Advantages

1. Two smooth moulded surfaces
2. Constant shape and weigh mouldings
3. Higher moulding quality than can be achieved with a one-part mould.
4. Ribs and other parts can be moulded in one operation.
5. Styrene emission is reduced since it is a closed mould process.
6. Cure is less susceptible to draughts and changes in workshop temperature.
7. Lay-up is cleaner and less wasteful.
8. Labour costs are reduced.
9. Rapid mould turn-around can be obtained.

Disadvantages

1. Accurately made matched moulds are needed and several may be required to keep the injection equipment fully utilised.
2. Capital costs of equipment and moulds are higher.

Pressure Injection

Pressure injection is virtually the same as resin injection. However, moulds are generally heavier and of more solid construction. Chrome plated matched metal moulds, generally with provision for heating, are used, mostly with epoxide resin systems.

One area where pressure injection is of prime importance is in the manufacture of radomes for aircraft. All civil aircraft and most military aircraft are fitted with nose radomes. These house radar transmitting and receiving equipment and are radar transparent. They are classified as Class 1 structural parts whose failure during flight, take-off or landing could jeopardise the safety of the aircraft.

Rigid matched metal moulds are used since radomes have to be constructed to very high tolerances. Radomes are usually of sandwich construction, with an inner and outer skin 1 mm thick and a non-metallic honeycomb of foam core about 9 mm thick.

Reinforcements are usually of the woven or knitted type, tailored to shape. Reinforcement and core material is placed in the suitably released mould, the mould closed and resin injected under pressure. Heat cure is accomplished by fitting heating coils to both the outside and inside of the mould. Great care is needed to ensure that bubble free mouldings are produced.

Vacuum Impregnation and Injection

Vacuum impregnation is an alternative process to resin injection. In some ways it is more suited to epoxide resin systems which contain no volatile monomers, than to polyester systems which contain volatile styrene; however, both resin systems may be used. Vacuum impregnation is used for the manufacture of nose cones, randomes and circuit breaker tubes from heat cured epoxide resin systems.

An alternative process, used with polyester resins, is vacuum injection. The only real different is the way in which the resin is drawn into the mould. Various processes are in use and are described below. These processes can be used for the manufacture of a wide range of products, including boats and train cabs.

Vacuum impregnation

Heated matched metal moulds ate used, with a highly polished or chrome finish. The mould surface is treated with an appropriate release agent such as a silicone. Reinforcement is then placed in position and the top half of the mould lowered over the bottom half. The reinforcements used may consist of woven or knitted glass cloth tailored to size. Quick release clamps are used to hold the two halves of the mould together.

Once the mould has been assembled it is either lowered into a resin bath or fitted in such a way that resin can be fed to the bottom of the mould. Vacuum is applied to the top of the mould to suck the resin system up through the reinforcement until it completely fills the mould. Care must be taken to ensure that there is an adequate supply of resin at the bottom of the mould to prevent any air from being drawn in. It is also important to ensure that the resin system has been degassed under vacuum prior to use, otherwise degassing will take place in the mould, resulting in void formation in the laminate. External or internal heating may be applied to the mould to effect gelation and cure of the resin system. Once cure has been completed, demoulding and trimming can take place.

Mouldings can be made to very high tolerances by this technique.

Advantages

1. Two smooth surfaces on the moulding.
2. Constant shape and weight mouldings to very high tolerances.
3. Closed mould process—no fume emission.

Disadvantages

1. If used with heated matched moulds these are expensive.

Vacuum injection moulding

The vacuum injection process is a combination of vacuum bag moulding and resin injection. It was developed by Hoechst to overcome the disadvantages of the other two processes. To take full advantage of the process, special moulds and resins are necessary. The process can be used for the production of boat hulls as well as many other types of moulding.

Moulds are made from GRP, the lower half being of rigid construction 6-8 mm thick, whilst the upper half is more flexible and only 3-6 mm thick. It is this flexible half which is the essence of the process. A vacuum channel is built into the mould around the periphery for mould closure.

A resin with a viscosity of about 200 MPa s at 20°C is needed for this process.

As with other moulding processes the mould surfaces are waxed, polished and coated with PVA release agent. If a gelcoat is to be used, this is applied to the mould surface and allowed to cure prior to filing the lower half of the mould with reinforcement. The use of a gelcoat does, however, increase production time.

The reinforcement is cut to shape and fitted into the lower half of the mould. Gasket material is placed around the edge of the mould to forma a channel and the top half of the mould lowered into position. The reinforcements used may be chopped strand mat with a styrene insoluble binder, continuous strand mat or a combination of chopped strand mat and woven rovings. Glass content of the finished moulding can range from 25 to 50 depending on the type of reinforcement used. Surface tissue may be included if desired. As with other moulding processes, foam panels, balsa wood and ribs can be moulded in.

Once the upper half of the mould is in position, vacuum is applied to the gasket channel to close the mould and render it airtight. Catalysed resin is next injected, either under pressure (0.05-0.2 MPa) or by gravity feed (1 m

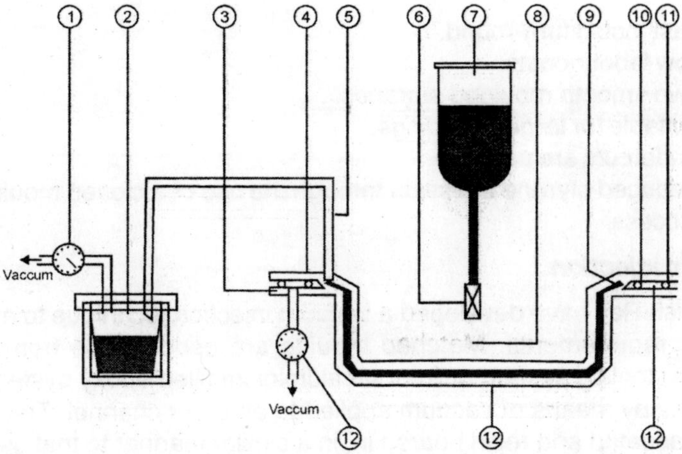

head), until the calculated amount has been added. The resin feed is then shut off. More than one injection point may be used on large moulds.. Finally the air remaining in the mould is sucked out, when the flexibie top half forces resin to flow through the reinforcement until the mat is thoroughly impregnated and compacted. Vacuum is maintained until the resin has cured. Demoulding and trimming is carried out in the normal way.

1 Pressure of 0.66–0.80 kp/cm^2 below atmospheric.
2 Trap for excess resin
3 Lower mould portion
4 Upper mould portion
5 Vacuum lead to resin suction channel
6 Cut-off valve
7 Resin supply reservoir
8 Injection connector
9 Peripheral resin suction channel
10 Peripheral sponge rubber gasket
11 Peripheral sponge rubber gasket
12 Pressure of ca. 0.13 kp/cm2 (130 mbar) below atmospheric
13 GRP moulding
14 Vacuum closing channel

Construction of two-part vacuum injection mould for the Hoechst process.

Advantages

1. Relatively low capital cost (similar to resin injection).

2. Fast mould turn-round.
3. Low labour costs.
4. Two smooth moulded surfaces. .
5. Suitable for large mouldings.
6. Undercuts are possible.
7. Reduced styrene emission through the use of a closed mould process.

Vacuum injection

British Rail have developed a vacuum injection technique to meet their specific requirements. Matched moulds are used, made from either a polyester tooling system or from an aluminium filled epoxy system. Mould closure is by means of vacuum applied to an outer channel. The mould is then evacuated and resin poured in, in a similar manner to that used in the Hoechst process. Gelcoats are used and inserts, such as plywood cores, may be included. By careful mould design, with loose mould pieces, undercuts may be moulded in.

Monoforming

This system is offered by J. Coudenhove GmbH, for use with polyester resin systems. Lightweight matched moulds are used with positive pressure resin injection and vacuum to hold the mould halves together and aid in consolidation of the laminate. The lower half of the mould is of rigid construction, supported on a suitable framework. The upper half is generally a sandwich of glass reinforced epoxy with a balsa wood core. Mould costs are claimed to be about three times those of a mould used for hand lay-up, but only one-filth to one- half of the cost of moulds needed for resin injection. Resin viscosity for use with the process should be of the order of 200-400 mPa s.

Foam Reservoir Moulding

Foam reservoir moulding (FRM) is a low pressure technique for the production of lightweight rigid composite structures with two smooth surfaces. Mouldings produced by this process have high strength to stiffness ratios. The process was initially developed for use with epoxide resin systems by Shell Research Ltd but can also be used with polyester resin systems. To date most applications and developments have been with epoxide resin systems.

Male and female moulds are required which, due to the low moulding pressure needed (0.1 MPa), can be manufactured from GRP for moderate temperature cure or lightweight metal for higher temperature cure. As with other moulding processes, care must be taken in preparing the mould surface and the application of release agent. Due to the nature of the process, moulding is always to stops.

The composite system used for this process consists of an open -celled flexible foam impregnated with resin system, sandwiched between two layers of glass reinforcement. The glass can be in the form of either chopped strand mat or woven fabric, depending on the shape and performance requirements of the moulding. Surfacing tissue may be included on either side if required. The foam used comprises two sheets of small open celled flexible urethane foam with a density in the region of 12-15 g/litre. One side of each sheet of foam is coated with the resin system, which may contain pigments and fillers, and the two layers sandwiched together, resin side inwards. This gives a resin foam sandwich which is dry to handle. Shelf-life depends on the resin system used and storage temperature,

To produce a moulding, glass or either reinforcement is placed in the mould followed by the resin foam sandwich, Further glass reinforcement is then placed over the foam and the mould closed slowly to stops, As the mould is closed resin is forced through the foam into the reinforement, displacing the air. Generally a compression ratio of 10: 1 is used. By careful selection of foam thickness and amount of reinforcement and resin system, a fully impregnated composite results. Heat is applied to cure the resin system. Pressure is maintained throughout the cure cycle. Once the resin system has cured the mould is cooled and demoulding can take place.

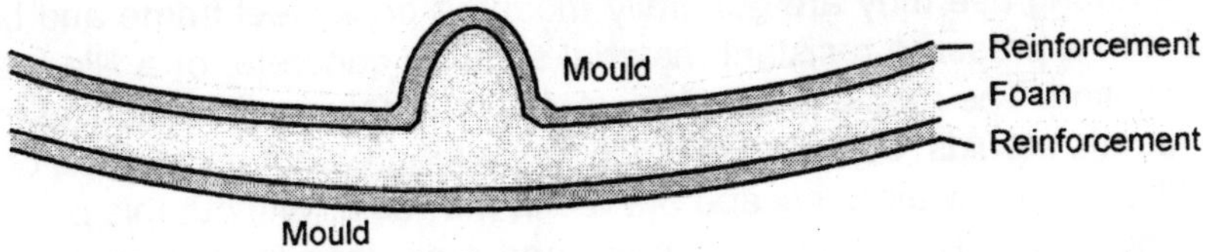

A typical FRM composite

Complex mould shapes can be readily produced since the foam takes up the mould shape and presses the reinforcement against the mould surface. Thus ribs can be moulded into one side of the laminate without having to add additional foam or reinforcement, making lay-up more sample. In this way optimum use can be made of the reinforcement.

Clearly, by varying the foam thickness and amount of glass reinforcement used, a wide range of composites with differing properties can be produced. Typical ranges for some properties are shown in table. Full details can be obtained from Shell Chemicals UK Ltd who licence the process.

Typical properties of FRM composites

Specific gravity	0.6–1.4
Flexural strength	60–625 MPa
Flexural modulus	0.8–35 GPa
Impact strength	2.5–12.75 J.

Cold Press Moulding

This is an intermediate process between contact moulding and hot press moulding. Inexpensive GRP tools are used and only a lightweight hydraulic press is necessary to produce mouldings with two smooth surfaces. Moulding pressure is not usually greater than 0.5 MPa.

Although called cold press moulding, mould temperatures are usually between 40 and 50°C. This is brought about by the heat of reaction of the resin system during gelation and cure. However, to ensure that consistent. mouldings are produced, the mould is often heated at the start of a production run. By utilising the exothermic heat produced during cure to heat the mould, the moulding cycle is reduced, mould life extended and reject rate reduced.

Moulds are frequently made from GRP, although light metal alloy moulds may also be employed. Average mould life for GRP moulds is 1000 releases, although 2000 releases have been known. To ensure that the moulds do not distort during use they are generally mounted on a steel frame and back filled with a pressure resistant material such as concrete, or a filled resin composition. The mould tools consists of accurately made matching male and female moulds, designed to pinch the reinforcement of the edge of the moulding, to allow air to escape but retain the resin. Without this pinching area there is a risk of air entrapment and resin loss leading to a higher percentage of rejects. For most mouldings this pinching area should allow for two mat thicknesses to be compressed. Unlike hot press moulding, the surplus reinforcement cannot be trimmed off the mould. Mould surfaces are best coated with a release agent which permits many releases without recoating so that acceptable production cycles can be achieved.

Moulding thickness is usually within the range 2-5 mm and is uniform throughout the whole moulding. Above 8 mm thickness, problems can arise through either excessive exotherm, resulting in a scorched or distorted moulding, or an excessively long cure cycle to prevent this. Undercuts are not practical since split moulds are prone to troubles.

The reinforcing material-which may be glass mat or woven fabric-is cut to shape and placed in the mould. With deep draw mouldings a preform is more suitable. A surfacing tissue may be used on one or both sides of the moulding to achieve a resin-rich surface free from fibre pattern. Whilst gelcoats may also be used, their use results in a much longer and generally unacceptable production cycle. Once the correct amount of reinforcement has been placed in the mould, the cold curing resin system is poured in and the press closed with a strong deceleration towards the end of the stroke. The resin displaces the air and impregnates the reinforcement. Since the resin system used should have a short gel time and a short cure time, it can only be mixed immediately prior to use. The exothermic heat generated during gelation accelerates the cure of the resin system and permits a relatively short moulding cycle to be used. This may be between 6 and 30 min depending on moulding size and thickness. Once the moulding has been released from the mould it can be trimmed. The glass content of the finished moulding can be up to 50% by weight. This is roughly twice that which can be achieved with contact moulding.

One way of obtaining a very short gel time with ease of mixing and very low material wastage is to use a two-component mix. One component is prepared with a cobalt accelerator and benzoyl peroxide catalyst, the. other with dimethylaniline accelerator and cyclohexanone peroxide catalyst. These two components are then mixed immediately prior to use to give a gel time of 3-4 min and a moulding cycle time of about 10 min. Both components are stable for at least one working day.

Hot Press/Matched Metal Moulding

This process is one of the most economical for the high volume production of small-to-medium sized components from either polyester or epoxide resin systems. Mouldings have two smooth surfaces and can be made to relatively high tolerances. Due to high tooling costs, this process cannot generally be justified for short runs.

Heated matched metal moulds are used, mounted in a hydraulic press fitted with automatic opening and closing and accurate speed control. Moulds are generally fabricated from tooling steel with flame hardened edges to trim the moulding during the press cycle. Moulds used with sheet moulding compounds often have ejectors fitted but these are rare on moulds used with liqudi resin systems. The mould surface should be highly polished and may be chrome plated to ease removal of the moulding. Such moulds generally have a life of about 100,000 releases. To prevent warping of the moulding the temperature difference over the whole mould surface should not exceed 2.5°C.

Mould design is of great importance *for* efficient production cycles and must take into account the material to be used. Also an adequate taper must be built into the mould to permit easy ejection of mouldings.

A high production rate can be achieved with cycle times ranging from 1 to 8 min. This is governed by moulding temperature and pressure, type of resin/ catalyst system used and moulding wall thickness. As a general guide a press time of 2 min is used for a wall thickness of 2 mm or less, above this it is general to allow 1 min per millimetre of wall thickness. Press temperatures *are* usually in the range 100-170°C, with temperatures of 100–130°C being more common with polyester resins. Pressures used vary between 0.5 and 15 MPa depending on mould dimensions and the material being processed.

Silicone release agents may be used to facilitate demoulding, although generally, once a mould has been 'run-in', particularly With moulding compounds where metallic soaps are used as internal release agents, further application becomes unnecessary. If a moulding is to be subsequently painted, great care must be taken in choosing a release agent that will not interfere with adhesion of the paint. This is also true if adhesives are to be used on the moulding.

Several methods exist for producing mouldings by the hot press technique; these are: liqudi resin/chopped strand mat; liquid resin/preform; sheet moulding compounds or prepregs; dough moulding compounds.

Liquid resin/chopped strand mat

This procedure is only suitable for simple relatively flat shapes. The chopped strand mat reinforcement is cut to shape and the required amount placed in the mould. A mat bound with a styrene insoluble binder is preferred since this prevents the fibres from being displaced during the press cycle. If desired a surfacing tissue may be placed on either side of the mat to give a resin-rich finish and to mask the fibre pattern. willi flat mouldings, woven cloths may be used, but these can distort if used with contoured mouldings.

The pre-mixed resin system is poured over the reinforcement and the mould closed. Mould closure is carried out rapidly at first but more slowly a final closure approaches, to allow air to escape and full impregnation of the mat to take place. By cutting the mat slightly larger than the moulding dimensions, the excess glass acts as a fllter to allow air to escape whilst retaining the resin. With correct mould design this excess is cut off during the final closure of the mould. Mould closure is usually regulated by stop to predetermine the moulding thickness and prevent too much resin from being squeezed out. Since a liquid resin system is used, a relatively low moulding pressure is all that is necessary (0.5-2.5 MPa).

To reduce moulding costs, increase the rigidity of the moulding and reduce shrinkage and hence improve surface finish, fillers such as calcium carbonate, china clay or talc may be added to the resin system.

For preference the resin system should be of high reactivity and medium-to-high viscosity at 25°C, to prevent it from running through the reinforcement and polymerising at the mould surface before the mould has been closed. With polyester resin systems, benzoyl peroxide is frequently used as catalyst without an accelerator. With this catalyst a large batch of resin can be prepared at any one time, since shelf0life at room temperature within the range 25-50%.

Liquid resin perform

With complicated shapes, to ensure a uniform distribution of glass, it is preferable to use a preformed glass mat rather than chopped strand mat. In this way even glass distribution is assured.

The equipment required for preforming consists of a chopper gun and a preform screen of the same shape and size as the mould, mounted on a turntable and connected to an exhaust fan. The preform screen is made from perforated steel sheet or wire mesh.

Continuous glass rovings are fed to the chopped unit and cut into lengths of between 5 and 50 mm. These fibres are blown by fan onto the preform screen whilst it is rotated and are held in place by a slight vacuum from an exhaust fan. Once the preform screen has been evenly covered to the required thickness, a small quantity of an aqueous emulsion binder is sprayed over the fibres to bond them together. This is to give the preform sufficient strength to be removed from the screen and handled. Emulsion binders may be made from polyester resin, urea-formaldehyde resin, polyvinyl acetate and acrylic resins. A styrene insoluble binder is often used to prevent displacement of the fibres during the pressing to strengthen the edge of the moulding.

Once the binder has been applied, the preform and screen are placed in a forced draught oven for 2-3 min at 125-140°C to dry. When cold the preform is removed from the screen and is ready for use. To aid production a large batch of preforms may be prepared first and stored ready for use.

An alternative method of making a preform is to prepare a slurry of chopped fibres and emulsion binder and draw the screen through this until the required thickness of fibres has been deposited. The screen is then removed from the slurry, drained and the preform dried as before.

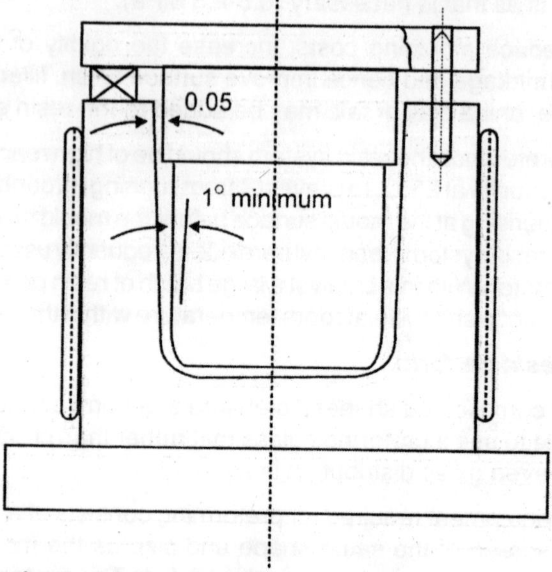

An inverted mould for hot press moulding

To prepare a moulding, the preform is placed in the suitably released mould and the correct amount of catalysed resin poured over it. The mould is then closed and excess resin squeezed out. The procedure used is then the same as that for liquid resin/ chopped strand mat moulding. Cure temperature and cure time depend on moulding size and resin formulation. With deep mouldings it is preferable to invert the mould to prevent the fibres from being squeezed into the bottom of the mould as closure takes places. With correct mould design, trimming takes place in the mould.

Sheet moulding compounds (SMC) and prepregs

These consist of reinforcement which has been preimpregnated with resin in sheet form. They may be dry and rigid or soft and tacky; made from chopped strands, woven fabrics or unidirectional filaments.

Sheet moulding compounds usually consist of a filled polyester resin system reinforced with chopped glass fibres, whilst prepregs consist of woven fabrics or unidirectional fibres impregnated with epoxide or other resin systems. Preparation details are given in chapter 16.

SMC or prepreg is cut to shape and the required number of layers sandwiched together, placed in the mould and pressed. Where necessary the mould should be treated with a mould release agent first. Pressure, temperature and cure time depend on the particular resin formulation used and component thickness. Cure time for a typical polyester sheet moulding compound is around 1 min per millimetre of wall thickness.

Moulding is usually to stops, to prevent excessive exudation of resin when pressure is applied. In certain cases contact pressure may be applied for a predetermined time to heat the prepreg and partially advance cure so that when full pressure is applied only limited resin flow occurs. This is more usual with epoxide resin systems than with polyester resins.

Mouldings produced from SMC are smooth on all surfaces and show almost no glass structure. Glass content is usually within the range 20-35%. Moulding thicknesses within the range 1.5-6 mm are common, while about 10 mm thickness delamination may occur. For this sections, dough or bulk moulding compounds are preferred.

With correctly designed moulds, trimming takes place within the mould, thus limiting finishing just to the removal of flash. Since SMC must deform to fill the mould cavity, pressures substantially higher than those used with liquid resin systems are necessary—typically 3-7 MPa. Ejectors and split moulds, to accommodate undercuts, are common practice, which with the high viscosity resin systems used for SMC rarely cause sticking problems. Release agents are unnecessary once the mould has been 'run-in' since internal release agents are incorporated in the formulation.

Low profile SMC can be used to improve surface finish where large flat area are to be moulded, by eliminating sink marks.

Epoxide resin based prepregs are used for the preparation of printed circuit board laminates for electrical applications. Here a sheet of copper foil, coated with a suitable oxide fIlm to assist adhesion to the resin system, is placed on one or both sides of the layers of prepreg before placing the whole sandwich in the press. Melinex or Cellophane film may be used as release agent to prevent damage to the copper fIlm and contamination with release agent. Pressing is invariably to stops between two parallel heated platens. Cure time depends on the system used but is generally longer than with polyester systems. Cure temperature may also be higher. Glass contents of up to about 70% by weight are usual.

Dough or bulk moulding compounds (DMC or BMC)

Dough moulding compounds (DMC) or Premix are dough-like materials consisting of a mixture of glass or sisal fibres, polyester or epoxide resin plus catalyst and a filler such as calcium carbonate. Similar types of phenolic resin based moulding compounds are also available. Fibre length is normally in the region of 3-12 mm with about 15-20% addition by weight. This material is referred to as Bulk Moulding Compound (BMC) in the USA.

The correct weight of compound is placed in the suitably released mould and the mould closed to stops. Pressures used range from about 4 to 7 MPa. With polyester DMC or BMC, moulding temperature is usually within the range 120-150°C and cure time about 2 min, although this may vary from about 45s up to about 8 min. With epoxide resin DMC, the cure temperature range is higher at 150-170°C, with cure time between 10 and 20s per millimetre of wall thickness.

With correctly designed moulds trimming takes place in the mould, leaving only flash to be removed after demoulding. Split moulds, fitted with ejectors, may be used and are similar to those required for processing SMC.

Transfer Moulding

Transfer moulding is used for the manufacture of small components and is particularly useful with multi-cavity tools and where small inserts are to be moulded in. Materials used are polyester and epoxide dough moulding com pounds, although a new liquid resin injection technique is reported.

Heated steel moulds, preferably hard chrome plated, are used, which may be of multi-cavity design. Tooling costs are higher than for compression moulding since appropriate gates and runners must be included in the mould.

A pre-weighted quantity of DMC is placed in a heated transfer pot by hand. A punch or ram com presses the material and causes it to flow into the heated tool cavity where it cures. The tool is mounted between the platens of a press.

Factors to be considered with transfer moulding are transfer and tool clamping pressures and transfer time. To reduce transfer time and increase overall efficiency the moulding compound may be pre- heated in an oven or high frequency pre-heater such as micro-wave oven.

Mould temperatures range from 155 to 170°C both for polyester and epoxide resin com pounds, with moulding pressures ranging from 5 to 100 MPa depending on the type of com pound to be processed, mould design and temperature. Cure time in the mould (excluding pre-heat time) is usually of the order of 10-30s per millimetre of wall thickness for both types of com pound.

Injection Moulding

Injection moulding, a technique used extensively for the processing of thermoplastic materials, has also been developed to process thermosetting resin systems. Due to high mould costs it is generally only suitable for the large scale production of small-to-medium sized components. Material processed in this way are polyester and epoxy DMC and also phenolics, ureas, melamine and diallyl phthalate moulding compounds. These latter materials are generally more difficult to process than either polyester or epoxy DMC.

Thermoset mouldings produced by injection moulding are used widely in the electrical and automotive fields, thus large production runs are common.

Injection moulding has advantages over both compression and transfer moulding in that the process is more automated and far higher production rates can be achieved. Although mould costs are higher than for compression moulding, overall finished component costs are generally lower. With small weight components, scrap from runners can be high com pared with com pression moulding but for large mouldings this becomes relatively insignificant. Injection moulding is also better for thick parts since, with the pre-heating of the DMC before injection into the mould, shorter moulding cycles are possible.

Whilst injection moulding machines designed specifically for processing thermoset materials are available, a number of manufacturers offer replacement screw and barrel assemblies and stuffer hoppers to convert conventional thermoplastic injection moulding machines to process thermosets.

Moulding compound is transferred in the cold state by pressure from the material hopper into the main injection chamber. Here it can be preheated before injection into the heated mould tool Injection, through a special nozzle, can be either by ram or screw pressure. If screw feed is used, the screw must be of the type designed to process thermosets as opposed to thermoplastics.

Early machines were designed with vertical clamping pressure on the mould but today horizontal machines are mostly used. Since thermosetting materials are liquid until gelation occurs, clamping pressure has to be maintained on the mould until the resin has cured. Unless this is done, excessive flash will form. Heated matched metal moulds are used, which may be of multicavity design. These moulds must be designed for use with thermosetting resins, taking into account the fact that thermoset mouldings are harder, more rigid and less easily deformed than thermoplastics.

A typical temperature sequence for injection moulding DMC would be feed hopper and feed zone—ambient temperature; metering section 50-60°C; nozzle 80-90°C; mould temperature 135-185°C for polyester DMC or 160-220°C for epoxy DMC; injection pressure 80-160 MPa. Cure time is generally of the order of 10-20s per millimetre of wall thickness. Very little finishing of mouldings is necessary. .

Where fully automatic moulding machines are used, hydraulic ejection with perhaps a 'joggle' facility is necessary, since thermosets have a tendency to stick in the mould.

Filament Winding

Filament winding is a technique used for the manufacture of pipes, tubes, cylinders and spheres and is frequently used for the construction of large tanks and pipework for the chemical industry. By suitable design, filament wound structures can be fabricated to withstand very high pressures in service. In general, products fabricate by filament winding have the highest strength to weight ratios and can have glass contents of up to 80% by weight.

The process is suitable for use both with polyester and epoxide resin systems and a variety of fibres including glass, carbon, aramid and metals, providing that these materials *are* available in continuous filament lengths. Glass fibre is by far the most common reinforcement used and will be used as the example in the description of the process.

Filament winding is basically a simple process, although numerous modifications have been developed to improve product quality. Mouldings can be produced by either a wet lay-up process or from prepreg.

In recent years filament winding has been extended to the continuous production of pipe using a continuous steel band mandrel. In this way continuous lengths of pipe can be produced, with diameters ranging from about 0.3 to 3.5m.

Wet lay-up

With the wet lay-up process glass rovings are drawn through a resin bath to impregnate them with resin. The impregnated rovings are then wound under tension round a rotating mandrel. Generally the feed head supplying the rovings to the mandrel traverses backwards and forwards along the mandrel.

The mandrel, which may be segmented for large diameter pipes, is generally wrapped with a release film, such as Cellophane, prior to wrapping with glass and resin. The mandrel may incorporate some means of heating the resin system, such as embedded electric heaters, or provision for steam heating. Alternatively, the fully wrapped mandrel and laminate may be transferred to a curing oven to effect cure.

In order to provide a resin-rich, corrosion resistant inner lining to the pipe, the mandrel may be wrapped with a surfacing tissue followed by one or two layers of chopped strand mat or woven tape prior to filament winding. This first layer is usually allowed to cure partially before winding commences to prevent the resin from being squeezed out into the main laminate.

The winding angel used during construction of pipes or tanks depends on the strength/performance requirements and may vary from longitudinal through helical to circumferential, as shown in figure. Often a combination of

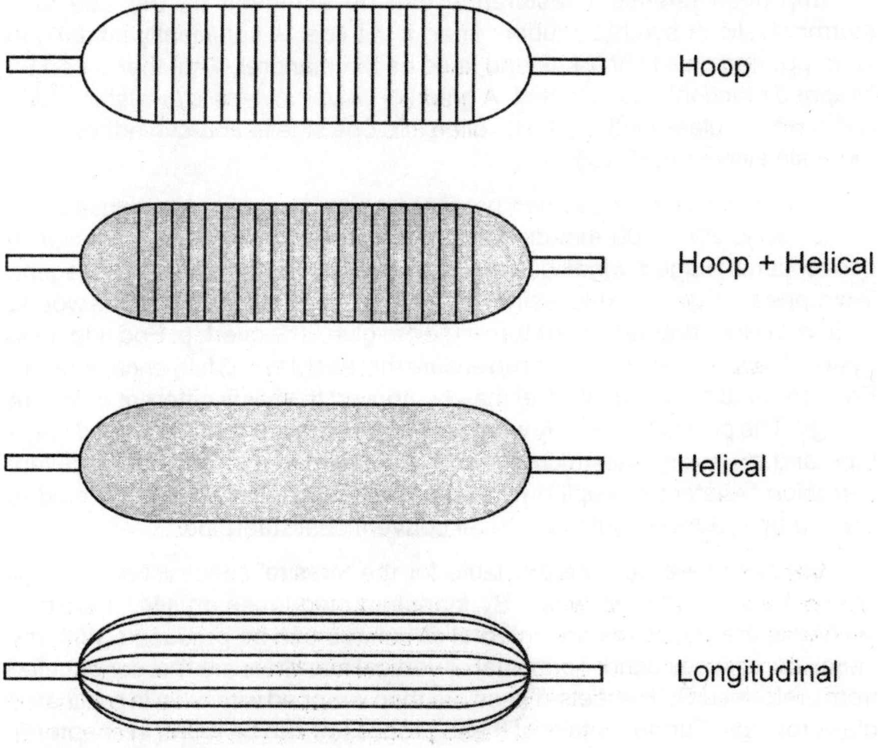

Filament winding patterns.

different winding patterns is used to give optimum performance. Accurate fibre alignment is possible.

For pipe construction, steel mandrels are generally used. However, where cylinders or spheres are to be made, an alternative material has to be used so that it can be removed once the resin system has cured. In these cases the mahdrel can be made from wax, a low melting metal alloy, or an inert plaster held together with a water soluble binder. Clearly, in these cases the mandrel can only be used once. Material choice for the mandrel will depend on the cure cycle needed for the resin system.

In addition to winding with continuous filament rovings, machines have been developed which permit winding with tapes or slit-width chopped strand mat and woven rovings. These reinforcements may be used alone of combined with continuous fllament rovings. Thus considerable design flexibility exists for the production of large simple shapes.

Improved chemical resistance can be achieved by the use of a thermoplastic or synthetic rubber liner. If the liner is sufflciently rigid if can be supported on a light frame and used as the mandrel, if not then it can be wrapped round the mandrel flrst. A grade of polypropylene is available which has a woven glass cloth partially rolled into one side to improve adhesion of the resin system (Celmar).

Dunlop has developed a new process for pipe production to produce pipes in the range 200-2000 mm diameter. Essentially the process is similar to conventional filament winding. A mandrel, suitably coated with release agent, is wrapped with an epoxide resin impregnated glas& tape. Over this is wound a 150mm high-strength steel strip angled to give 50% overlap. Epoxide resin system is applied to the steel strip to ensure that each layer is fully encapsulated. From three to 13 layers of steel may be applied to satisfy different pressure ratings. The pipe is finished by wrapping with further resin impregnated glass tape and the resin system cured. Pipe produced in this way has excellent corrosion resistance coupled with a high strength/weight ratio. It is said to provide up to 50% weight saving over conventional steel pipe.

Various processes are available for the 'on-site' construction of large filament wound storage tanks. By manufacturing these on site, transport problems are overcome and integral structures can be produced. With the various processes either horizontal or vertical mandrels are flrst constructed from preformed GRP sheets. These are then wrapped with resin in pregnated glass rovings. Further details of these processes can be found in chapter 8.

Prepregs

Filament would vessels can be produced from prepreg tapes and rovings. This technique is often used with carbon fibre to reduce fibre damage during the winding operation and to permit the use of resin systems which cannot be handled by wet lay-up techniques. Here, it. is essential to use a heated mandrel to melt the resin and hence displace air and consolidate, and cure the laminate. Resin content of the laminate can be controlled more accurately with prepreg since the prepreg can be made with exactly the right resin content. The use of prepregs also makes for cleaner operation.

Other applications.

Filament winding has been used to provide a protective laminate on the outside of steel pressure pipes where external corrosion can take place. An example of this use is in the protection of the splash zone of steel riser pipes used on sea based oil and gas production platforms. Here, care has to be taken in the design of such a composite structure since the coefficient of expansion of the filament would glass wrap can be lower than that of the steel core. If such a composite structure is produced using a heat cured resin system (say 120°C cure) and then subjected to subzero temperatures in use, the steel pipe can shrink away from the laminate and permit entry of water by capillary action. Thus the object of wrapping the pipe to prevent corrosion can be defeated, since corrosion can then still take place under the laminate. Once the bond has broken it can never be remade.

Centrifugal Moulding

Centrifugal moulding or casting is a method used for making cylindrical objects with uniform wall thickness. It is mainly used for the production of large diameter pipes, up to 5 m in diameter, from either polyester or vinyl ester resin systems, although epoxide resin systems may also be used. Pipes produced in this way are void-free and smooth on both the inner and outer surfaces. Threaded sections can be moulded into the external wall if required. More recently a system has been developed for producing tapered and curved poles by centrifugal casting.

Moulds need to be bored and polished to a mirror finish and of sufficient strength to withstand, without distortion, the high G-force exerted during spinning. A steam jacket or other means of heating may be built into the mould to cure the resin system, or alternatively hot air may be blown through the mould.

Release agents used include silicones, bake-on PTFE types or PVA, although silicones are generally preferred. If the exterior of the fmished pipe is to be painted than a silicone release agent should not be used.

Choice of resin system must depend on application and a heat cured resin may be used, particularly where chemical resistance is required. In addition, the process lends itself to thc use of several different resin systems incorporated in the one pipe, such as an abrasion resistant outer skin, a general purpose centre and a chemically resistant inner skin. The resin system used should have some degree of flexibility to give good impact resistance to the pipe, coupled with good chemical resistance. To achieve both of these requirements in the one resin system may require a compromise in properties.

Various methods of fabrication can be used. With large diameter moulds, glass and resin can be applied by the hand lay-up technique using a slow gel resin system so that the whole mould can be coated and the mould spun before gelation of the resin takes place. Here, it is necessary to tailor the reinforcement to shape to avoid overlaps.

Alternatively, the reinforcement may be wrapped round a mandrel, inserted into the mould and then unwound onto the mould surface. The mandrel is removed before resin is injection into the mould. With this technique a faster gelling resin system may be used. Woven fabrics and chopped strand mat are suitable reinforcements.

A third method, capable of being fully automated, is generally preferred. Here, resin and glass are applied to the mould surface utilising a travelling feeder arm fitted with a chopper and spray gun, which passes slowly backwards and forwards through the mould whilst the mould is rotated. The laminate can be built up in layers of 0.5-1 mm thickness per pass. Once the reinforcement and resin system have been placed in the mould it is rotated at up to 2500 revolutions per minutes (rpm) depending on mould diameter, the larger the mould diameter the slower the speed.

After the main resin system has gelled, a chemically resistant topcoat may pe applied while the mould is still rotating. Mould rotation is continued until all the resin has cured.

In all of the above techniques, a relatively flexible glass reinforced resin pipe is produced, with properties similar to some of those made by fllament winding. To produce stiffer pipes a modification to the spray technique has been developed and is in use commercially. Stiffer pipes, particularly in the larger diameter range, offer considerable advantages in handling and installation and maintain their shape during installation.

With this modified process, which is fully automatic, the mould is coated with release agent and rotated at a suitable speed. The feeder arm is designed in such a way that it can deliver programmed amounts of resin, chopped glass and a filler such as sand, to the mould surface as it moves in and out of the mould. In this way a layer of abrasion resistant sand filled resin system can be applied to the mould surface. Over this is applied a layer of glass reinforced resin. By suitable design of the chopper unit, fibre. orientation can be controlled. Next a layer of sand filled resin is applied followed by a further layer of glass reinforced resin. Depending on the type and size of pipe to be produced, several more layers of GRP altenated with filled resin may be added. Finally the inner surface is coated with a suitable chemically resistant layer of resin, which may be lightly filled or reinforced, to give a smooth corrosion resistant lining.

The equipment used can be programmed to feed materials to the mould to build up in pipe wall thickness at a rate of between.O.5 and 1 mm per pass and to compact the materials by centrifugal force throughout the whole production cycle. Once the final layer of resin has been applied, hot air is passed through the mould to assist curing of the resin system. The mould is cooled to ambient temperature to assist curing of the resin system. The mould is cooled to ambient temperature to assist removal of the finished pipe, which is pushed out using

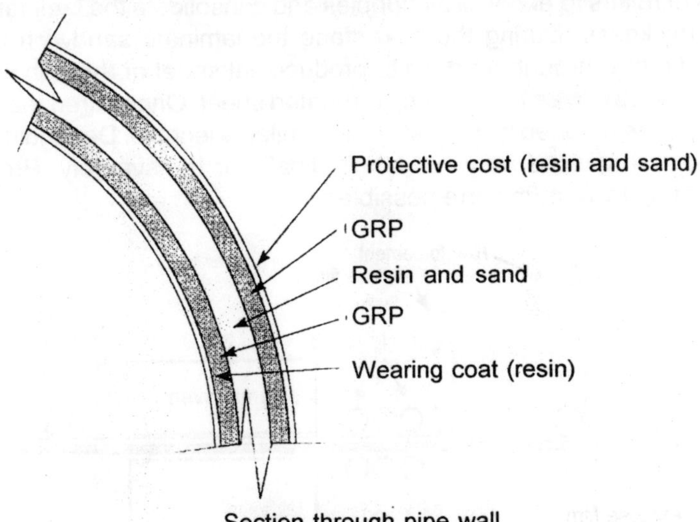

Construction of a typical rigid centrifugally cast pipe.

a hydraulically operated ram. Using this technique, rigid hard wearing pipes can be produced, tailored to meet and user requirements. A typical pipe construction is shown in figure. This is a simplified version of the pipes produced commercially, to illustrate pipe construction. In practice several more layers of glass and sand filled system may be incorporated in the pipe wall. A range of bends and joints is also available to meet most needs.

Continuous sheet Manufacture

Continuous machine processing is used for the production of most corrugated roof sheeting and also for flat clear, translucent and decorative sheeting. It should be noted, however, that the decorative laminates used in building and transport applications are in the main manufactured from melamine faced phenolic resin/paper laminates.

Several patented processes exist for continuous sheet production, all of which are similar in broad principle.

Resin and glass reinforcement are sandwiched between two sheets of release film, Such as Melinex, Mylar or Cellophane and passed through rollers to consolidate the laminate before curing in an oven. Resin is applied to the release fIlm either by spray or trickle process, care being taken to ensure that application is uniform, Glass reinforcement is laid in the resin and a second layer of release fIlm applied. This sandwich is passed through a series of rollers to expel all air bubbles and consolidate the laminate to the correct thickness. During the next stage the laminate sandwich is either passed directly through an oven to produce flat sheet or through rollers or dies and then an oven to produce corrugated sheet. Once cured the sheet is trimmed to the required width and cut into suitable lengths. Depending on the process, corrugations may run longitudinally or transversely. Production speeds of up to 12 m/min are possible

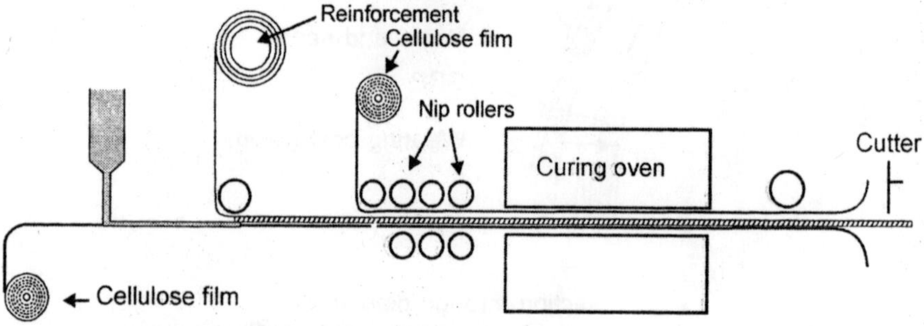

Continuous sheet manufacture

To produce clear sheeting the refractive index of the resin system must match that of the glass reinforcement.

Generally the glass reinforcement used consists of chopped strand mat with a soluble polyester powder binder or chopped rovings deposited directly into the resin film. However, for certain applications woven fabrics may be used. With the latter and to a much lesser extent with chopped strand mat, the glass cloth may be drawn through a resin bath and excess resin removed between doctor blades or rollers, before placing between two layers of release film and processing as before.

With high quality sheeting a surfacing tissue may be used to ensure a resin-rich finish. Such sheeting must be installed with the resin-rich surface exposed to the weather.

Resin systems are generally specifically formulated for each machine, since gel time and viscosity must suit the particular operating conditions or the machine. Resin systems used include those suitable for producing clear fire retardant sheeting.

By the correct choice of resin system, sheeting can be manufacturing which will not yellow to any extent after exposure to tropical weather conditions for several years. However, to ensure that this is the case the resin system must be chosen with care and must be fully cured. Also the release film must be removed before installation and the laminate should contain not less than 75% by weight of resin. In other cases the resin content of the laminate may fall between 65 and 75% by weight.

Decorative sheeting can be produced with an attractive printed patterned surface by incorporating a suitably patterned surfacing sheet. This surfacing sheet can consist of a glass surfacing tissue onto which the pattern has been specially printed or alternatively a dress fabric may be used.

Pultrusion

Pultrusion is a technique used for producing continuous fibre reinforced sections in which the orientation of the fibres is kept constant during cure. The process is suitable for use with both polyester and epoxide resin systems, reinforced with glass, carbon or synthetic fibres. An infinite number of profiles can be produced using appropriate dies and includes rods, tubes and flat and angled sections. All profiles have high strength and stiffness in the lengthwise direction, with fibre content generally around 60-65% by volume.

The reinforcements used consist of continuous fibres such as glass rovings or continuous carbon fibre tows, woven rovings or chopped strand mat or a combination of the two, depending on the strength and rigidity required in the moulded profile.

Two processes are available which use liquid resin systems. In the first the reinforcement is drawn through an impregnating bath containing catalysed resin. For this process, a resin system with a long pot-life at room temperature is necessary. The reinforcement is then drawn through a heated die which removes excess resin, determines the cross-sectional shape and cures the resin system.

In the second process the reinforcement, accurately positioned and under tension, is drawn through a heated metal die where impregnation of the fibres and cure of the resin system takes place. Here, by the use of appropriate resin injection equipment, a short pot-life system can be used. Typical resin injection pressures are between 0.1 and 0.5 MPa. To speed up cure, the reinforcement may be pre-heated to about 100°C before passing through the die. Production rate of 1 m/min can be achieved. By careful design of the pulling mechanism, consistent profiles can be produced with no bending or twisting of the fibres. With some resin systems a tunnel oven may be required after the die to give a suitable post cure.

Apart from the wet processes it is also possible to make pultruded sections from prepregs. The forming procedure is the same as that used with wet

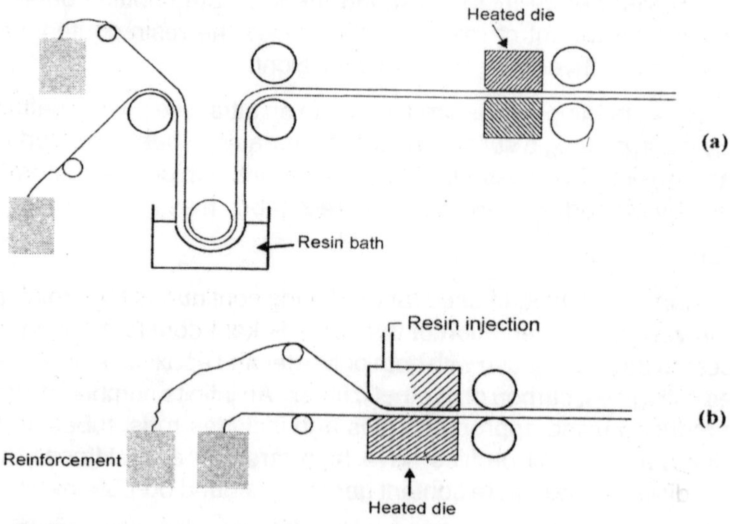

Pultrusion (a) using a resin bath; by resin injection

resin systems. The prepreg is drawn through a heated die which melts the resin,. compresses the prepreg into the required shape and cures the resin. This is a somewhat cleaner process than that using a resin bath.

The sandwich panels are being produced in the USA by pultrusion. In this process a plywood core is completely encased in a 3 mm thick glass polyester skin, resin penetrating the plywood during production to give increased bond strength and moisture resistance.

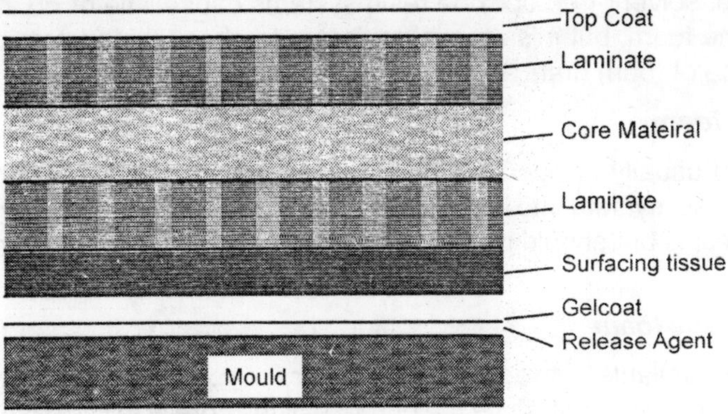

Typical sandwich construction.

Sandwich Construction

With sandwich construction, a core of some material is coated on both sides with a laminate. The effect of this is to produce a composite material with increases stiffness, increased thermal insulation and in many cases increased buoyancy. These factors must of course depend on the type and thickness of the core material used. Many articles are made by sandwich construction techniques utilising both polyester and epoxide resin systems. Some examples are aircraft floor panels, building panels, boats and surf boards.

Core materials used include balsa wood, plastic foam and honeycombs of paper, glass fibre or metal. Since several different types of plastic foam are available, some comments on these may be useful.

Expanded PVC

This is available in several different grades, both plasticised and unplasticised. If the foam has a surface skin this should be roughened to improve adhesion. Apart from this, unplasticised OVC foam requires no special treatment. With plasticised PVC foam, prolonged contact with polyester resin may cause attack and so the foam may require sealing first.

Expanded Polystyrene

This is severely attacked by the styrene present in polyester resins and must be sealed before use. This can be done with a solvent-free epoxide resin system, preferably reinforced with one layer of woven glass cloth. For maximum bonding of a polyester to an epoxide resin system, the polyester should be applied soon after the epoxy has gelled. If this cannot be done then the epoxy surface should be abraded before application of the polyester resin. Most solvent-free epoxide resin systems cause little or no attack on polystyrene foam, but it is always advisable to check the system out on a small piece of foam flrst.

Phenolic foam

This is usually of open cell construction and hence will absorb a low viscosity resin system into its pores. It is not attacked by either polyester or epoxide resins but should be sealed with a thixotropic resin system before use.

Polyurethane foam

This is available both as rigid and flexible foam. Generally the rigid foam is used as core material, since the purpose of the core is to increase rigidity. Pre-moulded slabs and blocks can be used, the only pre-treatment necessary being the removal of dust from the surface, providing that a closed cell foam is used. If an open cell foam is used this must be sealed with a thixotropic resin system first. If the foam has a skin on the surface this should be abraded before use.

Where blocks or slabs of foam are to be bonded to a pre-moulded laminate, an epoxide resin adhesive should be used, preferably abrading the laminate before application of the adhesive.

Urethane foams can also be foamed in situ, in which case no special surface treatment of the laminate is necessary except to ensure that it is clean, dry and grease-free.

Fabrication techniques

These include contact moulding, resin injection and compression moulding. Depending on the process and the type of core material used either liquid resin systems or prepregs may be used. Reinforcements used include glass, carbon and aramid fibres and may be in the form of chopped strands, woven fabrics of unidirectional fibres, depending on strength and rigidity requirements.

Moulding with Performed Materials

Two processes have been developed to speed boat building without the need for expensive moulds and patterns. Both patterns use lightweight wooden frames on which to construct the boat hull.

C-Flex planking system

F.G. Industries market C-Flex planking. This is designed to eliminate expensive mould and pattern making in boat construction. C- Flex planking consists of parallel rods of glass fibre reinforced polyester alternating with bundles of continuous glass fibre rovings, all held together by two layers of lightweight open weave cloth. It conforms to curves without having to be deformed. In use the C-flex planking is fixed to wooden frames spaced 450 mm apart. These frames from the shape of the hull or deck and may be of a temporary or permanent nature. Over this is applied one layer of chopped strand mat (225 or 300 g/m^2) impregnated with polyester resin. This is followed by, for example, two layers of Linrovmat (600:150) applied with the unidirectional reinforcement at right angles to the C-Flex planking. Next one layer of Fabmat (300: 150) is applied. The surface is then coated with a filled finishing compound, rubbed down and finished with a polyurethane paint.

'Duradense' building system

Tyler Mouldings have developed the 'Durandense' system of boat construction to eliminate the cost of producing a pattern and mould for one-off designs. In this process, pultruded GRP battens are fixed to wooden frames spaced about 450 mm apart. The outer surface is then laminated by hand lay-up using say three layers of 300 g/m^2 chopped strand mat and finished with a gelcoat. Once the resin has cured, the frames are removed from inside (except every flith frame to remain shape) and the inside is laminated in the same way as the outer skin. Bulkheads can be incorporated as required.

Properties of 'Duradense' battens

Pultruded GRP	
Glass content	65% wt
Widths	25 and 50 mm
Thickness	3.85 mm
Lengths	up to 12 m
Longitudinal tesnile strength	414 MPa
Longitudinal tensile modulus	22 GPa
Longitudinal flexural strength	515 MPa

Longitudinal compressive strength	193 Mpa
Impact strength	128 J/25.4 mm notch
Specific gravity	1.8
Water absorption	0.5%
Barcol hardness	45-60

Trimming and Finishing

Trimming and finishing should be carried out while the resin is still in the 'green' stage and the mould still in the mould. By suitable design and construction of the mould edge, this can be used as a trimming guide. Trimming can be carried out with a sharp knife held at right angles to the laminate, cutting towards the mould rather than away from it. Alternatively scissors may be used. Care must be taken not to distort the moulding at this stage.

Once fully cured, FRP products are difficult to trim and special cutting tools may be required.

To prevent delamination during trimming or drilling operations, the moulding should be supported and clamped as close to the cutting line as possible. Holes up to about 5 mm diameter may be drilled with conventional high speed drills but above the diameter and up to about 10 mm diameter, carbide tipped drills are preferable. Over 10 mm diameter, cutters should be used. Drilling should be started from the gelcoat side, with a block of wood or similar material firmly clamped to the back of the moulding.

For tapping and threading, high-speed nitrided and chrome plated tape are suitable. Holes and blanks can be punched in a similar manner to that, used with sheet metal.

All surfaces exposed by machining or drilling should be sealed with a suitable lacquer to prevent ingress of water or chemicals.

Most FRP products will be self-coloured and will not therefore require painting. However, occasions may arise when this is necessary, for exam ple to repair scratches or other blemishes, or to add a pattem or lettering, or with boats, to apply an antifouling paint. In all of these cases the moulding must be thoroughly cleaned to remove all traces of release agent or polish.

PVA release agent can be washed off with warm water. Normal wax release agents and polishes require washing off with white spirit or a similar proprietary clean. If a silicone containing release agent has been used then an abrasive cleaner will be required. Similar, if the moulding has been contaminated with oils or greases, then an abrasive cleaner may be required. In each case the final rinse should be with clean, fresh water.

A good check for the presence of a release agent is to apply clean, fresh water to the surface of the moulding. If the water breaks into small globules, there is a release agent present. If the water remains in a fairly uniform sheet,: the surface will take a fresh coat of paint. In all cases cleaning must be continued until the water no longer breaks into small globules.

Once the surface is thoroughly dry it can be painted. The first coat should be a suitably formulated primer. This may, be epoxy or polyurethane based and will be in either case a two pack system. After this the undercoat and topcoat can be applied, allowing the correct cure time between coats. Various suppliers offer paints designed for use on FRP mouldings. In all cases the paint manufacturer's recommendations should be followed completely to obtain a satisfactory finish.

6

Polyester Resins

Unsaturated polyester resins form the bulk of all resins used for laminating applications and are without doubt the best known for laminating. Many different types of resin are now available from a large number of suppliers. Many of these resins have been developed for specific end use applications or for use with specific processes such as continuous sheet production or resin injection.

Polyester resins

The basic materials used to make a polyester resin are a dibasic organic acid or anhydride and a dihydric alcohol (glycol). To obtain a polymer chain which can be cross-linked into a thermosetting resin, a proportion of the dibasic acid must contain an unsaturated group or double bond. This unsaturation must be non-aromatic otherwise cross-linking will not take place. For example styrene (vinylbenzene) will react through the pendent vinyl group in the presence of a peroxide catalysts, whilst and benezene nucleous does not react.

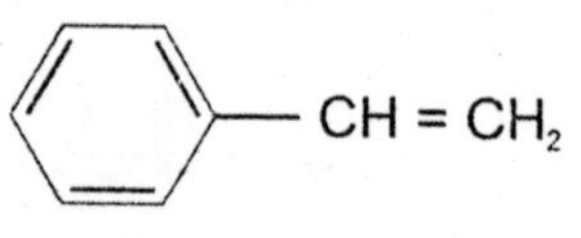

A simple polyester resin might be prepared from propylene glycol, meleic anhydride (unsaturated) and orthophthalic anhydride (saturated— in the context). By varying the ratio of the two anhydrides, the cross linking reactivity of the polyester resin contains a high proportion of unsaturation. The polymer formed in this way is a solid or semi-solid thermoplastic material which could be converted into a thermoset by the addition of a suitable catalyst; it would, however, be far two brittle for commercial use. By varying the glycol and dibasic acids used, a whole family of polyester resins can be made.

In order to convert this thermoplastic material into a usable resin for laminating, a furhter component is necessary. This is a low viscosity, unsaturated monomer such as styrene. This monomer acts as a solvent for the polymer chain, viscosity reducer and cross-linking agent. During cure the monomer links the polymer chains together through the unsaturated reactive groups, to give a usable product.

It can be seen that there are four components needed to produce a usable resin, namely:

1. a glycol,
2. an unsaturated dibasic acid,
3. a saturated dibasic and
4. a reactive monomer

One further component is needed to obtain a liquid polyester resin with an acceptable storage life and that is an inhibitor. This is added after the polyester resin has been manufactured, to prevent premature gelation during storage.

Each of these components will now be discussed briefly in turn.

Glycols

Many different glycols are commercially available, over a wide price range. Clearly, from a commercial point of view, the cheapest glycol, providing that it gives a satisfactory resin, will be chosen.

The simplest glycol is ethylene glycol. This can be used but gives polyester resins with a marked tendency to crystallise and which have limited compatibility with styrene.

The next glycol in the series is propylene glycol (propane-1,2-diol). This gives non-crystallising polyester resins completely compatible with styrne and is also relatively cheap. Thus it is used in the bulk of all polyster resins produced today.

Other glycols in use include the following:

Diethylene glycol	—	This gives resins with improved flexibility.
Dipropylene glycol	—	This gives some important in flexibility coupled with better chemical resistance.
Neopentyl glycol	—	This gives resins with improved chemical resistance, particularly to alkalis,and improved hydrolytic

stability. It may need blending with other glycols to improve the styrene compatibility of the resin.

Unsaturated acids

The unsaturated acid present in the polymer chain enables it to be cross-linked. The higher the proportion present, the higher the degree of cross-linking, the higher the heat distortion temperature of the cured resin, but the lower the elongation at break and tensile strength. This component also effect the reactivity of the resin. The higher the degree of unsaturation, the higher the reactivity of the resin.

Reactivity and curved properties can be modified by blending a saturated dibasic acid with the unsaturated dibasic acid. This procedure is adopted with most commercially available resins.

The most commonly used unsaturated acid is maleic acid (m.p. 132-140°C), generally used as the anhydride (m.p. 60°C) due to its lower melting point. An alternative acid is fumaric acid, the trans isomer of maleic acid. Although maleic acid isomerises to give fumaric polyester resins, those prepared from fumaric acid generally have higher softening points and a greater tendency to crystallise.

Saturated acids

The term saturated is used to describe those dibasic acids or anhydrides which do not contain double bonds which react in the presence of a peroxide catalyst. They may, however, contain an aromatic nucleus.

Monomers

The monomer serves two purposes :

1. to act as solvent for the polyester resin to produce a liqudi with a suitable handling viscosity and
2. to crosslink the polyester chain to give a fully cross-linked thermoset structure.

Styrene is the most frequently used monomer due to its low viscosity, low cost and ready availability. Another monomer, methyl methacrylate, or alternatively n-butyl methacrylate, may be used where cured resins with excellent clarity and UV stability are required. Such resins are used for the manufacture of transparent roof lights and corrugated sheeting, where their low refractive index, similar to that of E-glass, renders the glass virtually invisible.

Refractive indices of resins and glass

Material	Refrective index, n^{20}_{d}
Orthophthalic polyester/styrene	1.569
Orthophthalic polyester/styrene/light stabilised	1.560
Orthophthalic Polyester/methyl methacrylate	1.552
HET acid polyester	1.550
E-glass	1.548
C-glass	1.520

Diallyl phthalate is used as monomer in prepreg systems and some mouldings compounds because of its lower volatility than styrene. It is, however, difficult to cure at room temperature and so is restricted to heat curved systems. Curved systems are tougher than those containing styrene.

Resins containing a-methylstyrene are more flexible than those containing styrene and show lower shrinkage on cure. Thus a-methylstyrene is sometimes used in the formulation of potting and encapsulating compounds.

Helogenated monomers which have been considered for improving the flame retardant properties of polyester resins includes dichlorostyrene and dibromostyrene. Whilst these reduce flammability to a limited extent, their use has been restricted due to high price.

One of the best monomers found to impart self extinguishing properties to polyester resins is diallybenzene phosphonate. This gives excellent self-extinguishing properties with almost no effect on other properties. High cost has however, limited its use.

Triallyl cyanurate can be used as monomer to produce heat resistant polyester resins.

Inhibitors

Once the polyester polymer has been dissolved in a monomer, the system may gel at room temperature in the absence of a catalyst. Styrene is well known for its ability to polymerise on its own in the absence of an inhibitor. To prevent this from occurring and to obtain an acceptable storage life of the resin, an inhibitor is added. This is normally added after the polycondensation reaction has been completed and before the resin is dessolved in the monomer.

Inhibitors are generally reducing agents which absorb free radicals by donating hydrogen atoms and hence prevent those free radicals from polymerising the resin. Clearly, only an inhibitor has been exhausted, any further generation of free radicals will cause gelation of the resin.

When a peroxide catalyst is added to a preaccelerated resin the first reaction is to neautralise the inhibitor and it is this reaction which accounts for the initial period of apparent inactivity of the system. Where a longer gel time is required with no reduction in rate of cure, then additional inhibitor can be added to the system. This is preferable to reducing the catalyst or accelerator proportion, since then a slower rate of cure results.

Typical of the inhibitors used commercially are hydroquinone, t-bylccatechol and substituted benzoquinones. These are used in amounts ranging from 100 to 300 ppm. The actual amount of inhibitor needed to stabilise a resin will vary from one resin to another and whether or not the resin is for tropical use. In practice a mixture of inhibitors may be used to achieve optimum stabilisation whilst maintaining optimum reactivity.

Where an inhibitor is use to increase gel time, the amount added will be of the order of 1% of a 1% inhibitor solution. This is equivalent to 100 ppm of pure inhibitor. The effect of such an addition is to increase gel time from, say, 18 min up to amount 50 min without altering reactivity.

Commercial Resins

The various types of commercially available unsaturated polyester resins. These can be divided into eight different classes or groups as follows :

1. Gelcoat/topcoat resins.
2. General purpose resins.
3. Chemical resistant resins.
4. Reduced flammability resins.
5. Low styrene emission resins.
6. Low profile/low shrink resins.
7. Special purpose resins.
8. Casting resins.

Many of these resins are availbel in reactivities ranging from high through medium to low. They may also be available non-accelerated or preaccelerated–generally with a cobalt accelerator and with or without a thixotroping additive.

Other variations includ low, medium or high viscosity and additional stabiliser for tropical use.

Gelcoat/topcoat resins

The gelcoat is the first layer of resin applied to the released mould surface and forms and wearing surface of the finished moulding. It serves to protect the laminate against weather, moisture and chemicals and gives a decorative pigmented finish. In order to protect the laminate from damage during service the gelcoat must be resilient when cured so that it can withstand knocks and abrasions. Resilience is necessary since at most the gelcoat will only be reinforced with a surfacing tissue. Thickness is generally of the order of 0.4 mm.

Gelcoats may be clear or pigmented depending on application. Where high performance or high chemical resistance is required they are invariably reinforced with a surfacing tissue of either C-glass or synthetic fibre to provide additional protection to the underlying laminate and to mask the fibre pattern. In practice, the gelcoat may be applied in the normal way and backed up with a surfacing tissue so that a resin rich surface is obtained and the laminate protected by both the resin-rich layer and the surfacing tissue.

Most gelcoat resins contain tixotropic additive to prevent runs and sags from forming during appliction and cure. Generally they are available in two types,

1. for brush application and
2. for spray application

These usually only differ in viscosity and thixotropy.

Genegal purpose gelcoat resins are based on orthphthalic or isophthalic resins, the latter type offering improved water, chemical and impact resistance. Where superior weathering resistance is required, the gelcoat will invaribaly be of the isophthalic type and may contain a blend of methyl methacrylate and styrene as monomers.

Some manufactures offer fire retardant gelcoats based on HET acid or HET acid/ isophthalic blends, while others recommend their normal isophthalic resins. Care has to be taken in selecting a fire retardant gelcoat for outdoor applications since many of these exhibit inferior weathering resistance.

Where chemical resistance is required gelcoats are available based on isophthalic, isophthalic/HET acid, isophthalic/NPG and bisphenol A resins. Choice depends on the precise chemical environment and service temperature.

In addition to gelcoat resins, there is also a range of topcoat resins available. These are similar to gelcoat resins with one important difference and that is they do not suffer from air inhibition during cure. This is generally achieved by adding a wax to the resin which migrates to the surface during the initial stage of cure.

Topcoat resins serve to protect the underlying laminate, give a tack-free decorative finish and balance up the laminate by giving a resin-rich surface. The finish obtained is never of the sam quality as the gelcoat finish since it is not a moulded surface.

General purpose resins

These are mostly orthophthalic resins with good allround properties. They have for many years been used for boat building, but are slowly being replaced by isophthalic polyester resins due to the reduced water absorption of the latter.

Many different orthophthalic polyester resins are available, designed for a variety of application and processing techniques. They cover a wide range of viscosities reactivities and gel time and can vary from relatively soft to hard rigid cured resins.

Other resins which fall into the general purpose class are the terephthalic acid and some isophthalic acid based polyesters, although this letter group also come under the heading of chemical resistant resins.

Chemical resistant resins

For maximum chemical resistance any resin system used in a chemical environment must be fully cured, preferably at a temperature 10-20°c above that to which it will be subjected in service.

Clearly before any resin system can be selected, the service conditions, environment and temperature must be specified.Only then can a particular types of resin be chosen. With milk chemical environments several different types of resin may be available, but for severe conditions choice may be restricted to only one resin.

The weak link in the polyester molecule is the ester group and it is this that needs protecting from chemical attack. This can be accomplished by increasing the degree of cross-linking of the resin and by hindering attack by placing bulky groups around the ester links.

Intermediate levels of chemical resistance can be obtained with isophthalic polyester resins. These will vary somewhat in performance depending on their precise formulation.

A higher level of chemical resistance can be obtained by replacing the propylene glycol with neopentyl glycol to give an isophthlic /NPG resin. Chemical resistance can be further increased by using bisphenol. A derivatives or by using HET acid to make the resin.

Reduced flammability resins

Various ways of producing self-extinguishing resins were discussed. These can be summarised as follows :

a. By using a chlorinated or brominated monomer.
b. By using a chlorinated or brominated glycol.
c. By using a chlorinated or brominated acid, either saturated, unsaturated or both.
d. By using other types of fire retardant monomers.

Other materials such as chlorinated hydrocarbons, trichloroethyl phosphate or bromine containing compounds may also be incorporated into the resin to give some degree of flame retardancy. Not all of these methods are equally effective. There are also commercial reasons why all resins do not meet the most stringent fire requirements.

Flame retardancy can be enhanced by adding antimoney trioxide to halogen containing resins. This does, however, render than opaque. Other fillers, such as aluminium hydroxide and zinc borate, may also be used.

With all laminates resin/glass ratio and component design can effect flammability. In particular, the higher the glass content of a laminate the lower the flammability with any particular resin system.

A further way of aiding fire retardancy is to coat the laminate with an intumescent coating. This expands on contact with a fire and protects the laminate from flames for some considerable time, depending on the intensity of the fire. Direct flame contact converts the coating to a carbonaceous foam filled with an inert gas and in so doing reduces spread of flame.

Low shrink/ low profile polyester resins

With normal unsaturated polyester resins containing about 35% of styrene, shrinkage of about 8% usually occurs during cure. With large flat mouldings this high shrinkage results in sink marks and a geneally poor quality finish, unacceptable for many applications.

Whilst some reduction is shrinkage can be achieved by the use of alternative monomers, such as vinyltoluene and t-butylstyrene, higher viscosities and incompatibility can result.

Developments for low and zero shrink unsaturated polyester resins have centred around the use of thermoplastic additions. Since the first claim, made in a French patent in 1957, that thermoplastic soluble in or swollen by styrene could be used to reduce shrinkage, numerous patents have appeared, covering the use of practically all types of thermoplastic materials.

Examples of some of the thermoplastics presently being used are polyvinyl acetate homopolymers and copolymers, polycaprolactones from Union Carbide, cellulose acetate butyrate from Eastman Kodak and acrylic polymers from Rohm and Haas.

One theory for the low shrinkage, is that the low shrinkage of the cured polyester resin is due to void formation during cure, through monomeric styrene diffusing out of the thermoplastic leaving behind hollow microspheres. They consider this to be the mechanism in the case of polystyrene and polyethylene additions.

However, the voids are formed in the cured resin due to thermal expansion of the thermoplastic during cure of the unsaturated polyester resin. Subsequent cooling results in voids around the thermoplastic inclusions.

Whiever mechanism is correct, void formation seems to be either a necessary part, or a by product, or that mechanism. It also seems that there must be some incompability between the polyester and the thermoplastic to produce low or zero shrinkage.

In general, the recommended level of thermoplastic additive lies between 10 and 20% of the weight of unsaturated polyester resin, the exact amount depending on the particular additive used and its effect on process variables such as viscosity. The major use of such resins has been in formulating sheet and dough moulding compounds where shrinkage marks present a major problem.

Whilst many zero shrink compositions have been formulated few of these have overcome all the problems of moulding the low profile parts required by the automotive industry. Some additives result in surfaces with poor paint adhesion, whilst others give systems which are unsuitable for pigmentation. Also, difficulties can be encountered in achieving consistently high quality mouldings free from micro-porisities. Where ribs and bosses are moulded in, there is still a tendency for sink marks to appear on the moulded surfaces.

This is probably caused by the significantly higher exotherm developed during cure in these thicker sections.

Other factors which affect shrinkage are types and quality of filler, reinforcement, catalyst and thickening agent; moulding temperature and pressure; part shape and thickness. These must all be taken into account in addition to the selection of the low profile additive to be used.

As far a is known at present, none of the these low profile systems is suitable for room temperature cure; all require heat cure for the effect of the additive to be seen.

Various resins and additives are available commercially, as are low profile and zero shrink sheet and dough moulding compounds.

Special purpose resins

This classification is used to describe those resins which do not conveninetly fit into the previous categories or which have been designed for use with particular processes.

Flexible resins

Flexible resins are those which in the cured state are soft and rubbery. They are prepared by replacing part or all of the saturated acid with a dibasic aliphatic acid such as adipic or sebacic acid. In so doing, the chemical resistance of the cured resin is generally reduced and water absorption increased.

Their main applications are in increasing the flexibility and impact resistance of the more rigid laminating systems and in casting and encapsulating systems.

Resins for sheet moulding compounds

Various types of resin can be used for SMC production. All must be of consistent quality, with carefully controlled water content. Low viscosity resins are used which can be chemically thickened by the addition of calcium oxide or magnesium oxide. This pre-thickening characteristics must be consistent from batch to batch, with rapid thickening and stable final viscosity. The resin used must also be stable for several months in the presence of a catalyst, yet cure fast at elevated temperature to ensure a short moulding cycle.

Many sheet moulding compounds contains low profile additives to ensure that high quality mouldings can be produced free from sink marks.

Resins for dough moulding compounds

Various types of resin can be used for DMC and BMC. Whichever resin is used is should be capable of taking a high filler loading and remain sufficiently viscous to carry glass fibres and filler to all parts of the mould during the moulding cycle. The resin also needs to be stable for several months in the presence of a catalyst, yet cure rapidly at processing temperature to provide a short moulding cycle for high production rates. As with resins used for SMC, the resin must have consistent properties, both in the liquid and cured state, and consistent reactivity.

Many commercially available dough moulding compounds contain low profile additives to ensure that consistent high quality mouldings are produced, free from sink marks.

Resins for prepregs

Resins used for prepregs are generally of the heat resistant type, with a high viscosity brought about by the addition of up to 5% of a polyhydric alcohol during manufacture. Since prepregs are expected to have a shelf-life of several months at room temperature, a low volatility monomer is needed, this diallyl phthalate is used in place of styrene as monomer. Prepregs may be prepared by impregnating the reinforcement with an acetone solution of the catalysed resin. During manufacture the acetone evaporates to leave a slightly tacky prepreg.

Light cured resins

Unsaturated polyester resins are available which can be cured by exposure to visible light at the blue end of the spectrum, centred on a wavelight of 420 nm. These consist of conventional polyester resins incorporating a special catalyst system.

They are only suitable for use in open moulding processes and mostly for transparent laminates where light can penetrate the laminate. Small pigment loadings (0-5%) and some filler loadings can be tolearated, but light transmission decreases as filler loading increases. Thus cure time increases with filler loading. Aluminium hydroxide and Ballotini glass pheres are the most satisfactory fillers for use with these resins.

The advantages claimed for these resins are :

1. No catalyst addition necessary by the user, therefore no mixing errors are likely to occur.
2. Resin does not gel on brushes and rollers and so cleaning is easier.

3. Surplus resin can be used again since it will not cure until exposed to an appropriate light source.

Other speciality resins

Other speciality resins are available with good adhesion to acrylic sheeting for bath manufacture, or good adhesion to rigid PVC for the manufacture of chemical plant and pipes.

Where process requirements dictate, special reactivity of viscosity resins can generally be obtained from most suppliers. These may be of the standard type or chemical or fire retardant resins.

Further modifications, where resins are intended for the manufacture of roof domes and sheeting, are the incorporation of UV stabilisers and optical brightners.

Casting Resins

Polyester resins are widely used for button manufacture. Here the resin needs to be either colourless or every light coloured and colour stable after cure. When cured the resin should exhibit good hot water resistance, hardness and impact resistance. Also, the resin must exhibit good punching properties immediately after gelation and good machineability after cure.

For fast production rates, a high reactivity, low viscosity resin, with fast air release is needed. Various resins are available which meet all of these requirements.

Clear colourless resins are also used for encapsulation. Here the resin must exhibit rapid air release for bubble-free castings. Low viscosity resins are used, preferably with some degree of flexibility to withstand impact. The resin should also be resilient, crack resistant and have moderate to low shrinkage during cure, with low exotherm, where filled system are used, the colour of the resin is unimportant and brown or straw coloured resins may be used. For some applications good electrical properties are also required.

Where decorative castings are to be produced, such as paper weights, the objects to be encapsulated must be free from moisture, otherwise this will cause cloudiness in the cured resin system the objects to be encapsulated should be dipped in acetone for 5-10 min before encapsulation, followed by immersion in a mixture of equal parts of uncatalysed polyester resin and acetone, then in pure uncatalysed polyester resin and finally in the catalysed resin. A low catalysed level should be used to give a long gel time and hence negligible exotherm, to prevent damage to the specimen. A cure time to up to several weeks may be ncessary to achieve full cure. Where plants or animals are encapsulated, these may change colour or the colours may fade completely within a short period of time.

With the encapsulation of electrical components, either clear or filled resin systems may be used. Here, the colour of the resin system is generally unimportant and straw coloured or pale brown resins may be used. Fillers such as alumina, silica flour and calcium carbonate are often added to the resin system to disperse exothermic heat and reduce shrinkage during cure.

Electrical components may be embedded using metal or plastic moulds, or potted using metal or plastic containers which remain part of the finished components. In this latter case, thin walled metal or polystyrene containers may be used. With polystyrene, excellent adhesion to the polyester containers may be used. With polystyrene, excellent adhesion to the polyester resin is obtained and if a thin-walled container is used it follows the shrinkage of the resin on curing. Vacuum encapsulating is often used to ensure complete penetration of the resin into the component and bubble-free castings.

Castings resins are also used for making synthetic marble. Here, chunks of marble are encapsulated in polyester resin. When cured the blocks are sawn and polished and used in a similar way to whole marble slabs. By so doing, marble waste can be fully utilised. Resins used for this application must have good adhesion to marble, good impact resistance, good elasticity to precent sawing, minimum shrinkage and good polishability. They must also be heat resistant and resistant to most foodstuffs, since slabs cut from blocks are frequently used as table tops.

7

Catalysts, Accelerators and Inhibitors for Unsaturated Polyester Resins

The catalysts used are invaribly organic peroxides. Since these are chemically unstable as a class of compounds, of which some can decompose explosively in the pure form, they are mostly supplied as solutions, dispersion or pastes in a plasticiser or as a powder mixed with an inert filler to stabilise them. Often diluted peroxides are described as 'phlegmatised' with a plasticiser such as dimethyl phthalate. This indicates that they have been made safter to handle or stabilised with a plasticiser. Since organic peroxides are hazardous materials to handle, due note shoule be taken of the safety recommendations issued by the various manufacturers. More organic peroxides are used at between 1 to 4% based on the resin weight.

The most commonly used accelerators are either those based on a cobalt soap or those based on a tertiary amine. Other types of accelertors may be used for specific applications and include quaternary ammonium compounds, vanadium, tin and zirconium salts. Cure can also be accelerated by exposure to UV light. For certain applications mixed cobalt/tertiary amine accelerators are used to give very short gel times. Accelerators are usually used at between 0.5 and 4% based on the resin weight.

Catalysts and accelerators should never be mixed together since this will result in violent decomposition of the peroxide with the risk of fire and explosion.

Although the wide range of catalysts available gives considerable scope in selecting a system with the desired pot-life, occasions can arise when it is desired to lengthen the pot-life without altering gel and cure time so that demoulding is not affected. This can be accomplished by adding an inhibitor to the system. This is in addition to the inhibitor already present in the resin. Some inhibitors increase pot-life, gel time and cure time whilst others just extent gel time—such an effect is shown in figure.

In order to achieve the optimum cured properties from the resin system, the catalyst and accelerator must be chosen with care and the correct amount used. Suppliers generally recommend particular catalyst/accelerator combinations for use with each of their resins, together with recommended propertions. These systems have been arrived at by experimentation and when used as recommended will give cured resins with optimum properties—mechanical, chemical, etc. Often more than one catalyst/accelerator system is recommended to take account of the variety of processes which might be used in production.

The curing Reaction

Cure of unsaturated polyester resins takes place by free radical polymerisation through the unsaturated groups (double bonds) both in the polyester chain and the styrene or other monomer. This is shown schematically below. The free radicals are provided by the peroxide as it decomposes and it is the rate at which these free radicals are produced which governs the gel and cure time of the resin.

A polyester resin will begin to cure as soon as the catalyst has been added. However, with heat cured systems and, in particular, sheet and dough moulding compounds, to all intents and purposes cure does not progress until a certain minimum temperature has been reached. This is the activation or critical temperature of the organic peroxide. This temperature is lowered in the presence of an accelerator.

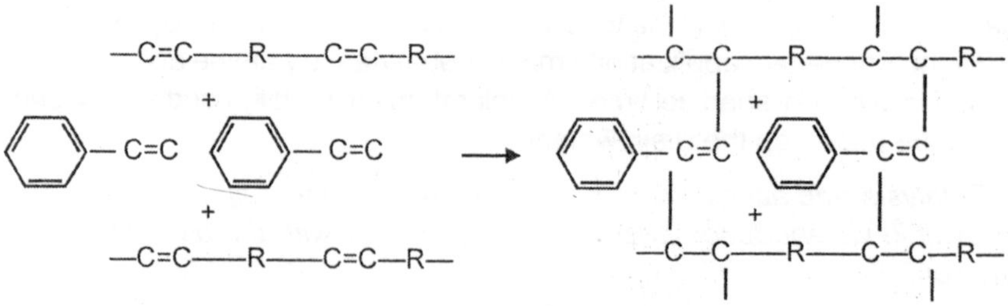

Once sufficient free radicals have been formed the resin starts to cross link. This reaction is exothermic and the heat evolved can raise the mix temperature to above 150°C very quickly. As the temperature increases so does the rate of production of free radicals. Under the worst circumstances this produces a run-away exotherm with an exponential temperature rise. If this happens while the catalysed resin is in bulk in the mixing pot, the exoterm can be violent enough to decompose the resin. The result is copious black smoke the possible ignition of the resin. In a laminate, the temperature rise may well be lower due to the smaller bulk of resin involved and the greater surface area available to conduct heat away. However, if an uncontrolled exotherm does occur this will result in a scrap moulding and possible damage to the mould.

The consequences of excessive exotherm during the moulding process can be discolouration and stress cracking – neither of which is acceptable in the finished moulding it is for these reasons that care must be taken in the selection and use of catalyst/accelerator systems.

Of important in determining which organic peroxide to use with which process are decomposition rate, half-life, critical temperature and active oxygen content of the peroxide. All but active oxygen content are interlinked.

Active oxygen content. This is the percentage of active oxygen (—O—O—) in the peroxide assuming it is 100% pure. It gives an indication of the number of free radicals available assuming normal decomposition. However, since double cleavage may also occur it can only be used as a guide. As an example, pure benzoyl peroxide has an active oxygen content of 6.60% but is more frequently supplied as a 50% paste with an active oxygen content of 3.2%. Various methods are used for determining active oxygen content.

Critical temperature. This is the minimum temperature at which a peroxide starts to rapidly form free radicals. Generally only those peroxides with critical temperatures within the range 60-130°C are used for cross linking polyester resins.

Half-life. This is a convenient way to express rate of decomposition of an organic peroxide at a specified temperature and is taken as the time for half of the peroxide originally present to decompose. This is generally determined on a 5 mol% solution in benzene. A dimethyl phthalate solution may also be used but this gives a different result. Other molar concentration solutions may also be used.

The curing of a polyester resin can be considered to take place in three stages.

1. Gelation— where there resin changes from a free flowaring liquid to a soft gel.
2. Hardening— where the resin cures from a soft gel to a hard material capable of being removed from the mould.

3. Final cure or maturing — where the resin achieves its full mechanical and chemical properties. This can take from several hours at elevated temperatures to several weeks at room temperature. This may also be referred to as post cure. For room temperature cured systems, maturing or post curing may be carried out at elevated temperature. Such post curing may be carried out immediately following the hardening stage while there is still sufficient residual peroxide available to complete the cure. If this is delayed for several days permanent undercure may result due to exhausted catalyst. Clearly different systems will require different post curing conditions.

Several parameters can be changed to modify the curing process. These can be summarised as follows :

A reduction in catalyst content will increase gel time.

A reduction in accelerator convent will increase gel time. The converse of these is also true.

Increasing the cure temperature reduces gel time.

Increasing film or laminate thickness reduces gel time.

The addition of fillers tends to increase gel time.

Catalysts or initators

Catalysts or initiators for unsaturated polyester resin systems consists of organic peroxides. These may be supplied as powders, pastes or liquids, all of which must be thoroughly dispersed in the resin to ensure uniform cure.

Organic peroxides can be divided into two broad classes— the true peroxides such as benzoyl peroxide and the hydroperoxides such as cumene hydroperoxide. Some, such as MEK peroxide are considered such as cumene hydroperoxide. Some, such as MEK peroxide, are considered to be mixed peroxides.

The most commonly encountered peroxide catalysts for room temperature cure are EMK peroxide, cyclohexanone peroxide and acetylacetone peroxide— each of which is used with a cobalt accelerator. In addition, benzoyl peroxide accelerated with a tertiary amine is sometimes used.

For elevated temperature cure benzoyl peroxide is more frequently used. There are, however, numerous other peroxides available for specific applications and specific temperature ranges. For example, where a non-yellowing system is needed a catalyst other than benzoyl peroxide is preferred. Here, t-butyl perococtoate may be used. Where a very high degree of care is required to avoid tainting of food stored in contact with a moulding, a mixed catalyst system may be needed.

Since pigments often contain traces of metals which can act as accelerators for peroxide catalysts, care has to be takn in selecting not only the pigment but also the catalyst used. Di-t-butyl peroxide and the perketals are generally unaffected by trace metals in pigments. Perketals can only be used for elevated temperature cure since no accelerator is known to promote room temperature cure.

When selecting any catalyst, consideration must be given to cure temperature and gel time with the particular resin to be used. The choice is further affected by moulding process and whether or not a short, medium or long curing cycle is required. With moulding compounds such as SMC and DMC, shelf-life of the catalyst system is also of importance. This can sometimes be adequately prolonged by adding additional inhibitor to the system.

Three broad processing temperature groups exist :

Room temperature cure (20—50°C)—

Contact moulding cold press moulding, resin injection.

Intermediate temperature cure (50–100°C)—

continuous laminating filament winding.

High temperature cure (100–160°C)—

hot press moulding, SMC, DMC

Peroxide catalysts can be conveninetly divided into six different chemical types.

Diacyl peroxides

General formula : $R{-}\overset{\overset{\displaystyle O}{\|}}{C}{-}O{-}O{-}\overset{\overset{\displaystyle O}{\|}}{C}{-}R'$

The most commonly encountered diacyl peroxide is benzoyl peroxide, or more correctly dibenzoyl peroxide. Others found in use include 2,4-dichlorobenzoyl peroxide, diacetyl peroxide and dicaprylyl peroxide. They may be used both in room temperature and elevated temperature cured systems, although an amine accelerator is needed to promote cure at room temperature.

1. Benzoyl peroxide

Molecular weight		242.2				
Action oxygen content		6.6%				
TLV		5 mg/m3				
Melting point		103-5°C				
Critical temperature		70°C				
Maximum storage		25°C				
Temperature						
Half-	Temperature	72	88	92	102	136
Life :	(°C)					
	Time (h)	10	2	1	0.5	0.017

The pure material is a white granular solid, soluble in a vareity of organic solvents but insoluble in water. It is normally stored damped with water or as a paste in phthalate plasticiser. It is also available as a paste in tricresyl phosphate where fire retardant properties are required. Care should be taken to ensure thorough dispersion of the paste in the polyester resin to obtain uniform cure.

Benzoyl peroxide is used without an accelerator for heat cured systems and finds application in SMC, DMC, filament winding, compression moulding and for the manufacture of continuous sheeting. For room temperature cure a tertiary amine accelerator is necessary. Cobalt accelerators are ineffective. The amine accelerated system can be used for hand and spray lay-up body stoppers and putties, and site applications.

Amine accelerated system have a tendency to yellow and craze on ageing, probably dur to the lower degree of cure obtained with these systems then with cobalt/hydroperoxide systems. In spite of this, the system has important uses in the temperature range 10–25°C. Normal usage in 2% by weight of a 50% paste.

2.2,4–Dichlorobenzoyl peroxide

Molecular weight	380
Action oxygen content	4.28%

Critical temperature		60°C			
Maximum storage temperature		25° C			
Half–Life :	Temperature (°C)	50	60	70	80
	Time (h)	17.8	8.2	1.4	0.5

2,4 Dichlorobenzoyl peroxide is used with an amine accelerator either alone or in combination with benzoyl peroxide to obtain gelation of polyester resins down to 0°C, providing that a post cure about 15°C is given to ensure full cure. It has a low peak exotherm when used below 70°C and can be used to produce fairly large crack-free castings. It finds use in contact moulding, hot press moulding and low temperature curing systems.

3. Dilauroyl peroxide

Molecular weight		404				
Action oxygen content		4.0%				
Critical temperature		65°C				
Maximum storage temperature		25°C				
Half-Life :	Temperature (°C)	50	62	70	80	100
	Time (h)	60	10	3	1	0.1

Dilauroyl peroxide is used in heat cured systems over the temperature range 60–80°C. It is effective some 10–15°C below the temperature needed to obtain full cure with benzoyl peroxide. It does not affect the yellowing of polyester resins. It is a powder which is directly soluble in the resin.

4. Diacetyl peroxide

Molecular weight	118
Action oxygen content	13.6%
Critical temperature	75°C
Maximum storage temperature	25°C

Half– Life :	Temperature (°C)	5070	100	
	Time (h)	190	7.3	0.2

Diacetyl peroxide is only suitable for use in heat cured systems and finds application in SMC and DMC. No yellowing of cured systems is obsered on ageing.

5. *Di-n-octanoyl peroxide (caprylyl peroxide)*

Molecular weight 286

Action oxygen content 5.6%

Critical temperature 60°C

Maximum storage temperature 10°C – refrigerated

Half– Life :	Temperature (°C)	50	70	100
	Time (h)	63	3.5	0.1

This peroxide finds use in hot press moulding and continuous laminating.

Ketone peroxide

General formula :

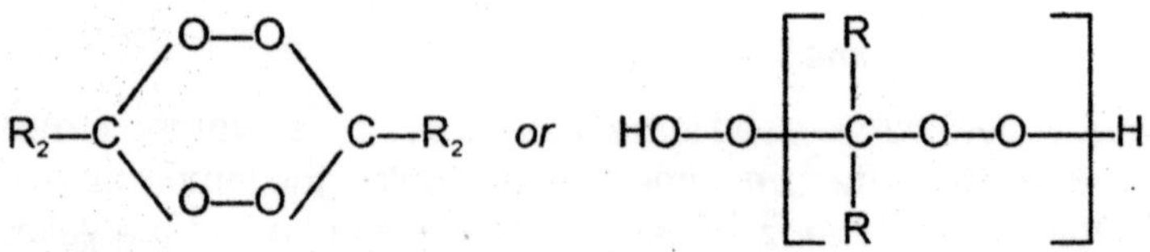

This is perhaps the most common class of peroxides used with polyester resins. Two commonly encountered ketone peroxide are methyl ethyl ketone (MEK) peroxide and cyclohexanone peroxide. These are used for cold curing polyester resins in the presence of a cobalt accelerator. Whilst they are described as peroxides they are in in fact mixing peroxides containging a number of different products. Cyclohexanone peroxide is also used at 150°C to prevent staining of metal moulds.

Other peroxides included in this class are acetylacetone peroxide, methyl isobutyl ketone peroxide and various ketone peroxide mixtures. The typical chemical structure for the pure ketone peroxide is shown on the left above whilst the hydroperoxide structure is shown on theright.

1. *Methyl ethyl ketone peroxide*

Molecular weight	176
Action oxygen content	18.2%
TLV	0.2 ppm (1.5 mg/m³)
Critical temperature	80°C
Flash point	65–104°C
Maximum storage temperature	25°C

Half-Life				
	Temperature (°C)	100	120	150
	Time (h)	16.2	6.0	0.2

MEK peroxide is very explosive in its pure form and is therefore always supplied diluted with a plasticiser such as dibutyl phthalate. It is used for the room temperature cure of polyester resins in conjunction with a cobalt accelerator, over the temperature range 15–25°C. It slowly decomposes at room temperature with the evolution of gas and should be strored in vented containers. Many different grades are available with different reactivities. Dyed solutions are also available to assist in mixing. Often a blue dye is used which disappears during cure. Normal usage is 1–2% for laminates and 2–4% for gelcoats.

2. *Cyclohexanone peroxide*

Molecular weight	228
Action oxygen content	13.1%
Critical temperature	88°C
Melting point	75°C
Maximum storage temperature	25°C

Half–Life :	temperature (°C)	70	80	90	100	120
	Time (h)	140	34	9	7.7	0.9

Cyclohexanone peroxide is available as a pure powder a 50% paste in a phthalate plsticiser and in solvent solution. Like MEK peroxide it is a mixture of different compounds. It is used with a cobalt accelerator over the temperature range 0-25°C but, if used below 15°C, a post cure above this temperature is necessary to achieve full cure. Tertiary amine accelerators can also be used but polyesters cured in this way have a tendency to yellow and age. It is often used in body stoppers with a mixed tertiary amine/cobalt accelerator. It can also be used without an accelerator to cure polyester resins at temperatures above 160°C.

Very long pot-life systems can be obtained by using a manganese accelerator. Another accelerator sometimes used in vandium octoate.

Cyclohexanone peroxide offers several advantages over MEK peroxide. It generally gives a lower peak exotherm, is less sensitive to cure temperature and has a lower tendency to yellow in transparent sheeting. It is also preferred when a low stress cure is desired.

3. *Acetylacetone peroxide (3,5-dimethyl-3,5-dihydroxy-1,2-dioxolane)*

Molecular weight		134		
Action oxygen content		11.9%		
Critical temperature		95°C		
Maximum storage temperature		25°C		
Half-Life	Temperature (°C)	142	170	233
	Time (h)	10	1	0.017

Acetylacetone peroxide is used with a cobalt accelerator to give very fast cure even with levels of 0.5% peroxide. When used at the same level as MEK peroxide a slightly shorter gel time is obtained, with demoulding possible less than 1 h after gelation. In this respect it behaves somewhat like a bezoyl peroxide /tertiary amine system but without the yellowing effect. Due to its heat of reaction it is not recommended for laminates thicker than 3–4mm. Since cure progresses rapidly through the soft to hard stage, trimming with a knife is virtually impossible.

Acetylacetone peroxide catalysed resin without an accelerator present has a far longer pot-life than the equivalent MEK peroxide system and has been described which is extremely shock, sensitive.

It finds application as acatalyst in general room temperature cured systems and in particular in resin injection systems.

4. *Methyl isobutyl ketone (MIBK) peroxide*

Molecular weight		232
Action oxygen content		13.8%
Critical temperature		50°C
Flash point (as supplied)		75°C
Maximum storage temperature		25°C
Half–Life :	Temperature (°C)	100
	Time (h)	19.6

Polyester resins catalysed with MIBK peroxide have very long gel times at room temperature with rapid cure above 60°C, so this catalyst is generally used in the temperature range 60–120°C. It is often combined with benzoyl peroxide, t-butyl peroxtoate or 1,1 – bis (t-butylperoxy) –3,3,5-trimethylocyclohexane. It is particularly useful in the manufacture of corrugated sheeting and for filament winding due to its low critical temperature and relatively low exotherm. It can be used at room temperature with a cobalt accelerator. The effect of various catalyst blends on cure time at 80°C is shown in table

Effect of different catalyst blends on cure time at 80°C

Catalyst	***Accelerator 1% Co (% wt)***	***Kickoff temp (°C)***	***Curetime (min)***	***Peakexotherm (°C)***	***Potlife (min)***
1.5% MIBKP	—	60	6.0	196	8
1.5% MIBKP	0.5	55	4.7	179	1
1.0% MIBKP + 0.5% t butyl peroctoate	—	60	6.0	182	10
1.0% MIBKP + 0.5% t-butyl percotoate	0.5	55	4.8	184	1

Catalyst	***Accelerator 1% Co (% wt)***	***Kickoff temp (°C)***	***Curetime (min)***	***Peakexotherm (°C)***	***Potlife (min)***
1.0% MIBKP + 0.5% Benzoyl peroxide	—	60	6.0	182	10
1.0% MIBKP + 0.5% benzoyl peroxide	0.5	55	4.8	180	1

5. Ketone mixtures

Various mixed ketone peroxides are available based on unspecified ketones. These have generally been formulated for specific applications.

Hydroperoxides

General formula : $R_3—C—O—O—H$

Only two hydroperoxides are found in common use, namely, t-butyl hydroperoxide and cumene hydroperoxide. Both can be used with cobalt or vanadium accelerators.

1. *t-Butyl hydroperoxide*

Molecular weight		90			
Action oxygen content		17.7%			
Critical temperature		88°C			
Maximum storage temperature		25°C			
Half-Life:	Temperature (°C)	100	120	130	150
	Time (h)	170	12	3.2	0.4

This was one of the earliest hydroperoxides in use but is not so widely used today due to its lower stability compared with MEK peroxide or cyclohexanone perioxide. It can be used with a vanadium accelerator for surface coating and dip coating applications. It can be inhibiting effect on MEK peroxide/cobalt systems and lowers peak exotherm. It can be used alone for elevated temperature cure.

2. *Cumeme hydroperoxide*

Molecular weight		152		
Action oxygen content		10.5%		
Critical tempeature		100°C		
Maximum storage temperature		25°C		
Half-Life :	Temperature (°C)	115	130	150
	Time (h)	472	113	10

Cumene hydroperoxide can be used in high temperature cured dip moulding compounds or combined with benzoyl peroxide for intermediate cure temperatures. For example, with a blend of these two peroxides used to cure a polyester resin at 70°C, the benzoyl peroxide starts to cure the resin and when the temperature reaches 100°C the cumene hydroperoxide takes over.

Cobalt and vanadium accelerators can be used with cumene hydroperoxide to give systems with long working times and good final cure. Such systems find application with air drying topcoat resins.

Dialkyl and diarakyl perioxides

General formula : $R_3—C—O—O—C—R_3$

Several examples of this group of peroxides are in use to cure polyester resins, mostly with heat cured sheet and dough moulding compounds.

1. *Dicumyl peroxide*

Molecular weight	270
Action oxygen content	5.9%
Critical temperature	100°C
Maximum storage	25°C

temperature					
Half-Life	Temperature (°C)	100	120	135	150
	Time (h)	100	6.8	1.0	0.2

Dicumyl peroxide is generally used in potting compounds and sheet and dough moulding compounds. It has an exceptionally long pot-life coupled with good elevated temperature cure. It cannot be accelerated.

2. Di-t-butyl peroxide

Molecular weight		146		
Action oxygen content		10.9%		
Critical temperature		100°C		
Maximum storage		25°C		
Maximum storage temperature		25°C		
Half - Life :	Temperature (°C)	100	120	150
Time (h)		210	20	0.8

Di-t-butyl peroxide is used for hot cured systems where a long catalysted pot-lifeis needed. Pot life is not influenced by pigments. As supplied, di-t-butyl peroxide is a highly volatile liquid; this limits its storage life and hence its use.

3. t-Butyl cumyl peroxide

Molecular weight		208		
Action oxygen content		7.7%		
Critical temperature		110°C		
Maximum storage temperature		25°C		
Half- Life :	Temperature (°C)	110	130	150
	Time (h)	35	3.6	0.42

t-Butyl cumyl peroxide gives systems with a long pot-life coupled with good elevated temperature cure. It finds use in SMC, DMC and hot press moulding systems.

4. *2,5-Dimethyl-2,5-bis(t-butylperoxy)hexane*

Molecular weight		290		
Action oxygen content		11.0%		
Critical temperature		100°C		
Maximum storage temperature		25°C		
Half-Life :	Temperature (°C)	119	138	175
	Time (h)	101.0	0.017	

Whilst this peroxide gives systems with a very long pot-life and good mechanical strength of moulded parts, it requires a high moulding temperature. It finds use in SMC, DMC and hot press moulding compounds.

Peroxyesters

General formula : $R_3—C—O—O—\underset{\underset{O}{\|}}{C}—R$

Several different types of peroxyesters are found in use, mostly for hot press moulding and sheet and dough moulding compounds. They can be used over a wide range of processing temperature arom about 70°C to above 150°C.

1. *t-Butyl peroxybenzoate*

Molecular weight		194		
Action oxygen content		8.2%		
Critical temperature		90°C		
Maximum storage temperature		25°C		
Half-Life :	Temperature (°C)	90100	120	150
	Time (h)	7017	1.6	0.05

t-Butyl peroxybenzoate can be used alone as a catalyst for hot press moulding in the temperature range 130-150°C or accelerated with cobalt or vanadium salts at somewhat lower temperatures. If gives systems with a longer shelf-life than those containing benzoyl peroxide. It is also used to cure diallyl phthalate resins.

2. t-Butyl peroxydiethylacetate

Molecular weight		188			
Action oxygen content		8.5%			
Critical temperature		65°C			
Maximum storage temperature		10°C- refrigerted			
Half-Life :	Temperature (°C)	5070	90	100	
	Time (h)	330	19	1.7	0.46

This peroxide catalyst fins use in SMC, DMC and hot press moulding compounds.

3. t-Butyl peroxyester

This peroxide catalyst is used for filament winding, hot press moulding and continuous sheet manufacture over the tempeature range 60–100°C.

4. t-Butyl peroxyisononanoate (t-butyl peroxy-3,5,5-trimethylhexanoate)

Molecular weight		230			
Action oxgyen content		6.9%			
Critical temperature		80°C			
Maximum storage		20°C			
Half-Life :	Temperature (°C)	70	100	120	130
	Time (h)	700	14.7	1.5	0.3

This peroxide catalyst can be used as an alternative to t-butyl peroxybenzoate for filament winding and hot press moulding.

5. *t-Butyl perocotate (t-butyl peroxy-2-ethylhexanoate*

Molecular weight		216			
Action oxgyen content		7.4%			
Critical temperature		70°C			
Maximum storage Temperature		20°C			
Half-Life :	Temperature (°C)	5070	90	100	
	Time (h)	330	16	1.4	0.5

t-Butyl perocotate is used for hot curing above 60°C. It finds application in filament winding continuous sheet manufacture, hot press moulding and SMC and DMC. It gives less yellowing than bezoyl peroxide. It can be used with cobalt and vanadium accelerators.

6. *Di-t--buityl diperoxyphthalate*

Molecular weight		310		
Action oxygen content		10.3%		
Critical temperature		95°C		
Maximum storage temperature		25°C		
Half-Life :	Temperature (°C)	100	120	150
	Time (h)	211.2	0.01	

This peroxide catalyst gives systems with a long pot-life. It is used for hot press moulding at temperatures above 150°C.

7. *t-Butyl peroxypivalate*

Molecular wegith	174
Action oxygen content	9.2%
Critical temperature	50°C
Maximum storage temperature	0°C – refrigerator

Half-Life :	Temperature (°C)	5070	90
	Time (h)	231.9	0.16

t-Butyl peroxypivalate is used for hot press moulding in the temperature range 90–110°C where it gives a short cure cycle. It can also be used for continuous sheet production. If accelerated with a cobalt or vanadium accelerator it can be used in the temperature range 50-70°C. It gives less yellowing than benzoyl peroxide. The major disadvantage is that it requires refrigerated storage.

8. 2,5 Dimethylhexane-2,5 -diperoxybenzoate

Molecular weight		386		
Action oxygen content		8.3%		
Critical temperature		—		
Maximum storage temperature		25°C		
Half-Life :	Temperature (°C)	100	118	155
Time (h)		10	1	0.017

This catalyst finds application in hot press moulding compounds with a short cure cycle.

9. 4,4 Di-t-butyl peroxy-n-butyl valerate

Molecular weight		302			
Action oxygen content		10.6%			
Critical temperature		80°C			
Maximum storage Temperature		25°C			
Half-Life :	Temperature (°C)	70	90	100	120
	Time (h)	630	135	12	1.5

This catalyst finds application in hot press moulding compounds, SMC and DMC.

Perketals (peroxyketals)

General formula :

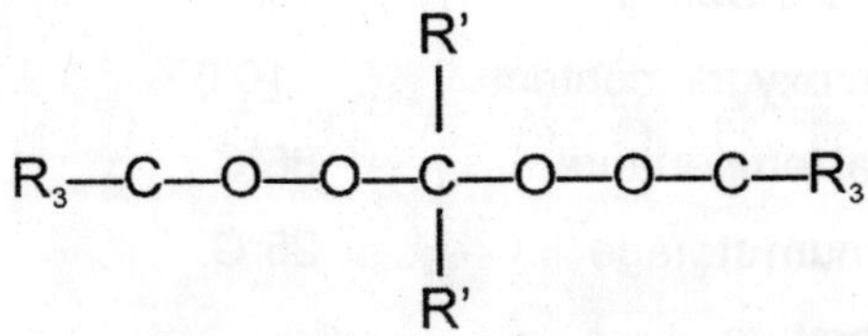

Perketals are used as catalysts in hot cure moulding compounds. They are less sensitive to metal compounds, pigments, etc., than t-butyl perbenzoate and are therefore very suited to use in pigmented moulding compounds, SMC and DMC. They can be used at elevated temperatures with a vanadium accelerator but no accelerator are known to promote cure at room temperature.

1. *2,2-Bis(t-butylperoxy)butane*

Molecular wegiht		234		
Action oxygen content		13.6%		
Critical temperature		100°C		
Maximum storage temperature		25°C		
Half-Life :	Temperature (°C)	110	115	130
	Time (h)	10	2	0.3

This catalyst finds application in hot press moulding SMC and DMC

2. *1,1-Bis(t-butylperoxy)cyclohexane*

Molecular weight		260		
Action oxygen content		12.3%		
Critical temperature		85°C		
Maximum storage temperature		25°C		
Half-Life :	Temperature (°C)	95	113	130
	Time (h)	10	1	0.13

This catalyst finds application in hot press moulding SMC and DMC.

3. *1,1-Bis(t-butylperoxy)-3,3,4-trimethylcyclohexane*

Molecular weight		302		
Action oxygen content		10.6%		
Critical temperature		86°C		
Maximum storage temperature		25°C		
Half-Life :	Temperature (°C)	85110	115	130
	Time (h)	273.8	0.71	0.17

This catalyst finds application in hot press moulding, SMC and DMC.

Accelerators and Promoters

These are materials which when used in conjunction with an organic peroxide catalyst increase the rate at which that peroxide breaks down into fee radicals. Thus they accelerate the cure of the polyester resin in a controlled manner. They are mainly used to enable otherwise unsuitable peroxides to be used to cure polyester resins at ambient temperature, although they may also be used to reduce the cure temperature of heat cured systems. They can be divided into two classes of materials— metal compounds and tertiary amines.

Metal compounds such as cobalt naphthenate are excellent accelerators for hydroperoxides and mixed peroxides but have little or no effect on true peroxides. Tertiary amines, on the other hand, work well with peroxides and are often used in conjunction with cobalt naphthenate as coaccelerators for mixed peroxides such as MEK peroxide.

Generally the pre-accelerated resins available commercially contain a cobalt salt as accelerator.

Accelerators must at all times be kept well away from organic peroxides and never mixed with them since violent decomposition of the peroxide will result.

Metal compounds

These are usually metal salts or soaps supplied in solutions of various concentrations to plasticisers, solvents or styrene. Cobalt salts are the most common ones used although vanadium salts may also be encountered. Other metal soaps such as manganese and copper may sometimes also be used.

These, however, tend to give gel times of several hours at room temperature and are best used with heat cured systems where a short gel time can be obtained, coupled with a long pot-life. With all metal salts, solutions, in phthalate plasticixers generally have better storage lives than those in styrene.

Cobalt accelerators

These are based on such materials as cobalt siccatolate, naphthenate or octoate. Solutions are available with cobalt concentrations ranging from 0.5-10%. The more concentrated solutions are either diluted before use or added directly to large batches of resin to reduce the amount of diluent or plasticiser added. The typical level of cobalt used with a normal polyester resin is between 0.5 and 2% of a solution containing 1% of cobalt. Cobalt accelerated resins tend to be pale pink in colour.

Manganese accelerators

Manganese salts are occassionally used as accelerators for polyester resin systems. They give long gel times at ambient temperature when used to accelerate ketone peroxides.

Vanadium accelerators

Vanadium accelerators are used to accelerate ketone peroxide catalysed polyester resins for low temperature cure or peroxyester and perketal catalysed systems at elevated temperatures. They give faster hardening with ketone peroxides than can be achieved with cobalt accelerators. Normal dosage is between 0.2 and 4% of a 0.5% solution, based on the resin.

The effect of cobalt and manganese accelerators on gel time of a general purpose polyester resin.

	Gel time (min)					
	50% Cyclohexanone peroxide paste, addition			50% peroxide addition 2%	MEK 2%	
Temperature (°C)	**20**	**40**	**50**	**20**	**40**	**50**
Accelerator						
Cobalt salt (1%) Co	22	13	9	18	13	8
Manganese salt (1% Mn)	316	55	25	495	88	41

Tertiary amine accelerators

Generally only three tertiary amines are used as accelerators, the most common being dimethylaniline. They are used to accelerate peroxide catalysts such as benzoyl peroxide to give ambient temperature cure. Dimethylaniline is also used as a co-accelerator in cobalt accelerated systems with ketone peroxide catalysts. Tertiary amines are generally used at between 1 and 4% of a 10% solution. One disadvantage of amine accelerated systems is their tendency to yellow with age.

An indication of the difference in accelerating effect shown by the three commonly used tertiary amines can be seen in table.

Effect of different tertiary amines on gel time of a general purpose polyester resin

Material	Proportions (parts by weight)		
General purpose polyester resin	100	100	100
Benzoyl peroxide, 50% page	2	2	2
Diethylaniline	1.5	—	—
Dimethylaniline	—	1.5	—
Dimethyl-p-toluidine	—	—	1.5
Approx. gel time at 20°C (min)	100	20	5

NN-Dimethylaniline

This is normally referred to as dimethylaniline. It gives normal gel times and quick cure when used to accelerate diacyl peroxide catalysed systems. It can also be used as a co-accelerator with cobalt accelerated ketone peroxide caalysed systems to reduce gel times. In this respect it is of particular use in cold press moulding and resin injection systems.

NN-Diethylaniline

This is normally referred to as diethylaniline. It gives long gel times coupled with fast cure at room temperature when used as an accelerator in bezoyl peroxide catalysed resin systems.

NN-Dimethyl-p-toluidine

Dimethyl-p-toluidine gives short gel and cure times in conjunction with benzoyl peroxide catalysed resin systems. It is used where short moulding cycles are needed with ambient temperature cure.

Mixed metal salt/t-amine accelerators

These provide extremely short gel and cure times when used to accelerate ketone peroxide catalysed systems. They are particularly suitable for use in could press moulding and resin injection systems where fast mould turn round is required. They generally consist of a plasticiser solution containing 2% cobalt and 10% dimethylaniline. Their effect on gel time is shown in Table.

Effect of mixed accelerator on gel time of a general purpose polyester resin system.

Material	Proportions (parts by weight)					
Genegal purpose polyester resin	100	100	100	100	100	100
cyclohexanone peroxide (50%)	2	2	2	2	—	—
MEK (peroxide (50%)	—	—	—	—	1	1
Cobalt naphthenate (1% Co)	1	1	1	1	1.5	1.5
Dimethylaniline (10%)	—	0.1	1	—	—	0.75
Dimethyl-p-toludine	—	—	—	1	—	—
Gel time at 20°C	36	23	16	18	—	—
at 25°C	—	—	—	—	8	2

Inhibitors

When polyester resins are manufactured, inhibitors are added to ensure adequate shelf-life of the resin. However, occassions may arise where the pot-life of a system needs to be prolonged. This can be achieved by adding a further small quantity of inhibitor to the system. Some inhibitors increases gel time and cure time as well as pot life, whilst others just increase pot-life without influencing gel and cure times, so that demoulding can still take place soon after gelation. if pot-life is lengthened by decreasing accelerator proportion rather than by using an inhibitor, then gel and demoulding times are both prolonged.

Two inhibitors which are used to prolonged pot-life are t-butyl catechol and di-t-butyl-p-cresol.

8

Epoxy Resins

Epoxy resins are materials which contain two or more epoxide groups  or more generally glycidyl groups 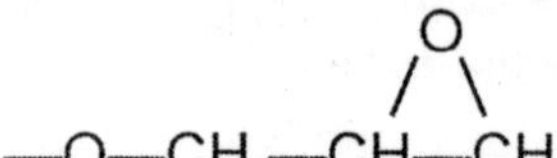 per molecule. The same terms are however, also used to describe the cured materials. The uncured resins range from free flowing liquids to high melting solids, which can be cured or cross-linked into hard infusible materials by reaction with an appropriate curing agent.

The curing reaction is brought about by the addition of a suitable di- of poly-functional curing agent to the resin. Typical curing agents include primary and secondary amines, polyamides and organic anhydrides. These are generally used in roughly stoichiometric proportions with the resin and may require heat to effect cure. Other curing agents used are the catalytic curing agents such as the boron trifluoride complexes. These are used in catalytic amounts and may require either ambient temperature or heat cure. No by products are evolved during cure. The resultant cured resins are generally hard thermoset materials with excellent mechanical, chemical and electrical properties.

Epoxide resins are widely used in coating, adhesive, flooring, laminating and casting applications. Hardly any industry today does not use an epoxide resin composition of some sort; indeed they are even found in many hones in the form of a two-pack adhesive-perhaps the best known being the 'Araldite' adhesives from Ciba Geigy Plastics and Additives Company.

For many applications the straightforward reaction of a resin with a curing agent gives a product suitable for immediate use. For other applications basic formulation may need to be modified to improve handling and curing characteristics, mechanical or other properties. Such modifications can be brought about by the addition of diluents, flexibilisers, fillers and pigments, reinforcements, fire retardants and accelerators. The effect of some of these on resin properties will be dealt with later in this chapter and also in the following chapter on curing agents.

One of the main advantages which epoxide resins have over polyester resins is their low shrinkage during cure. This is generally between 1 and 2% but can be reduced to virtually zero by the addition of fillers.

Epoxy resins are usually classified according to their epoxide equivalent weight or Epoxy Molar Mass (EMM). This is the equivalent weight in grams of resin containing one epoxide group. Alternatively this may be expressed as epoxide content, which is the number of equivalents per kilogram of resin. Thus an epoxide equivalent or EMM of 500 is the same as an epoxide content of 2.0 Epoxide equivalent is determined by direct titration of a solution of resin in an appropriate solvent with hydrobromic acid or perchloric acid using crystal violet as indicator.

Resins used for laminating applications fall into two broad classes :

(a) the liquid resins-used mostly for wet lay-up and site applications, although some are used for prepregs, and

(b) The low molecular weight solid resins-used in solution for making prepregs.

The unmodified bisphenol A resin (diglycidyl ether of bisphenol A-DGEBA) are generally used for heat cured wet lay-up systems. These, when cured with an amine such as diaminodiphenylmethane (DDM), have excellent mechanical and electrical properties, with a heat deflection temperature above 150°C. They also have excellent chemical resistance.

With site applications, the viscosity of the basic resin is generally too high for convenient use and so a diluent is added to lower the viscosity. This can also serve to improve ambient temperature cure by increasing the mobility of the system. Most ambient temperature cured epoxide resin systems have a heat deflection temperature of about 50°C. This can, in some cases, be raised by giving the system an elevated temperature post cure. This is often accomplished when the laminate is put into service.

Resins used for electrical laminates may be liquid or solid depending on whether a wet lay-up or prepreg techniques is used. For prepreg manufacture either a liquid resin, EMM 190-250, or a fairly low molecular weight solid resin, EMM 450-900, is used. These can both give rigid tack-free prepregs. Where tacky prepregs are required liquid resins are always used. Flame retardant laminates the generally prepared from brominated resins. For convenience, resins and diluents are discussed in this chapter and curing agents and accelerators in the next.

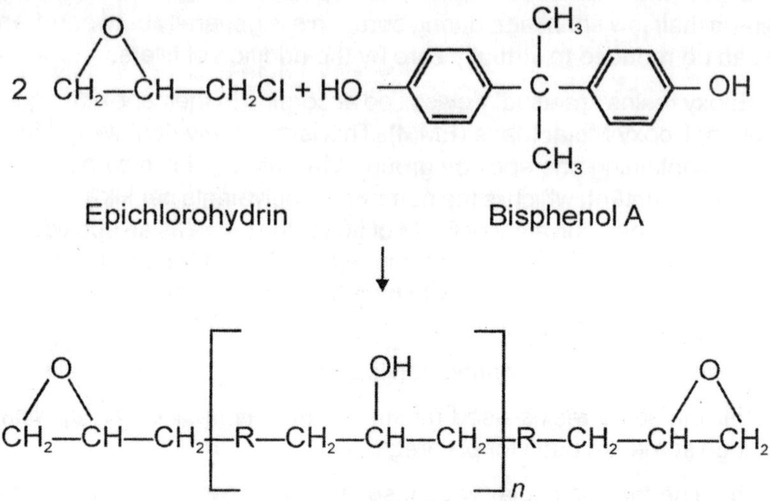

Diglycidyl ether of bisphenol A

$n = 0, 1, 2, 3$, etc

$n = 0$ represents the pure diglycidyl ether of bisphenol A

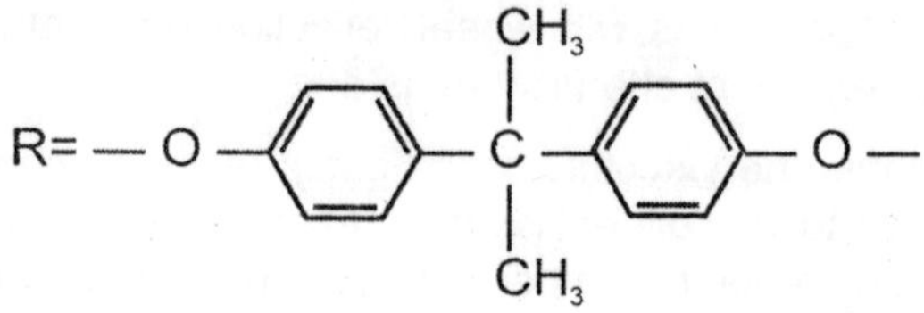

The resins

Bisphenol a based resins

These were the first resins to be produced commercially and form some 95% of all epoxide resins available today. They range from medium viscosity liquids through to high melting solids and are all prepared by the reaction between epichlorohydrin and bisphenol A. the different resins are formed by varying the proportions of the two reactants. With some ten times excess epichlorohydrin the product is virtually pure monomer, i.e., two molecules of epichlorohydrin plus one molecule of bisphenol A. as the proportion of epichlorohydrin is reduced, so the molecular weight of the resin is increased. All the resins produced in this way consist of mixtures of different molecular weight species and it is this molecular weight distribution which governs the viscosity/ melting point of the resin.

Glycidyl ester resins

The structure of a typical glycidyl ester resin is as follows :

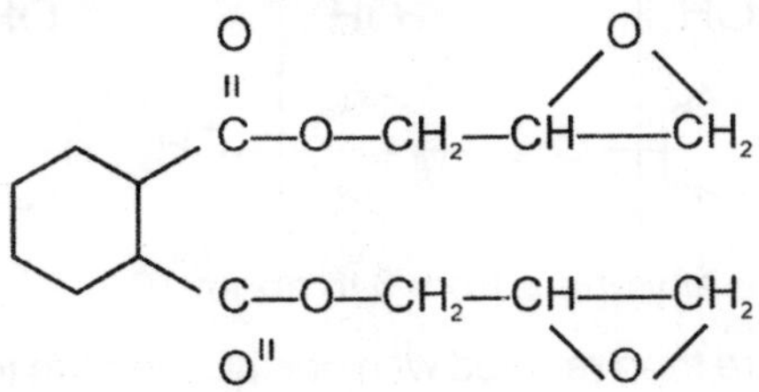

Resins of this type are used with anhydride curing agents, to give systems with viscosities and reactivities ideally suite to vaccum impregnation, laminating and casting applications. These resins cannot generally be used with normal ambient temperature curing agents due to lack of adequate cure.

Glycidyl amine resins

The general structure of a tetra-functional glycidyl amine resin is as follows :

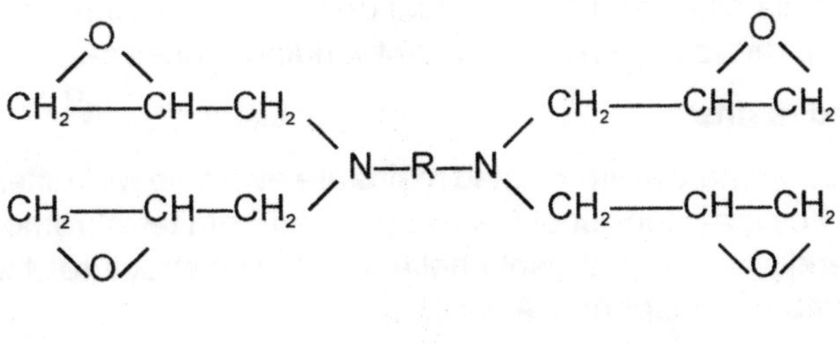

Such resins can be made from most diamines and may be liquids or solids. One such resin is the tetraglycidyl amine of 4,4'-diaminodiphenylmethane. Other resins may be based on secondary amines such as hydantoin, where a diglycidyl amine resin results.

Few resins of this type are commercially available. Those which are available are mostly cured with anhydrides to give rproducts with good high temperature strength retention and good resistance to nuclear radiation. These systems are used for wet lay-up laminating and filament winding.

Glycidyl ethers of novolac resins

Novolac resins are produced when phenol and formaldehyde react together in acid solution. The simpliest novolac is bisphenol F. Most, however, have higher molecular weights, thus :

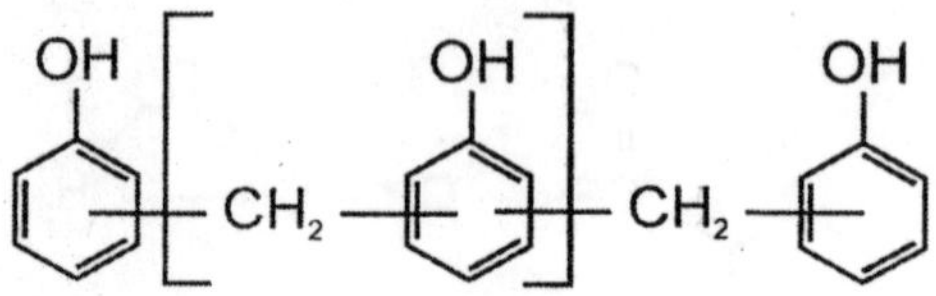

Where n can be anywhere from 0 to about 10.

These resins are then reacted with epichlorohydrin to form glycidyl ether novolacs. The bisphenol F resin is a liquid while the higher molecular weight resins are solids.

Such resins, when cured, offer high temperature stability and good chemical resistance but have the disadvantage, with certain curing agents, of having a low strain at break (1–1.5%). Thus they can fail by interlaminar shear if used in 90° cross-plied carbon fibre composites, due to the strain induced by the negative coefficient of thermal expansion of the fibre along its length.

Norrnally the curing agents used with epoxy novolac resins for pregpregs are aromatic diamines and boron trifluoride complexes. Anhydrides are used for wet lay-up (head cured) and filament winding processes.

Brominated resins

Various commercial brominated resins are available with different bromine contents. They may consist of resins prepared from tetrabromobisphenol A alone or blends with normal bisphenol A resins. The structure of the diglycidyl ether of tetrabromobisphenol A is :

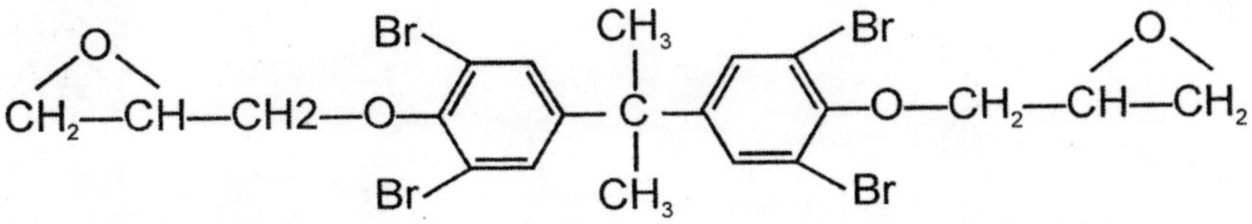

These resins are used to confer flame retardancy to composites. They are mostly used in the manufacture of fire retardant printed circuit boards, for example to NEMA Grade FR4 specification, where cure is effected with dicyanidiamide.

Diluents

Diluents are added to epoxide resins primarily to lower viscosity and thus improve handling characteristics. They also modify the cured properties of the resin. In general terms, the higher the proportion of diluent added to the resin the lower the viscosity and the lower the mechanical properties and chemical resistance of the cured system the level at which properties start to drop dramatically varies from one diluent to another. Most cause little concern up to between 10 and 15% addition.

Diluents can be divided into two classes :

(a) the reactive diluents such as the monoglycidyl ethers and

(b) the non-reactive diluents

The reactive diluents are the most widely used, since they form an integral part of the cured structure and cannot be leached out.

Most resin manufacturers supply a range of diluted resins designed to meet specific end-user needs. These cover a wide range of viscosities, with diluent concentrations generally within the range 0-20%. Many of these resins have been specifically formulated for end uses other than laminating.

9

Curing Agents for Epoxide Resins

Most curing agents promote this curing reaction by opening the epoxide ring and become chemically bound into the resin in the process. Others, the catalytic curing agents, cause self-polymerisation of the epoxide resin through the epoxide groups. These reactions may occur at room temperature with some curing agents or at elevated temperature with others.

The curing reaction is an exothermic process, which with some systems, may cause an exothermic process which, with some systems, may cuase an unacceptable rise in temperature resulting charring and possible ignition of the system, whilst in others the exotherm is insignificant. Cure may be accomplished in as little as 30s or take severl days or even weeks. With ambient temperature curing systems, full cured properties are not generally reached from 1-2 weeks.

Although the epoxide group will react with some 50 or so other chemical groupings, for the most part, particularly in laminating and adhesive applications, only four groupings are encountered. These can be classified as amines (both primary and secondary), organic anhydrides, catalytic curing agents and polyamides. This last group are used more for adhesive and coating applications than for laminating.

The reactivities of epoxide groups differ depending on their location. They may be ring situated, internal or terminal. Terminal epoxide groups also differ in reactivity depending on whether they are glycidyl ethers, glycidyl easters or glycidyl amines. IN some cases accelerators may be required to ensure that adequate cure occurs.

In addition to the straightforward range of chemical compounds used as curing agents, numerous formulated products are available. These may consist simply of blends of amines with other amines or diluents, adducts with epoxide resins or glycidyl ether diluents, or more complicated formulations. Many such formulations also contain an accelerator to promote or speed-up cure at ambient temperature. These products are frequently formulated for specific end use applications, where simple compounds prove inadequate.

Selection of Curing Agents

In selecting of curing agent the first consideration must be given as to where the laminate is to be made. For site applied in situ laminates, an ambient temperature curing system will be needed. This restricts the choice, for most practical purposes, to liquid amine curing agents. Here, several formulated aromatic amine based curing agents are available which combine low viscosity, reasonable pot-life and good handling characteristics with excellent cured properties and chemical resistance.

A system developed as an alternative to polyester systems for ambient temperature moulding is XD 927 from Ciba-Geigy with gelcoat XD 928. This system provides excellent in the uncured state.

With ambient temperature cured factory prepared laminates, various other formulated amine curing agents are available from resin and curing agent suppliers. Here the choice must depend on the properties required of the finished laminate.

These may be good electrical properties, good mechanical properties, high HDT, high impact strength, light colour or some combination of these. Details of some of these systems are given later in this chapter.

Amine Curing Agents

Amine curing agens may be primary or secondary amines, aliphatic, alicyclic or aromatic. In simple terms the reaction with an epoxide resin is an addition reaction where the amine links directly with the epoxide group to form a combined polymer, with hydroxyl groups formed during the reaction. Thus the amine needs to be present in a roughly stoichiometric proportion to ensure full cure. In practice, this proportion may need to be modifed slightly to achieve optimum cured properties.

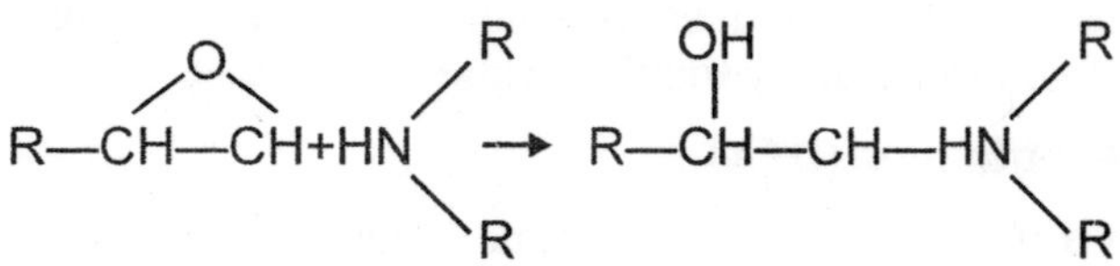

The primarly aliphatic amines react with DGEBA resins at room temperature to give products with excellent properties, but only react slowly with nonglycidyl ether resins. Those amines which are commercially available are generally polyamines and may contain both primary and secondary amine groups.

The alicyclic amines may contain primary, secondary and tertiary amine groups and may also require an accelerator to ensure full cure at room temperature. Examples of these materials are N-aminoethylpiperazine (AEP) and isophoronediamine (IPD). Salicylic acid and phenol are frequently used as accelerators for these materials.

The aromatic amines are generally used alone for heat cured systems or in solution, with an acclerator, for room temperature cure. They are widely used for laminating applications and give cured products with excellent mechanical, electrical and chemical resistance up to fairly high temperatures. Typical examples of aromatic amines in common use are 4,4'-diaminodiphenylmethane, m-phenylenediamine, and diaminodiphenylsulphone. All these are solids and so need to be dissolved in the resin prior to gelation.

Care should be taken when handling all amine curing agents and in particular the aliphatic and alicyclic amines, which can cause skin dermatitis. All normal precautions should be taken to avoid skin contact and inhalation of vapours.

1. Ethylenediamine (EDA)

EDA is a mobile, fuming liquid which is used to cure liquid DGEBA resins at room temperature. It is unpleasant to handle and so is mostly adducted with resin and used for coating applications, frequently in solution.

2. Trimethylhexamethylenediamine (TMD)

TMD is a colourless, low viscosity, aliphatic branched chain diamine consisting of a blend of two isomers. It can be used to cure liquid DGEBA resins alone or more generally a an activator for IPD. TMD is often partially adducted with resin and the viscosity of the adduct reduced with benzyl alcohol. Salicyl acid can be used as accelerator for room temperature cure. It is mostly used for coating and flooring applications.

3. Diethylenetriamine (DTA)

DTA is a mobile, almost colourless, fuming liquid used to cure liquid DGEBA resins at room temperature. It can be used for tooling and laminating applications and is often blended with polyamides for adhesive applications.

It is not as unpelasant to handle as EDA. Cure under high humidity conditions causes surface bloom.

Handling can be improved by reacting DTA with ethylene oxide to give 2- hydroxyethyldiethylenetriamine.

4. 2- Hydroxyethyldiethylenetriamine (T)

This is often referred to as Amine T. It is an almost colourless low viscosity liquid used to cure liquid DGEBA resins at room temperatue. It is more pleasant to handle than DTA but can still give rise to bloom on cured surfaces under high humidity conditions. It is used for casting, adhesive and wte lay-up laminating—often with diluted resins.

5. Dipropylenetriamine (DPTA)

DPTA is a colourless to pale yellow mobile liquid used with liquid DGEBA resins for coating and casting applications. If used immediately after mixing, the surface is prone to bloom. It can be adducted with resin to reduce this tendency.

6. Triethylenetetramine (TETA)

TETA is a mobile pale yellow liquid used to cure liquid DGEBA resins at room temperature. It is used for casitng tooling and wet lay-up laminating applications, often with diluted resins. HDT of the cured system can be increased by giving an elevated temperature post cure. Cured properties are similar to those obtained with DTA. Cure under high humidity conditions can result in bloom on the surface.

7. Tetraethylenepentamine (TEPA)

TEPA is a liquid aliphatic polyamine with reactivity and cured properties similar to those of TETA. It is mostly used for coating applications from solution.

8. Diethylaminopropylamine (DEAPA)

DEAPA is an aliphatic amine containing a tertiary amine group which acts as a catalytic curing agent at room temperature. For this reason it is used at only 4–8 phr rather than the level expected from calculation based on two active hydrogens. It is often used in adhesive formulations.

9. Dimethylaminopropylamine (DMAPA)

DMAPA is a similar curing agent to DEAPA and is used for similar applications.

10. m-Xylylenediamine (mXDA)

mXDA is a colourless low viscosity liquid amine which gives excellent cured properties with DGEBA resins after heat cure, but which requirs the addition of an accelerator and diluent to complete cure at room temperature. It is mostly adducted with a resin or glycidyl diluent to overcome problems of amine bloom. The adducts are used for coating and wet lay-up laminating application and cure well at room temperature.

11. N-Aminoethylpiperazine (AEP)

AEP is a mobile liquid giving cured systems with excellent impact resistance after full cure. Whilst cure will take place at room temperature, a post cure of 2 h at 100°C is necessary to develop full properties, particularly impact resistance. It gives a short pot-life and high exotherm with liquid DGEBA resins. It is often used in formulated amine curing agents.

12. Isophrone diamine (IPD) (3-aminomethyl-3,5,5-trimethylcyclohexylamine)

IPD is a colourless low viscosity liquid at room temperature. It gives excellent cured properties with liquid DGEBA resins after heat cure, but requires the addition of a diluent and accelerator to produce a usable system for room temperature cure. It can be used for casting and laminating applications.

13. Cyclohexylpropylenediamine.

This is colourless low viscosity cyclo-aliphatic polyamine used for casting and laminating appliations. Heat cure is required to acheive optimum properties, although when used with an accelerator, co-curing agent or diluent, cure will take place at room temperature. It can be used with liquid DGEBA resins and gelled at room temperature it is intermediate in reactivity between the aliphatic and aromatic amines. Typical accelerators for room temperature cure are salicylic acid, phenol and triphenyl phosphite.

14. 3,3'-Dimethyl-,4'-diaminodicyclohexylmethane

This is a colourless low viscosity, cyclo-aliphatic diamine used for casting and laminating applications. Heat cure is necessary for optimum cured properties but it will cure at room temperature in the presence of accelerators, co-curing agents or diluents. Typical accelerators for room temperature cure are salicyclic acid, phenol and triphenyl phosphite. It must be stored in closed containers to prevent reaction with carbon dioxide and it may crystallise during storage at room temperature. It can be melted by gently warming. It can be used as an alternative to DDM for heat cured systems.

15. 4,4'-Diaminodiphenylmethane (DDM)

DDM is also known as methylenedianiline (MDA), although this latter name is mostly used in the USA. DDM is an off-white solid at room temperature and is supplied either as a powder or flake. Normal mixing procedure is to melt the DDM at bout 100°C and add to the resin, also at 100°C. Once the resin and curing agent have been thoroughly mixed the blend can be cooled to about 50°C to prolong pot-life. At 50°C with a liquid DGEBA resin, pot life is about 2h.

DDM can be used for wet lay-up laminating, casting or prepreg separation. For prepreg preparation both the resin and curing agent are dissolved in solvent– either methyl ethyl ketone or acetone.

DDM dissolved in a liquid DGEBA resin will react at room temperature in the absence of solvents or accelerators, to form a tack-free 'B-stagged' system. This is a system which is partially reacted but which will metl and flow with the application of heat. It is on this basis that tack-free prepregs can be prepared. Shelf-life of such prepregs is between 1 and 3 weeks at room temperature but can be considerably prolonged with refrigerated storage.

One major advantage that DDM has over many other curing agents is the ability to cure liquid DGEBa resins down to about 0°C in solution in the presence of an accelerator such as phenol or salicylic acid. Several pre-accelerated solutions of DDM are commercially available. These are used for a variety of applications, including site applied laminates for repairs to oil storage tanks. The solvents generally used are high boiling ones, such as cresols, sulphalane, etc., which remain in the cured resin system as plasticisers. To prevent precipitation of the DDM during storage of such solutions, a small quanitity of resin or monoglycidyl ether diluent may be added to form a partial adduct with the DDM. Depending on the level of accelerator used, cure can proceed slowly with low exotherm or rapidlly with a high exotherm. Cure rate can be controlled far better than with the alphatic amine cured system.

16. m-Phenylenediamine (MDP)

MPD is a colourless crystalline solid at room temperature which rapidly darkens on exposure to light. It can either be added as a powder to resin at 80°C and dissolved with stirring or both resin and MPD can be heated to about 65°C and thoroughly mixed. In either case irritating fumes are given off. Once mixed the blend should be cooled to room temperature to prolong pot-life, Skin and clothes turn brown on contact with MPD. These stains resemble those obtained from walnut shells and are very difficult to remove.

Although MPD can be used both for wet lay-up and prepreg manufacture, it finds limited use due to its unpleasant handling characteristics.

17. 4,4'-Diaminodiphenylsulphone (DDS)

DDS is a free flowing pinkish powder with a fairly high melting point. It is usually used at about 10% excess of stoichiometric proportion in unaccelerated systems. It can be accelerated with boron trifluoride complexes, typically $BF_3$400-a boron trifuloride—monoethylamine complex.

The mixing procedure normally used for casting or wet lay-up laminating is to warm the resin to about 130-140°C and add the DDS slowly with stirring until it is all dissolved (about 20 min). Pot life at 130°C is about 1 h. If an accelerator is to be used the blend should be cooled to below 100°C before adding it.

DDS is used more as curing agent in prepreg systems than for wet lay-up. Here the resin and DDS are both dissolved in a ketone solvent such as acetone or MEK. Prepreg without an accelerator whould normally by dried for about 20 min at 150°C while if an accelerator is present, drying time would be about 15 min at 115°C. During this drying period partial reaction occurs between the resin and curing agent.

Anhydride Curing Agents

These consist of organic anhydrides and are use in roughly stoichiometric proportions with epoxide resins. The cured systems generally exhibit better thermal stability and radiation resistance than amine cured systems, with heat deflection temperatures as high as 305°C. In most cases an accelerator, such as a tertiary amine, is required to promote cure since, without it, the anhydride will not react directly with the epoxide group.

Whilst stoichiometric proportions of anhydrides can be used, in practice it has been found that optimum cured properties are usually achieved when a molar ratio of anhydride to epoxide resin of 0.85:1 is used. This is usually increased to 1:1 when a tertiary amine accelerator is added. With many anhydrides, due to the complexity of the resin/anhydride reaction, cured properties are they dependent on cure schedule and final cure temperature. The factors which govern cured properties are gel time and temperature. The factors which govern cured properties are gel time and temperature, post cure-time and temperature, type and amount of accelerator, hydroxyl content of the resin, proportion of anhydride used and amount of free acid present in an anhydride.

Of the wide variety of anhydrides available only a few are in common use and many of these are variations on a theme, e.g. the methylated and hydrogenated derivatives of phthalic anhydride. Some of the anhydrides in use are listed in together with typical cure schedules.

Anhydride curing agents can be divided into three categories based on handling convenince : (a) the liquids—which can be blended with liquid epoxide resins just by mixing (b) the low melting solids- such as hexahydrophthalic anhydride-which require melting before adding to warm resin, and (c) the high melting solids-these are generally used in solution for prepreg preparation or in powder form in powder coating systems.

Properties of anhydride eutectic blends

Anhydride blend		*Crystallisation temperature (°C)*	*phr*	*HDTa (°C)*
HHPA/NMA	(60/40)	–20	85	112
HET/NMA	(40/60)	+15	95	112
HET/HHPA	(40/60)	+10	85	128

[a]1 phr accelerator with liquid DGEBA resin EMM 190.

Since anhydrides have a tendency to pick up moisture during storage and are thus converted into the free acids—which act as accelerators—they should always be stored in dry sealed containers.

Anhydrides can be used both for wet lay-up in prepregs and, in many cases, give systems with low viscosities and long pot-lives. High temperature resistance can often be improved by using resins other than those based on bisphenol A.

1. Phthalic anhydride (EPA)

This was the first anhydride used to cure epoxide resins. It is a solid which readily sublimes on heating and is difficult to incorporate in epoxide resins for this season. The normal procedure used is to add the solid phthalic anhydride to resin at 120°C and stir until all the anhydrid has dissolved. Adequate ventilation must be provided to remove the subliming anhydride. Due to this problem phthalic anhydride is only used for casting applications.

2. Tetrahydrophthalic anhydride (THPA)

THPA is a white powder with a melting point of 100°C and a vapour pressure below 0.5 mm Hg at temperatures up to 130°C, thus sublimation is negligible under normal conditions. It can be incorporated into the resin by melting at 115–120°C and adding to resin at a similar temperature. After mixing, the blend can be cooled to about 90°C to prolong pot-life. Alternatively, THPA can be added to resin at about 90°C with continuous stirring until all has dissolved. It can be used for prepreg preparation from acetone solution (55-60% concentration).

3. Methyltetrahydrophthalic anhydride (MTHPA)

MTHPA is a low viscosity liquid and can therefore be stirred into liquid resins at room temperature. At 25°C pot-life varies from 2.5 to 7.5 h depending on accelerator level. Initial mix viscosity is of the order of 0.5-0.8 Pa s.

4. Endomethylenetetrahydrophthalic anydride (nadic anhydride -NA)

Nadic anhydride is a crystalline solid soluble in liquid DGEBA resin at 100-130°C, but it precipitates out below 80°C. It can be used for wet lay-up and prepreg preparation. To achieve maximum HDT a long high temperature post cure is necessary.

5. Methyl endomethylenetetrahydrophthalic anhydride or nadic methyl anhydride (NMA)

NMA is a pale yellow liquid at room temperature which, in the absence of an accelerator, will give a pot-life of several months at room temperature with liquid DGEBA resins. Maximum HDT varies considerably with cure schedule, as do mechanical properties. NMA can be used both for wet lay-up and prepreg preparation. HDT up to 280°C can be achieved with some of the high functionality resins. NMA is used in electrical laminating and filament winding applications.

6. Chlorendic anhydride (HET) (hexachloroendomethylenetetrahydrophthalic anhydride)

HET anhydride is a high melting white powder used to confer fire retardant properties on epoxide resin systems. Such systems, however, have limited thermal stability. It can be used with antimony trioxide to improve fire resistance. It can be dissolved in a liquid DGEBA resin at 100-120°C. For prepreg preparation HET anhydride can be dissolved in an MEK/toluene (8.8:1) mixture. No accelerator is necessary with HET anhydride. Whilst HET anhydride used to be used for the preparation of fire retardant prepregs, it has been superseded by brominated resins.

7. Hexahydrophthalic anhydride (HHPA)

HHPA is a waxy solid melting at about 35°C. It is generally stirred into resin at 40-45°C when it easily dissolved to give a homogeneous low viscosity mix (0.25–0.35 Pa s at 40°C). HHPA can be used to make prepregs as well as for wet lay-up laminating. It is also frequently used for casting applications.

8. Methylhexahydrophthalic anhydride (MHPA)

MHPA is a liquid at room temperature and can be mixed with liquid DGEBA resins over the temperature range 20-80°C. Pot life at 20°C is about 1 week. It is normally used with a tertiary amine accelerator for casting and laminating applications.

9. Trimellitic anhydride (TMA)

TMA is a white crystalline powder with a melting point of 168°C. It can be dispersed in a liqudi resin by stirring, in which case the system has a pot-life of about 3 days at room temperature. Alternatively it can be added to resin at 125°C when it dissolves. Pot-life at 125°C is only about 10 min. The use of an accelerator is unnecessary due to the presence of a free carboxylic acid group. Resins cured with TMA exhibit good elevated temperature properties. For prepreg systems TMA can be dissolved in acetone. TMA is often used in powder coating formulations.

10. Pyromellitic dianhydride (PDMA)

PDMA is a slightly off-white crystalline material with a high melting point. It is soluble in liquid DGEBA resins at elevated temperatures but, due to its high reactivity, the system may gel before all the anhydride has dissolved. For this reason it is often used in blends with other anhydrides such as meleic anhydride or phthalic anhydride, the maleic anhydride /PDMA blend showing superior heat resistance.

With mixed anhydrides the resin should be heated to about 70°C prior to addition of the anhydride, followed by continuous stirring and warming to 120°C. Once all the anhydride had dissolved, the mix should be cooled to 90°C to prolong pot-life. Some properties of mixed anhydride systems are given :

Properties of some PDMA/anhydride blends

DGEBA resins EMM 190	100	100	100
PDMA	31	20	20
Maleic anhydride	-	20	-
Phthalic anhydride	-	-	28
Pot-life at 90°C (min	<10	10	20
HDT (°C)	290	290	207
Tensile Strength (MPa)	22	26	31

Tensile modulus (GPa)	2.7	2.9	3.7

PDMA is often used in solvent solution for making prepregs. Solubility of PDMA in various solvents is shown.

Solubility of PDMA in various solvents

Solvent	*Temperature (°C)*	*PDMA (g per 100 g solvent)*
Acetone	20	7
	56	9
Dimethyl sulphoxide	20	20
	120	95
Dimethyl formamide	20	16
	140	100

11.Dodecenylsuccinic anhydride (DDSA)

DDSA is a pale yellow, low viscosity liquid (0.3 Pa S) at room temperature which can be stirred into liquid resins with little difficulty. It provides a long pot-life system and gives a flexible cured resin with a low HDT. It is usually blended with other anhydrides to provide flexibility without significantly altering electrical properties. It requires an accelerator to effect cure.

Acceleratorsfor anhydride cured systems

Various accelerators can be used with epoxy/anhydride systems to promote cure. they include tertiary amines, organic ammonium salts and imidazoles. They are generally used in the range 1-5 phr. Some examples of accelerators in use are :

Benzyldimethylamine (BDMA)

Tris (Dimethylaminomethyl) phenol

1. Methylimidazole (DY 070 from Ciba-Geigy)

N-Butylimidazole

2-Ethyl-4-methylimidazole

Triamylammonium phenate (DY 063 from Ciba-geigy)

The imidazoles generally give systems with higher HDTs than either BDMA, K54 or DMP-30, can be seen.

Effect of different accelerators on exotherm and HDT

Accelerator	Proportion (phr)	Time to Peak exotherm (min)	Peak Temp (°C)	HDT (°C)
K54 or DMP -30	0.6	12	192	—
	1.0	9	199	124
BDMA	0.6	14	176	—
	1.0	9	198	126
1-	0.6	9	249	143
Methylimidazole	1.0	7	258	—

Polyamide Curing agents.

The polyamides used to cure epoxide resins are all reactive compounds with free amine groups. they may be amidopolyamines, aminopolyamides or imidazolines. They are mostly used in coating systems and to a lesser extent in adhesive formulations. They are rarely used for laminating.

Manufacturing procedure depends on the type of polyamides to be produced. In general they are derived from polyamines reacted with mono-or dibasic carboxylic acids. The carboxylic acids used are mostly those obtained from fats and oils such as soya, tall oil, castor oil etc. A typical dicarboxylic acid used is the dimer acid prepared from linoleic acid by a Diels—Alder reaction. Imidazolines are prepared by the high temperature reaction of a polyamine with a carboxylic acid to cause ring closure.

Numerous polyamide curing agents are commercially available, including water dispersible ones, ranging from low viscosity liquids to semi solids. Most can be used over a wide range of mixing proportions. For example. Versamid 125— a typical aminopolyamide — can be used in proportions from 50 to 100 phr with a liquid DGEBA resin; however cured properties vary considerably over this range.

Other Curing Agents

Several other types of curing agents are used with epoxide resins for laminating applications or in moulding compounds. One of the frequent requirements is for good shelf-life or one-pack systems. This is of particular importance with prepregs and moulding compounds. To achieve this it is often necessary to use blocked compounds, that is ones which decompose or re-arrange on heating to produce a reactive material. Examples of these include the boron trifluoride complexes and dicyandiamide. Other curing agents not classified elsewhere are the substituted imidazoles. Several examples of these curing agents are described in this section.

1. Dicyandiamide (Dicy)

Dicyandiamide is a solid agent used with solid DGEBA resins for the preparation of prepregs from solution. It is only sparingly soluble in solvents and so the ones which have to be used are 2-methoxyethanol, acetone/water (3/2) or dimethylforamide, the former being preferred. Prepreg has a shelf life to up to 6 months at room temperature and is generally used for the preparation of printed circuit boards (NEMA Grade G.10). Although cure takes place fairly rapidly in the temperature range 150—170°C, accelerator would be BDMA used at 0.1-0.4 phr, with a typical cure schedule of ½h at 165°C.

2. Boron trifluoride complexes

A number of different boron trifluoride complexes are used as curing agents for epoxide resins. The most important one for laminating applications is the boron trifluoride monoethylamine salt. These materials are all catalytic curing agents and are therefore used in small proportions. They may be used as sole curing agent or as accelerators for other curing agents. Depending on which compound is used, cure can take place at room temperature or elevated temperature.

3. Boron trifloride monoethylamine

Born trifuloride monoethylamine, often referred to as BF_3MEF or BF_3400 is a white crystalline solid melting close to its dissociation temperature (about 90°C). It hydrolyses and becomes inactive as a curing agent on exposure to moisture. It can be dissolved in liquid DGEBA resins at about 80-85°C for small batches or made into a paste with resin at 50°C for larger batches. Alternatively it can be used in solution for prepreg preparation. It should not be dissolved in acetone since this solvent is invariably wet and can cause deactivation of the curing agent under some circumstances. Methyl ethyl ketone presents no such problems.

10

Reinforcement Agents in Polymers

Fibrous Glass as Reinforcement Agent

Most glass fiber reinforcements are made from either of three different types "E", "C" and "S" glass.

"E" (electrical) glass is the most common glass composition used for yarns and reinforcements. It provides superior electrical characteristics, resistance to water and alkali, and high heat resistance properties that are particularly suited for electrical insulation applications.

"C" (chemical) glass has superior resistance to corrosive action of acids, and is used for such applications as industrial batteries.

"S" (high tensile strength) glass is used for lamination in high performance structures, such as aircraft and missile components. Strength-to-weight ratios exceeding those of most metals can be reliably achieved. "S-2" glass has the same glass batch composition as "S" glass, but a different size system S-2 glass is also used in aerospace applications and in some commercial applications where high tensile strength is required.

The batch of glass is fed into a furnace where it is melted at high temperature Fine, precisely controlled filaments are drawn, or pulled rapidly, from streams of the molten glass. These filaments are given a chemical size treatment which protects the individual fibres and provides chemical bonding—glass-to-resin matrix— when used for reinforcement. Finally, the filaments are wound and packaged for further fabrication.

Glass fiber reinforcements and their uses in reinforced plastics

Nominal form	General Description	Processs	Nominal glass content of typical laminates %	Typical Application
Rovings	Continuous strands of glass fibers	Filament winding continuous panel, preforming (matched die moulding), spraying, pultrusion SMC	25 to 80	Pipe, automotive, rod stock, rocket motor cases, ordinance, bathroom Components
Chopped strands	Strands cut to lengths of 1/8 to 2in.	Premix moulding, wet slurry preforming injection moulding	15 to 40	Electrical and appliance parts, ordinance components automotive
Reinforcing mats	Continuous or chopped strands in random matting	Matched die moulding hand lay-up, centrifugal casting, pultrusion	25 to 45	Translucent sheets, truck and auto body panels, marine
Surfacing and overlaying mats	Nonreinforcing random mat	Matched die moulding hand lay-up, and filament winding	5 to 15	Where smooth surfaces are required— automobile bodies, some housings

Nominal form	General Description	Processs	Nominal glass content of typical laminates %	Typical Application
Woven fabrics	Woven cloths from glass fiber yarns	Hand lay-up, vacuum bag auto-clave, hig pressure laminating	45 to 65	Aircraft, structures, marine, ordinance, hardware, electrical flat sheet and tubing
Woven roving	Woven glass fiber strands-coarser and heavier than fabrics	Hand layup	40 to 70	Marine, large containers
Nonw oven fabrics	Unidirect ional and parallel rovings in sheet form	Hand layup, filament winding	60-80	Aircraft structures

This manufacturing process produces both continuous filament is an individual fiber of such length that it extends substantially throughout the length of a continous filament strand. A strand is composed of many continuous filaments that are drawn from the molten glass at high speeds.

Both continuous and staple fibers can be fabricated into yarns and cords through conventional twisting, plying, and cabling operations. The various available forms of fibre glass reinforcements are listed above, which also describes in general the use of each reinforced plastics and summarizes applications.

The streng'h of fibrous glass-reinforced plastics are proportional to the concentration (volume) and orientation of the reinforcements. The form of the reinforcements and type of plastic matrix also affect strength.

Rovings. Fiber glass roving consists of number of untwisted glass strands grouped to form a continuous ribbon of multiple strands. Spun roving is made by looping a continuous single strand upon itself many times, and holding it with a twist.

Rovings are used in sheet molding compound (SMC) for matched metal die molding, continuous panel filament winding, sprayup, and pultrusion processes.

Rovings can also be converted into chopped strand mat, preforms, and woven roving, or can be chopped into fibers for use in moulding compounds.

Rovings are rated by the following characteristics.

1. *Strand integrity*– degree to which filaments are held together in the strand.
2. *Ribbonization*–degree to which strands are held together in the roving bundle.
3. *Catenary*–degree of sag, or differences in length, between the individual strands that make up the roving bundle.
4. *Chopping characteristics*– ease of chopping, strand integrity retention, number of long strands, and static problems. Chopping characteristics vary with the size used; for example, silane-sized roving offer greater resistance to cutting than to chrome sized rovings.
5. *Wetout*–speed and degree to which the roving is wet by the resin. Wetout also in dependent upon the size used. Wetout the laminate clarity often are confused, but are not necessarily related. However, good clarity cannot be attained without good wetout, although many systems will yield a milky laminate even if thoroughly wetted out.

Reinforcing mats. There are two basis fibrous glass mat types; chopped strandmat and continuous strand mat. Both offer essentially the same degree of reinforcement, but have different molding and handling characteristics.

Mats provide nondirectional reinforcement, and are used in hand layup, matched metal die molding, continuous laminating (panel), and pultrusion processes. Excepting woven roving, mats are lower in cost than woven products, and are slightly higher in price than bulk chopped strand or roving.

Characteristics or fibrous glass mats such as conformability, molability, resin holding power, wetout, and porosity are important for various applications. Mats are available in many thicknesses described in terms of weight per square foot, ranging from 20 gms to 100 gm/sq. ft. for chopped strand mat.

Surfacing and overlay mats are actually thin nonreinforcing mats used with reinforcing mats to obtain a resin-rich surface on a reinfored plastics part. Surfacing mats are relatively strong and stiff, and are used only on flat sheets and simple shapes. Overlay mats are fluffy, extremely drapable, and can be used on many types of complex shaped parts.

Stiffness, wash resistance, and color of mats depend upon the binder used to hold the mat together. There are two general binder types, soluble and insoluble. Insoluble binders are used on fibrous glass mats for matched metal die and pultruded reinforced plastics moldings. Soluble binders are used for hand layup and panel processes.

Woven roving is generally supplied with a silane type sizing for fast wetting action and maximum laminate strength in both dry and wet service applications. Heavier woven roving styles, where applicable, supply the most reinforcement for the least cost. The lighter styles are often preferred because of their low cost per square foot in comparison with the cost of other fabrics.

The yield of the roving is varied to meet specific weight and strength requirements. Weights range from 300 gms to 1 kg/sq. mts. thicknesses ragne from 0.05 and 0.1 mm. Woven roving is most often used in combination with mat.

Uniformity varies with the style of the woven roving. Close weave styles have good conformability, with little danger of weave shifting. Loose weave styles are not recommended, because they can shift position, leaving resin-rich areas and poor uniformity.

Chopped strands. Continuous or spun rovings are chopped into short lengths, then used in premix and wet slurry thermoset compounds and thermoplastic reinforcements. Chopped strands are available in lengths from 3 mm through 50 mm, and with different chemical sizes for compatibility with most plastics. Chopped strands often are classified on the basis of strand integrity.

Woven fabrics. Fibrous glass fabrics are woven from glass yarns into a variety of styles, thicknesses and weights. The styles can be varied so that the laminate strength can be either undirectional or orthotropic. Fabric weights range from approximately 40 gm-650 gm/sq.mts.

Fabrics generally are woven from yarns having a starch-oil sizing. after weaving the fabric is heat cleaned and finished with a resin-compatible material (e.g. Volan, A-1100, etc.). In the case of S904 fabrics, however, which are regarded as high performance materials, the yarn is made with a compatible size, and is woven directly into immediately usable reinforcements that eliminate the need for heat cleaning and finishing before the fibrous glass meets the resin.

Milled fibers. Continuous strands are milled into short nodules of glass filametns ranging in lengths from 1 mm to 12 mm, the length referring to the diameter of the screen openings used in the processing. A variety of sizes is available, compatible with polyester, epoxy, and other resins. Milled fibers are widely used for encapsulation in the electrical industry, as well as in thermoplastic and silicone compatible compounds, adhesive, patching compounds, and putties.

Yarns, Twisted strands of yarns are used, primarily in the weaving of fabric reinforcements and have limited use as a difect reinfrocement for plastics.

Factors affecting processing of fibre reinforcement Thermoplastics

The machine varible such as mixing configuration and screw speed effect the material properties and process efficiency. The properties of composites can be assessed by measurement of the fibre length distribution and tensile strength.

The use of strong brittle fibres to reinforce thermoplastics has become an established practice the full potential offered by such fibres is never reached in commercial products because of methods used to incorporate the fibres into thermoplastic. In continuous compounding there is a severe degradation of fibre, reducing its effectiveness as a reinforcing agent.

The strength of composite can be written as and

$S = CX + CY + Z$

C = Orientation factor

X = Sub critical fibres

Y = Super critical fibres

Z = Polymers

The importance of fibre length and fibre matrix band is clearly illustrated by above equation. It is possible to preserve the length of the fibres passing through compounder by reducing the amount of mixing, but this may lead to poor distribution and wetting out of the fibres poor distribution of fibres may leave fibre-fibre bonds in the finished articles these are weak and break under load. When fibre surface is not well wetted out with polymer the strength will be low. Depending on magnitudes of these effects, the benefit of preserving the fibre length may therefore be more than offset from the reduction in the fibre bond strength. For any process it is important to find the magnitudes of these effects and evaluate a consensus in balancing the desired properties.

The average fibre length and fibre matrices bond are affected by conditions under which fibres are mixed into the polymer. When the mixing of the glass fibres in polymers is performed in Twin Extruders, it is the length of the mixing section that has the most significant effect on both these parameters. As the mixing length increases the fibre length will decrease, while the fibre matrix bond will improve, rapidly at first, then levelling off. The screw speed had a limited influence on fibre breakage or fibre matrix bond, it greatly affects production rate for a given set of operating conditions, the specific energy consumption was proportional to mixing length, so for energy efficiency it is undesirable to operate with mixing length, beyond that required to achieve the maximum fibre/matrix bond strength.

If the injection moulding cycle causes considerable fibre length degradation, then a compound where the fibre, matrix bond is strong, rather than one wher the fibre length has been maintained at the cost of this band, will give a stronger product, as injection moulding will reduce their average fibre length to the similar value.

The optimum processing conditions will make significant differences to product quality and line efficiency. Not only compounding procedure and operating conditions but also injection moulding techniques are to be developed to give maximum desirable properties to the product.

Polyvinyl Alcohol Fibres as Reinforcing Agent

Water insoluble grade in P.V.A. fibres are mostly used along with glass filled resins to upgrade the desired properties in industrial end use application where impact strength and abrasion resistance requirements are critical and high demanding. P.V.A. fibers are used in injection moulded rail-Tie retainers which has been used in Japanese National Railroad for more than severn year. These P.V.A. fibers reinforced polyester moulding are reported to have withstood exposure to sunlight and to the stress caused by trans trading at over 200km/hrs.

P.V.A. polyester laminate is also being used in green house glazing and other applications of glass P.V.A. blends premix include bath tubs and electrical circle breakers. P.V.A. cloth and mat are being used as a surface veils to improve impact strength weatherability and abrasion resistance.

Physical properties in comparison with Glass Fiber

		Percentage increase or decrease
1.	Tensile strength	Decrease 275%
2.	Specific Tensile strength	Decrease 40%
3.	Tensile elongation	Increase 300%
4.	Impact strength	Increase 700%
4.	Heat resistance	Decrease 300%

The P.V.A. Fibers claims following impressive advantages.

1. No need of coupling agents.
2. Superior impact resistance overother reinforcement agents.
3. Light weight compared to glass fibers.
4. No break under high break of shear in injection mouldings.
5. Thermal expansion coefficient similar to must of the polymers.
6. Flexibility at moulding temperature to yield smooth fresh on moulded part.

P.V.A. fibers make suitable premix blends with fibers. Such a premix will improve flow properties. These properties will depend upon composition of premix and moulding conditions. Optimum fiber blend ratios can be found out by practical applications.

Whiskers as Reinforcement Agent

The strongest fibers that have been observed to date are in the form of single crystal filaments, usually reffered to as shiskers. In some instances, these filaments approach the theoretical strength of solids. Such whiskers are quite attractive as reinforcing media for polymers. Not only do whiskers have an unusually high strength, but in the case of some ceramic whiskers this high strength is also associated with low density, high elastic modulus, and excellent high-temperature strength.

The ultrahigh strength of whiskers is attributed to their crystalline prefection and small dimensions, which minimize the occurrence of the defects that are responsible for the relatively low strength of massive materials. In Table I are room-temperature strength and elastic moduli of selected materials in whisker form.

Whisker diameters are typically a few microns or less. Their strength generally is inversely related to the diameter. They possess an extremely high degree of crystal perfection, the major defect type being an axial screw dislocation which has no adverse effect on fiber strength. In comparing the tensile strengths of whiskers with those of other reinforcing fibers such as glass and boron a several-fold increase in basic fiber strength is evident.

To achieve maximum strength in a whisker/resin composite, the whiskers must be properly oriented relative to the applied load. The simplest orientation (other than random) is that of uniaxial alignment, but even this is not easy to obtain on a useful scale, particularly if the whiskers are very small and entangled with other whiskers as a result of the conditions of growth. It is celar that (1) cleaning (2) separation (3) orientation, and (4) compaction of whiskers are all essential if high strength, high modulus composites are to be achieved. Of these requirements, orientation and compaction are probably most important.

A number of processes have been developed for orientation of whiskers, some of which involve forming a continuous yarn for ease of handling. Most such techniques are just in the advanced development stage, and these include fluid spinning, air elutriation, glycerine flow alignment, rotary deposition, extrusion in a removable binder, and electrostatic and vibratory orientation. Commercial equipment has recently been made available that permits the automatic cleaning and grading of whiskers by length. Extrusion processes are successful with short fibers, while spinning techniques can be accomplished only with the longer wook-like fibers. Sapphite whiskers tend to occur in a tree-like or branching crystalline growth structure that is extremely difficult if not impossible to orient unidirectionally, when present.

Physical properties of whiskers

Material	Density gm/cm3	Melting Point, °C	Tensile strength p.s.i. x 10^6	Young's modulus p.s.i. x 10^6	Strength density p.s.i 10^6
Aluminium oxide	3.9	1890	2-4	100-350	14-28
Aluminium nitride	3.3	1920	2-3	50	13-21

Material	Density gm/cm3	Melting Point, °C	Tensile strength p.s.i. x 10^6	Young's modulus p.s.i. x 10^6	Strength density p.s.i 10^6
Beryllium oxide	3.0	2410	2.0-2.8	100	18-27
Boron carbide	2.5	2280	1	65	11
Graphite	2.2	3320	3	142	37
Magnesium oxide	3.6	2610	3-5	45	27
Silicon carbide (alpha)	3.2	2130	3-5	70	26-44
Silicon nitride	3.4	1775	0.5 1.5	55	4.1-12

Whisker-reinforced composites have been succesfully fabricated using both thermoplastics and thermosetting matrices. A typical ABS resin with a 6 vol.% addition of silicon carbide whiskers demonstrated a tensile strength increase of 50%, and a flexural modulus increase of 200%. Epoxy resin composites with 60 vol% sapphire whiskers have given tensile strength of 86,000 p.s.i. flexural strength of 142,000 p.s.i. and tensile modulus of 31 million p.s.i. These properties are only a fraction of potential that exists. A need remains for fabrication techniques that will ultimately permit full translation of whisker strength and stiffness.

Carbon and Graphite fibers as Reinforcement Agent

Two general classes of carbon based fibers are available in a variety of forms and constructions. Although elementally the same and sharing similar manufacturing technology,mechanical properties and applications differ dramatically. For users dealing with both types of materials, and those using the newer high-performance fibers, it is becoming common to identify carbon fibers, as those materials with a Young's modulus (tensile modulus) less than 10,000,000 p.s.i. and those above 10,000,000 p.s.i, as graphite fibers, although the former group also includes types with high graphitic content. This practice is followed in this discussion.

Carbon and graphite fibers are made from carbonaceous, fibrous raw materials that can be pyrolysed in an air or other atmosphere to a char, without melting. Further processing in an inert atmosphere produces the final product.

By restraining or stretching the fibers curing processing steps a high degree of orientation of the graphite layers parallel to the fiber axis is achieved and results in the higher strength and modulus characteristics of graphite fibers.

Carbon fibers

Properties of carbon fibers are gnerally in the range of 6 to 10 x 10^6 p.s.i. tensile modulus, 30 to 180 x 10^3 p.si.i tensile strength, with an elongation at break of 1 to 2%. Elastic recovery is 100% within the family of carbon fibers, the low graphitic content materials have higher surface area, electrical resistivity, and water pick-up and lower thermal conductivity than do the higher graphitic content carbon fibers. Carbon fibers were commercially available in 1959 as woven fabrics, and in 1963 continuous filament yarns became available. Other product forms include felts and chopped fibers.

Carbon fibers are employed as high temperature, thermal insulating materials usable in some cases to over 3000°C. They are used as filter media and catalyst supports, and are often the fibrous reinforcement in corrosion, resistant packing in composite structures having high thermal resistance, thermal shock resistance. The low electrical resistivity of the fibers and fabrics has lead to use in flexible, heating elements and other applications in which a flexible non-metallic conductor is desired.

Graphite fibers

Commercially available graphite fibers are in the range of 25 to 80 x 10^6 p.s.i. tensile modulus, 250 to 240 x 10^3 p.s.i. tensile strength and have 0.25 to 1.2 elongation to break. Elastic recovery is 100% Material forms include continuous fiber yarns, tows, and woven constructions. In addition,long filament and chopped fibers are available.

Graphite fibers with high strength to-weight and high modulus to-weight ratios offer reinforcements for structural applications five to 10 times as stiff and three to nine times as strong as titanium, steel, and aluminium when compared on a weight basis. Structurally, the major advantage of high modulus graphite reinforcements is the large increase in stiffness, for other materials are available offering greater strengths.

Development of high-performance graphite fibers in the 1960s was, in part under the need of high performance products, and initial applications have been in aircraft, spacecraft, and similar hardware requiring high performance-to-weight. Other applications make use of the slightly negative thermal coefficient of expansion of graphie fibrs to fabricate large carticles with essentially zero thermal coefficient of expansion of graphite fibers to fabricate large articles with essentially zero thermal coefficient of expansion. Other desirable properties include ease of fabrication in complex configurations and ease of machining.

Wear resistance of non-lubricated components exceeds well lubricated steel on steel, and in addition, ultra-high modulus components do not wear the steel counterface.

The future of these materials is attractive because of the combination of high performance, ease of fabrication, and continually dropping costs, all of which contribute to an inceasing spectrum of applications that are cost effective.

Typical property ranges of carbon and graphite fibers

Property	Carbon[a]	Graphite
Filament tensile strength, x 10^3 p.s.i.	30000-80000	250,000-450,000
Tenacity, g./denier	5.3-6.2	—
Young's modulus, x10^6 p.s.i.	6-10	30-80
Elongation at break, %	1-2	0.25-1.2
Elastic recovery, %	100	100
Density,g./cc.	1.3-1.8	1.4-2.0
Filament shape	Irregular	varies with mfr.
Effective diameter, microns	8-9	6-9
Moisture regain (20°C, 56% r.h.)	2-14	0
Thermal Conductivity, Btu/ft./hr./ft^2/°F	11-22	34-90
Volume electrical resistivity, ohm-cm. x 10^6	3500-6000	700-1200
Specific heat,		
70°F., Btu/lb.,°F	0.17	0.17
Mean 70°F to 2700°F	0.40	0.40
Surface area, m.2/g.	4-130	1-4
Forms available	continuous filament	Continuous filament

Property	Carbon[a]	Graphite
	yarns, woven fabric, felts chopped fiber	yarns and tows, long fiber tows (40-50 in.), chopped fiber

Comparison of structural materials

Material	Densi ty gm/c c	Tensile Strength h x 10^3 p.s.i.	Tensile modulus x 10^6 p.s.i.	Modulus/ density x 10^6 in.
High strength graphite fiber	1.51	450	30	545
Boron fiber	2.62	450	60	632
"S" glass	2.48	550	12	133
Steel wire	7.82	410	30	106
Aluminium	2.56	70	11	118
Titanium	4.4	200	17.5	109
Carbon steel	7.8	155	30	106

Boron Filaments as Reinforcement Agent

A considerable volume of boron reinforcing filaments have been made for development and evaluation purposes in various aircraft, gas turbine engine, helicopter, and missile applications. Many items from these programmes are being test flown on aircraft to gain service experience, and are demonstrating 25.50% weight savings over materials previously used for the applications.

Present boron filaments are made by chemically vapor depositing boron from a boron trichloride (halide) and hydrogen gas mixture on to a 1.2-mildiameter tungsten wire substrate. The product of this operation is a 4 mil-diameter continuous filament having a density of about 2.65 g/cc, a modulus of 55.57x 10^6 p.s.i and tensile strengths of about 450,000 p.s.i.

Investigations of larger-diameter boron filaments, from both performance and economic standpoints, have resulted in the development and marketing of 5.6 mil boron filament. This filament meets or exceeds the properties of the conventional 4-mil material at a substantial reduction in cost.

Boron filaments are usually used in the form of prepreg tapes to which the filaments are carefully collimated and tensioned to provide a 1-filament-thick tape. Common widths of these tapes are 3 mm and 75mm, with a variety of other sizes and configurations being made for test or special purposes. Generally these tapes are composed of 65-70% by weight filaments and 30-35% epoxy resin, although some work with epoxy novalaks, phenolics, and polyimides is also being done.

Industry activity has been initiated to develop and quality the necessary prepreg material systems required to place the 5.6-mil filament in a competitive position for structural applications, and in some instances, acceptance has been gained for initital application.

Fabrication of components using these tapes has been primarily by the hand layup methods. However, significantly advances have been made using tape-winding and tape-laying techniques. In thecase of tape winding narrow (3 mm.) tapes are used when fabricating bodes of revolution but when flat or slightly curved parts are to be the product, the tape-laying technique is preferred. Some very sophisticated, numerically controlled, high-speed machines are currently in the process of being developed for this purpose.

Interest in metal matrix composites, primarily boron/aluminium and derivatives thereof, is on the increase, but still lags and born/epoxy technology development. The introduction of larger-diameter boron filament has reduced the cost of the material system, and appears to offer an increase in composite transverse tensile strength, both of which make its use more attractive for structural appliations.

Aramid Fibers as Reinforcements

It was introduced in 1972, Kelvar aramid fibres has broad application where light weight, high strength stiffness, resistance to stretch, vibration damping and resistance to damage are important. The fibre originally was developed to replace steel in radial tyres and is finding increasing use in the belts of radial car types and body of radial truck tires where it saves weight and increase strength and desirability.

Dupont Co manufacture and sells continuous filament yarns and roving and chopped fibres of Kevlar 29 and Kevlar 49 Kevlar 49 yarns in 195, 380, 1140, 1420 and 2130 denier sizes are supplied to commercial weavers who make board woven fabric, woven rovings and narrow woven tapes for plastic reinforcement application.

Kevlar 29 is designed for ballistic protection, slash and cut resistance, ropers, cables and coated fabrics and inflatables and architectural fabrics.

Kevlar 49 aramid isused in high performance composite applications where light weight, high strength and stiffness, damage resistance, resistance to fatigue and stress rupture and vibration damping are key properties. Reinforced composites can save upto 40% of the weight of glass fibre. Composite of greater stiffness.

The aramid composite resist chattering upon impact and the presence fo the fibres inhibits propagation of cracks. Aramid composites are non conductive and exhibit no galvanic reaction when in cotnact and metals. The tensile behaviour is linear and failure occurs at high stress. Aramid composites exhibit ductile behaviour when subjected to compressive and flexural loads and the ultimate strength in lower than that of either glass of graphite composites. Aramid can be combined with glass or graphite in hybrid composites. Hybrids allows the design engineer to achieve a balance of properties not available from single reinforcing fibre.

Aramid fibres are compatible with epoxy ortho isophthalic polyester and vinyl ester polyesters. Polyamide and phenolic resins.

Aramid fillers can be processed in essentially the same ways as glass and graphite to produce composite. High performance pressure vessels and missile engine cases are filament wound with rovings. Rovings can also be used in pultrusion allowing continuous manufacture of parts of constant cross sectional area. Vacuum by moulding of fabric prepregs is most often used in air craft industry. Rovings of Kevlar 49 are available in 4560 and 7100 dinier sizers. In the marine industry fabric and woven roving of aramid are used in the wet hand lay up method.

Because of the inherent toughness of the fibre special tools are required to cut fabric and woven rovings and to efficient by machine composite. Scissors and power cultures are available to cut fabrics and woven rovings, as are tools for cutting and machining composites.

Aramid find use in aircraft industry to save weight and incumbent metal or glass fibre components. Filament wound structures are used on the space shuttle. In the marine market composites are used in the hulls of canoes, kayckes, sailboats and large and small power boats to product light weight hull structures.

Aramid fibre now is used in variety of sports equipment is surf boards, fishing rods and skies for light weight stiffness, strength and vibration damping. The great efforts are need in the automotive industry to identify and manufacture prototype components where the use of light weight plastics composite can contribute to fuel economy in future automobiles.

11

Fibre Glass Reinforced Plastic Pipe

Fibreglass reinforced plastics, has revolutionised the piping market all over the world, it has chemical industry, petrolium, petrochemical, gas, water transporation, sewerage and many more vital applications. FRP has taken its place of pride in the above mentioned industries, among consultants because of its unique inherent advantages. FRP is an engineering material of construction. It is a composite material in which Glass Fibre reinforcement provides strength and stiffness while resins, viz., unsaturated polyester, epoxy, etc., provide the matrix, bonding them together and distributing the applied load to the reinforcing fibers.

Flexibility of design of FRP pipe has made it absolutely of versatile material for different applications. The strength requirements, whether it is axial strength or circumferential strength, can be achieved by varying the glass content, choosing the right type of Glass fibre reinforcement and changing the orientation of Glass Fibre Rovings during winding process. In the filament winding process for fabrication of FRP pipe, the ideally suited reinforcement in single and Glass Fibre Rovings. These rovings impart excellent runnability, fuzz and catenary-free service. These rovings are available in different linear densities from 150 km/kg to 4800 g/km and with different chemical coatings to suit different resin matrix systems.

The selection of resin matrix is very important towards the life of the pipe. Depending on the fluid to be handled, temperature of the fluid system and external environment, proper resin selection will ensure a long maintenance free life or FRP pipelines. Chemical resistance of FRP pipes is further improved by giving a resin-rich inner layer on the pipe using surface veil, mostly polyester surface veil/glass tissue mat. The external surface of the pipe can also be given additional protection by using a similar liner.

FRP pipe has become the system of choice because of the following factors.

a. Chemical Resistance;

b. Durability;

c. Freedome from maintenance;

d. Light Weight;

e. Ease of Installation;

f. Product Flexibility;

g. Higher Flow Capacity;

h. Ease of Shipment;

i. Lower life Cycle Cost;

j. Lower capital cost in manufacturing

In transportation of fluids, viz., water, petroleum fuels, etc., the frictional resistance produces the largest component of operating cost. Flow resistnace in steel pipe increases with time due to corrosion on the internal surface. The rate of frictional increase varies with the fluid being pumped. Unlike steel, the internal surface roughness of FRP pipe does not change the time since it does not corrode in most water applications.

The smooth bore of FRP pipe allows to downsize the pipe diameter without altering the flow rate. Smaller diameters result in more economical purchase. For the same pipe diameter FRP will consume less horse-power for a given flow rate.

FRP pipes are cheaper, saves lot of maintenance cost, protects environment preventing leakage of precious oil, chemicals and hazardous fluids through leaking pipelines into the soil. It saves money by preventing loss of precious oil, gas and chemicals,it is yet to achieve its true potential in Indian industrial scene. Studies reveal that loss due to corrosion in India in chemical industry is of the order of Rs. 10,000 crores per annum. It is also suggested that atleast 20 to 25% of this can be saved by adopting proper corrosion control measures. For the national interest and for the benefit of all, we cannot ignore the revolutionary material, i.e. fibreglass Reinforced Plastics, before it is too late.

12

Acrylic Sheet and Moulded Products

Acrylics are known for their sparking crystal clarity and outstanding surface hardness. Together with superior weatherability and good chemical resistance, these characteristics have made them the material of choice for a wide range of applications. Acrylics can be cast into sheet form. Cast sheet is produced from methylmethacrylate, which is polymerised during casting. Acrylic sheet can be transparent, translucent or opaque. It may be obtained in various colours and shades. The outstanding characteristics of acrylic sheets are that it has optical clarity, good outdoor weathering characteristics, high strength to weight ratio, good dimensional stability etc.

Sheet and profiles made of acrylic can be cut with power saws. Special blades improve the appearance of the cut and reduce the time required to polish the item. Conventional metal working and wood working equipment is used in the fabrication process. Extruded sheet in recommended when the thermoformed parts require intricate details with a difficult draw. Parts can also be joined by the hot blade, ultrasonic or spin welding techniques.

PROCESS OF MANUFACTURE

The process involves the following steps.

1. Recovery of monomer from the acrylic scrap.
2. Refining of fresh monomer.
3. Preparation of molding syrup.
4. Mould preparation.
5. Filling of the mould & curing
6. Finishing of product and quality control

PLANT ECONOMICS OF ACRYLIC SHEET AND MOULDED PRODUCTS

RATED PLANT CAPACITY		10 SET/Day
LAND & BUILDING	Rs.	5,00,000.00

PLANT & MACHINERY

1. Buffing Machine
2. Cutting Machine
3. Lathe Machine
4. Grinder and polishing Machine

FIXED CAPITALS

1. LAND & BUILDING	Rs.	5,00,000.00
2. PLANT & MACHINERY	Rs.	1,25,000.00
3. OTHER FIXED ASSETS	Rs.	79,500.00
TOTAL	Rs.	7,04,500.00

RAW MATERIALS

1. Acrylic Sheets
2. Packing material

TOTAL WORKING CAPITAL/MONTH

1. RAW MATERIAL	Rs.	2,25,000.00
2. SALARY & WAGES	Rs.	21,125.00
3. UTILITIES & OVERHEADS	Rs.	27,200.00
TOTAL	Rs.	2,73,325.00

TOTAL CAPITAL INVESTMENT

TOTAL FIXED CAPITAL	Rs.	7,04,500.00
TOTAL WORKING CAPITAL FOR 1 MONTHS	Rs.	2,73,325.00
TOTAL	Rs.	9,77,825.00

TURN OVER/ANNUM

By sale of Acrylic accessories and cabinets etc.,	Rs.	42,00,000.00

PROFIT SALES RATIO = Profit / Sales x 100 = 16%

RATE OF RETURN = Operating profit / T.C.I x 100 = 67%

BREAK EVEN POINT (B.E.P) = 43%

13

Bath Tub (Acrylic)

Acrylics are known for their sparking crystal clarity and outstanding surface hardness. Together with superior weatherability and good chemical resistance, these characteristics have made them the material of choice for a wide range of applications.

Acrylic bath tubs can be obtained in variety of colour and shades.

Their most outstanding characteristics being optical clarity, good outdoor weathering characteristics high strength to weight ratio and good dimensional stability.

MANUFACTURING PROCESS OF ACRYLIC BATH TUB

Acrylic bath tubs can be readily made when the monomer (polymethyl methacrylate) is heated to 150-170°C when it is soft and pliable. If no stretching is required the material is simply draped over the required form and allowed to cool. If stretching is necessary matched mold are used.

Methyl Metha Acrylate along-with Pearl essence, Colour, Benzoyl Peroxide (Catalyst) is stirred for about 10-15 minutes. Then the liquid monomer is transfer to mould for shaping bath tub.

These mould are half sunk in water and rotated at a speed of about 180 rpm. The temperature of the water is kept at 80°C initially for about half an hour. Then the temperature is decreased to 65 to 70oC and is maintained for about one and half hour.

Again the temperature is increased to 80oC. It is kept for 5 minutes for curing and then the mould are taken from the tank. Dip the moulds in the cold water for cooling. Open the mould and remove the acrylic bath tub so formed and later is finished by edge trimming and cutting.

The product is now packed and sent for marketing.

MANUFACTURE OF MONOMER

First of all acrylic scrap is heated in deploymerizing unit at a temperature of about 400 - 450oC. Black monomer is obtained by condensing the vapour which contains various impurities.

These impurities are removed by distillation process. Black monomer is heated to a temperature of about 80oC in a air tight vessels. At the boiling point of the monomer, vapour are formed which are condensed by fractional distillation. Pure monomer is obtained by condensation and black waste is lift in the vessel which is thrown away. The clean monomer is then washed by 2-4% conc caustic soda solution in water. This will clean the monomer thoroughly and will remove all the impurities. The monomer being lighter than caustic soda solution, will float above the solution. Monomer is now separated and then put in a clean vessel. This monomer contains traces of water.

Traces of water are removeal by adding calcium chloride or sodium sulphate. The monomer prepared is now ready for use.

PLANT ECONOMICS OF BATH TUB (ACRYLIC)

RATED PLANT CAPACITY 40 NOS./Day

LAND & BUILDING
(Land Area 1000 sq.mt.) Rs. 21,50,000.00

PLANT & MACHINERY

1. Depolymerising Unit
2. Steam heated distillation unit
3. Baby Boiler
4. Aluminium Moulds for bath tubes
5. Intermediate tank
6. Mixing tank
7. Vacuum Tank
8. Cutting machine
9. Piping & Instrumentation
10. Weighing machine
11. Laborating Testing Equipment

FIXED CAPITAL

1. LAND & BUILDING	Rs.	21,50,000.00
2. PLANT & MACHINERY	Rs.	7,00,000.00
3. OTHER FIXED ASSETS	Rs.	1,00,000.00
TOTAL	Rs.	29,50,000.00

RAW MATERIALS

1. Methyl mathacrylate monomer
2. Acrylic scrap
3. Benzoyl peroxide
4. Caustic Soda
5. Synthetic pearl essences
6. Calcium Chloride
7. Dye Colours
8. Packaging Materials

TOTAL WORKING CAPITAL/MONTH

1. RAW MATERIAL	Rs.	12,36,400.00
2. SALARY & WAGES	Rs.	57,615.00
3. UTILITIES & OVERHEADS	Rs.	79,650.00
TOTAL	Rs.	13,73,665.00

TOTAL CAPITAL INVESTMENT

TOTAL FIXED CAPITAL	Rs.	29,50,000.00
TOTAL WORKING CAPITAL FOR 2 MONTHS	Rs.	27,47,330.00
TOTAL	Rs.	56,97,330.00

TURN OVER/ANNUM

By sale of Acrylic bath tubs 12,000 Nos.	Rs.	2,40,00,000.00

PROFIT SALES RATIO = Profit / Sales x 100 = 27%

RATE OF RETURN = Operating profit / T.C.I x 100 = 114%

BREAK EVEN POINT (B.E.P) = 21%

14

Dough Molding Compound (DMC) Bulk Moulding Compound (BMC) Sheet Moulding Compound (SMC)

Premix is generally known as Dough Moulding Compound (DMC), flow mix or Bulk Moulding Compound (BMC). Premix has been defined as " A fiber reinforced thermoset molding compound not requiring advancement of cure, drying of volatiles, or other processing after mixing to make it ready for use at the molding press". To this might be added "and which can be molded without reaction by products under only sufficient presssure to flow and compact the material"*. If the word "mixing" in the above is changed to "manufacture" the definition can apply equally to sheet molding compound. The principal differences between premix and SMC are in the manufacturing methods and in the form in which they reach the molder. Each can be formulated of the same basic ingredients.

Premix is formulated by combining all the ingredients in an intensive mixing process. It emerges from the mixer in a fibrous putty form, and it can be used directly, the operator merely weighing out charges. Some formulations can be compacted and extruded into bars or "logs" of simple cross section to facilitate handling.

* In contrast to phenolic melamine or urea compounds that have water as a reaction product and require high pressure to prevent steam formation and consequent voids in the molding.

DMC COMPOUNDING METHOD

While much of the compounding practice, procedure and equipment is common to premix there are sufficient differences to consider them separately.

Premix:- Although premix has been compounded by a semicontinuous process because of severe limitations on the type of compound and questions of economics, consideration will only be given here to so-called "batch" mixing.

In most instances the mixing is done in two stages. In the first a prebatch of the resin, colorant, catalyst, release agent and possibly part of the filler are thoroughly blended. In the second stage the balance of the filler and the reinforcement are added. The mixing intensively and time up to the addition of the reinforcement can never be too long or too intense. However, when glass fibres are the reinforcement, extreme care must be taken to mix them only long enough to insure their uniform distribution. A typical mixing schedule for a general purpose premix would be as follows :

A. In Cowles Dissolver (or similar mixer) blend :

Resin
Catalyst
Release agent → Mix 10 minutes.
Colorant

B. Add 50 percent filler. Mix 5 minutes.
C. Transfer to double arm mixer.
D. Add balance of filler. Mix 10 minutes.
E. Add reinforcement. Mix 3 minutes.

PLANT ECONOMICS OF DOUGH MOULDING COMPOUND

RATED PLANT CAPACITY		500 Kgs/Day
LAND & BUILDING		
(Land Area 750 sq. mts.)	Rs.	19,30,000.00

PLANT & MACHINERY

1. Mixer Sigma Blade
2. Weighing Balance platform type
3. Bucket Elevator
4. Chopping Machine
5. Extruder
6. Laboratory testing equipments
7. Miscellaneous equipments, tools, jigs, fixtures etc.
8. Process Control equipments

FIXED CAPITAL

1. LAND & BUILDING	Rs.	19,30,000.00
2. PLANT & MACHINERY	Rs.	18,05,000.00
3. OTHER FIXED ASSETS	Rs.	6,50,000.00
TOTAL	Rs.	43,85,000.00

RAW MATERIALS

1. Polyester Resin
2. Benzoyl Peroxide
3. Zinc Stearate
4. Asbestors Floats
5. Calcium Carbonate
6. Glass Fibre
7. Packaging Materials

TOTAL WORKING CAPITAL/MONTH

1. RAW MATERIAL	Rs.	6,72,082.50
2. SALARY & WAGES	Rs.	77,000.00
3. UTILITIES & OVERHEADS	Rs.	85,500.00
TOTAL	Rs.	8,34,582.50

TOTAL CAPITAL INVESTMENT

TOTAL FIXED CAPITAL	Rs.	43,85,000.00
TOTAL WORKING CAPITAL FOR 1 MONTHS	Rs.	8,34,582.50
TOTAL	Rs.	52,19,582.50

TURN OVER/ANNUM

By sale of (DMC) Polyester Dough moulding compound 1,50,000 kgs.	Rs.	2,10,00,000.00

PROFIT SALES RATIO = Profit / Sales x 100 = 46%

RATE OF RETURN = Operating profit / T.C.I x 100 = 187%

BREAK EVEN POINT (B.E.P) = 17%

15

FRP Products

INTRODUCTION

The growth of Fiberglass Reinforced Plastics (FRP) in the world has been rapid, particularly in USA and UK. The FRP products are still new items in India where immense growth potential exists. FRP is not a substitute for for steel or any other metals, but a unique material in its own right.

The main construction materials of fibreglass reinforced products are fibregalss and resin of different types and grades. Basically, heated 'bushings' through a number of types a continuous filament from at a speed of several thousand feet per minute. The filaments are than wound as a single untwisted strand. Therefore, the strand is made into different types of Reinforcement - Chopped Strands, Surfacing mat and Rovings. The combination of resin and various glassfibre reinforcements, thus produced, moulded by different methods, results in a material having distinc properties of its own such as high tensile strength, low weight, chemical inertness, good insulating properties and case of moulding. This explains the very rapid growth in the use of this material all over the world and its application in a wide variety of items in the following main markets:-

1. Building and construction
2. Marine Engineering
3. Chemical Plant
4. Electrical Industry
5. Rail and Road Transportation
6. Aerospace Applications
7. Different Engineering Parts
8. Consumer Articles

MANUFACTURING PROCESS

There are about ten common processes used to produce FRP products. Following is the list of processes commonly used.

1. Dough Moulding Compound
2. Sheet Moulding
3. Filament Winding
4. Injection Moulding
5. Hand Layup
6. Spray up
7. Process for Intermediate cure
8. FRP foam structure
9. Vacuum Moulding
10. Pressure bag.

PLANT ECONOMICS OF F R P PRODUCTS

RATED PLANT CAPACITY 80.00 NOS/Day

LAND & BUILDING

(Land Area 600 sq.mt) Rs. 20,10,000.00

PLANT & MACHINERY

1. Hand operated Hydraulic press
2. Power operated hydraulic press
3. Tile press
4. Band Saw machine
5. Hand shearing machine
6. Bench drilling machine
7. Electrical operated drying oven
8. Shaping machine, length of storke
9. Precision centre lathe centre
10. Universal Milling machine
11. Pedestal Grinder, grinding wheel
12. Piller drilling machine
13. Power operated hack saw machine

FIXED CAPITAL

1. LAND & BUILDING	Rs.	20,10,000.00
2. PLANT & MACHINERY	Rs.	7,10,000.00
3. OTHER FIXED ASSETS	Rs.	2,20,000.00
TOTAL	Rs.	29,40,000.00

RAW MATERIALS

1. Glass
2. Resin
3. Gel coat
4. Accelerator
5. Catalyst
6. P.A.V.
7. Thinner
8. Colour
9. Titanium dioxide
10. Filler (Silica flour)

TOTAL WORKING CAPITAL/MONTH

1. RAW MATERIAL	Rs.	3,55,420.00
2. SALARY & WAGES	Rs.	96,562.50
3. UTILITIES & OVERHEADS	Rs.	99,750.00
TOTAL	Rs.	5,51,732.50

TOTAL CAPITAL INVESTMENT

TOTAL FIXED CAPITAL	Rs.	29,40,000.00
TOTAL WORKING CAPITAL FOR 3 MONTHS	Rs.	16,55,197.50
TOTAL	Rs.	45,95,197.50

TURN OVER/ANNUM

1. By sales of 10,000 Helmets
2. By sale of 5,000 wash basin
3. By sale of 6000 Roofing sheets
4. By sale of 3,000 seats

TOTAL	Rs.	89,00,000.00

PROFIT SALES RATIO = Profit / Sales x 100 = 15%

RATE OF RETURN = Operating profit / T.C.I x 100 = 30%

BREAK EVEN POINT (B.E.P) = 53%

16

Fibre Glass Sheet

By now fibre glass reinforced plastic/Fibre corrugated sheet industry is about 20 year old. There were two or three small moulding companies which were fabricating items like bath tubs, helmets and corrugated sheets in the year 1960. In that period both resin as well as glass fibre were imported. In 1962-63, Bakelite Hylam Ltd., started producing fibre glass since then the fibre glass Reinforced Plastics Industry has made tremendous stride. The fibre glass Reinforced Plastics Industry owes its progress to the enthusiasm of the raw material manufacturers, designer's and moulders and of course the end users. The Reinforced Plastic Industry has Justified the confidence that the corrosion protection industry has reposed on it by enabling import substitution, earing of foreign exchange through export and new development of products. Fibre Glass Reinforced Plastics

(FRP) are essentially structural materials of composite materials. As a matter of fact, modern composites owe's their genesis to glass-fibre reinforced polyester developmention the 1940's.

FRP have several features that mark them as out standing engineering material for a wide range of applications. Firstly they have excellent engineering properties which naturally are as competitive as, or even better than other conventional materials secondly and very important, FRP can be easily moulded into any size and shape, a property not so easily or cheaply achieved in other construction materials like metals, stones or timber,

finally FRP offer's considerable flexibility in the design of structure. A designer can within limits tailor his composite material to give the required mechanical properties by correctly selecting the phase materials and by adjusting these in proportion and micro structural geometry.

If he wants, he can also vary the strength and stiffness in different direction. Thus a structural design engineer working with FRP has the advantage of creating his own material custom tailored to fulfil the design specification of the structure.

PLANT ECONOMICS OF FIBRE GLASS SHEETS

RATED PLANT CAPACITY 34 NOS./Day

LAND & BUILDING

(Land Area 2000 sq.mts.) Rs. 33,50,000.00

PLANT & MACHINERY

1. Resin mixing tanks
2. Resin spray plant
3. Spray Guns for Release agents
4. Moulding Table
5. Drying oven
6. Miscellaneous equipt.& accessories washer roller hand tools trimmer's sander,air compressor.

FIXED CAPITAL

1.	LAND & BUILDING	Rs.	33,50,000.00
2.	PLANT & MACHINERY	Rs.	10,15,000.00
3.	OTHER FIXED ASSETS	Rs.	1,90,000.00
	TOTAL	Rs.	45,55,000.00

RAW MATERIALS

1. Polyster Resin
2. Fibre glass rovings
3. Catalyst Benzoyl peraoxide
4. Acceleartor (dimethyl Aniline)
5. Colors and dyes
6. Gel coat (Alumina trihydrate)
7. Miscellaneous Chemicals Viz. polyvinyl Alcohols

   (Mould realising - agents)
8. Miscellaneous,

TOTAL WORKING CAPITAL/MONTH

1. RAW MATERIAL	Rs.	8,73,965.00
2. SALARY & WAGES	Rs.	54,230.00
3. UTILITIES & OVERHEADS	Rs.	29,600.00
TOTAL	Rs.	9,57,795.00

TOTAL CAPITAL INVESTMENT

TOTAL FIXED CAPITAL	Rs.	45,55,000.00
TOTAL WORKING CAPITAL FOR 2 MONTHS	Rs.	19,15,590.00
TOTAL	Rs.	64,70,590.00

TURN OVER/ANNUM

Receipt By sale of 10,200 Nos. Fibre Glass sheets	Rs.	1,93,80,000.00

PROFIT SALES RATIO = Profit / Sales x 100 = 34%

RATE OF RETURN = Operating profit / T.C.I x 100 = 102%

BREAK EVEN POINT (B.E.P) = 20%

17

Fibre Reinforced Plastics

INTRODUCTION

Fibre Reinforced plastics are essentially structural materials that belong to the larger family of composite materials. Fibre-Reinforced plastics (FRP) have been born out of sheer necessity - necessity imposed by the straight requirements of present day technology and in particular aerospace technology. Engg. materials for the present day high technology must combine very special mechanical, electrical,thermal, chemical properties etc. and at the same time have good aesthetic characteristic very often, the same material has to combine several desired quantities like light-weight, high strength, high stiffness, toughness, chemical resistance,electrical properties, aesthetic appeal etc.

FRP have several features that mark them as outstanding engineering materials for a wide range of applications. Firstly they have excellent engineering properties which naturally are as competitive as, or even better than, other conventional materials. Secondly and very important, FRP can be easily moulded into any size and shape, a property not so easily or cheaply achieved in other construction materials like metals, stones, or timber. Finally FRP offers considerable flexibility in the design of structures. A designer can within limits tailor his composite material to give the required mechanical properties by correctly selecting the phase materials and by adjusting thus proportion and micro structural geometry.

If he wants, he can also vary the strength and stiffness in different directions. Thus a structural design engineer working with FRP has the advantage of 'creating' his own material custom tailored to fulfil the design specifications of this structure.

The current applications of FRP range from bathtubs, wash basins and suitcases to the heat shield of a satellite-launch vehicle, the nose cone of the SST concord and the hull of the mine sweeper HMS milder. About 60,000 different items have been dentified that can be made out of FRP.

FRP TECHNOLOGY AND ITS RELEVANCE TO INDIA

FRP and its technology have already been recognised as an important area listed under the National Science and Technology Plan. No doubt FRP technology is one of the sophisticated fields of study. But it provides a typical example of how modern technology can be utilised for the progress of a developing nation like India. The FRP products find applications in the area right from the satellite-launch vehicle down to the

manufacture of high quality plough or light weight bullock-cart. The excellent chemical resistance of FRP makes it ideal for combating the corrosion problem that drain our national resources. Many products made of imported special purpose metal can be moulded or die-cast out of FRP. At the same time it is a labour intensive industry and it can give employment to many.

FORMULATION & PROCESS OF MANUFACTURE

Formulation is the 'designing' of a compound to bring about the desired properties in the finished moulding, Compounds may be formulated to provide strength, stiffness, toughness, electrical insulation fire resistance, etc. and often two of more qualities but the primary requirement is, however, mouldability.

To become mouldable, the compound must to maximum degree remain homogeneous as it flows through, especially to the extremities of the mould, i.e. the resin filler and reinforcement should not separate. If they do, serious variations in properties will occur throughout the moulding and much of the contribution of the reinforcement will be lost.

The flow properties of the compound are determined by the degree to which the resin is absorbed by the fillers and glassifibre. Each of the drying ingredients employed has its own particular resin absorption, or drying effect on the resin. The drier the compound, the lower the plasticity of flow. Not do the fillers vary in resin absorption, but resin in their ability to

wet the fillers depending on their viscosity, basic chemical construction, type and quantity of monomers, etc.

The answer to the problem of formulating a compound that will have satisfactory flow and maintain reasonable homogeneity Šlies mostly in the selection of the resin and fillers combination. A high viscosity resin will carry reinforcement and filler well but made mixing more difficult. Combinations of smaller amounts of high absorption fillers, such as china clay and asbestos, with low absorption one such as calcium carbonate or silica works fairly well to solve both the flow and homogeneity problems.

A chemical thickening process can also be used as a flow control device. A resin with low initial viscosity permits addition of large quantities of filler or reinforcement with a suitable thickening subsequent to mixing.

Table Show Some typical formulations for premix

	General Purpose	Electrical high arc resistance	Water resistance	Appearance grade
Resin	28%	25%	30%	18%
Low Shrink modifying resin	—	—	—	7%
Glass fibre	15%	12%	15%	15%
Release agent	1%	1%	1%	1%
China Clay	10%	5%	3%	5%
Calcium Carbonate	45%	—	—	53%
Talc	—	—	50%	—
Alumina trihydrate	—	56%	—	—
Catalyst	0.3%	0.3%	0.3%	0.25%
Calcium hydroxide	0.7%	0.7%	0.7%	1%

Compounding or mixing of premix is mostly carried out in batches. In most instances the mixing is done in two stages. In the first, a batch of resin, colourant, catalyst and release agent are thoroughly blended. This is usually done on simple blade type stirrers.

The main mixing of the resin, filler and glass fibre is done in a sigma or spiral blade mixer. These should be heavy duty with a blade/trough clearance of 1/4" to 3/8". The mixing chamber should be jacketed for cooling water and the two blades should be geared to rotate at different speeds of 20 to 40 rpm respectively (lower for larger mixer-50 kgs. and over) and the blades should be capable of reverse movement to facilitate emptying and cleaning.

The mixing procedure involves the following steps:

1. Weight all powdered filler ingredient in the same container and charge into mixer. Mix for 5 minutes.
2. Take an appropriate quantity of resin-mix (preactivated in the first stage) and add part (about 3/4 to the mixer and mix for 5-100 minutes. Ensure that the filler and the resin blend into a free flowing paste. Add the remaining quantity of resin and mix for 3-5 minutes.
3. Weigh the glass fibre into a separate container and charge to the mixer as quickly as possible. Allow to mix for no more than 5 minutes.

This completes the mixing cycle. Empty the mixer and pack compound in air-tight container to prevent loss of monomer.

Catalysts and Accelerators

In order to convert the resin to a hard and infusible solid within a reasonably short time so as to make their moulding a commercial possibility, catalysts/accelerator are added to resin shortly before the use.

For the hot curing system i.e. where external heat is applied to the moulding in the range of 80 - 130oC a peroxide catalyst such as benzyl peroxide is widely used.

Colouring material & Pillers

Polyester resins are usually coloured by dispensing in them inorganic pigments or pigment lookes to give self coloured mouldings.

Fillers used with Polyester resin include calcium carbonate, silica, slate powder, mica flour, alumina etc.

The mixer after preparation is passed through an injection moulding machine. In this machine FTP pellets are fed into the machine through a hopper, heated and melted and forced with through a nozzle at the far end of the machine cylinder under pressure. In the mould, the polymer melt cools and hardens until fully set up. The mould is then opened and the moulded part removed.

PROCESSING CONDITIONS

In commercial practice, while moulding Fibreglass Reinforced Thermoplastics, the maximum shot size is 50-75% of the rated capacity of the machine. Injection pressures are higher than those used while moulding unreinforced polymers, to allow for the higher melt viscosities of the reinforced polymers. High injection speeds give better surface finish, weld line integrity and reduce orientation of the glassfibre. The injection speeds

should, however, not be maintained at such high levels where flashing in the tool can occur.

The screw speed should be 30 - 6- rpm and back pressure around 50 psi. With reinforced Nylon 66, near zero back pressures, just enough to ensure that the screw flights pick up the material (rather tha allow the material to slide past), are recommended. The mould temperatures used are also higher than used for unreinforced polymers. The surface finish, shrinkage, appearance of weld lines, tendency to warp, are all influenced by mould

temperature. The mould is heated by circulating hot oil through independent controls. The two moulds halves can be maintained at different temperatures to help avoid warping of the moulded piece.

The moulded article of FTP may be annealed to relieve stresses, although this is not absolutely essential. Annealing may be done in hot oil on removing the article from the mould. The annealing temperature may be around 120oC - 140oC and the time about 5 minutes per mm of thickness of article. The cooling, to follow the annealing should be gradual and at the rate of 20 - 40oC per hour.

Sprues, runner and rejects can be reground, using a grinder, and reused along with virgin material. The percentage of reground material being used with virgin material should not exceed 20%; if the quality of the regrind is not good, this percentage should be even lower.

PLANT ECONOMICS OF FIBRE REINFORCED PLASTIC

RATED PLANT CAPACITY 500 KGS/Day

LAND & BUILDING

(Land 500 sq.mt.) Rs. 4,20,000.00

PLANT & MACHINERY

1. Disintegrater
2. Simple-mixer suitable
3. High speed mixer
4. Weighing machine
5. Water storage tank (FRP)

6. Miscellaneous like pipe, fitting valves etc.
7. Injection moulding machine with all accessories

FIXED CAPITAL

1. LAND & BUILDING	Rs.	4,20,000.00
2. PLANT & MACHINERY	Rs.	7,85,000.00
3. OTHER FIXED ASSETS	Rs.	1,33,450.00
TOTAL	Rs.	13,38,450.00

RAW MATERIALS

1. Polyester Resins
2. Glass fibre
3. Release agent as calcium stearate
4. Calcium carbonate
5. Methyl ethyl ketone peroxide
6. Calcium hydroxide
7. China clay

TOTAL WORKING CAPITAL/MONTH

1. RAW MATERIAL	Rs.	3,71,875.00
2. SALARY & WAGES	Rs.	36,480.00
3. UTILITIES & OVERHEADS	Rs.	33,279.00
TOTAL	Rs.	4,41,634.00

TOTAL CAPITAL INVESTMENT

TOTAL FIXED CAPITAL	Rs.	13,38,450.00
TOTAL WORKING CAPITAL FOR 1 MONTHS	Rs.	4,41,634.00
TOTAL	Rs.	17,80,084.00

TURN OVER/ANNUM

By sale of 150 MT of FRP mix	Rs.	75,00,000.00

PROFIT SALES RATIO = Profit / Sales x 100 = 23%

RATE OF RETURN = Operating profit / T.C.I x 100 = 95%

BREAK EVEN POINT (B.E.P) = 33%

18

Fibre Glass

The use of glass combined with mica to form insulating tapes and cloth for slot and phase insulation offers both mechanical and electrical advantages and conserves the use of presently scarce mica materials. Also, the use of glass fiberous as a basis for phenolic laminated material has proved tc be a sound development, because the extremely low moisture absorption of fibrous glass gives such compostire materials high resistance to deterioration and excellant behavior under abnormal physical and electrical stresses.

Industrial uses ranges over a wide field. Glass cloths and tapes are used as a lagging or wrappng over pipe insulation and duct work in hot locations or in tropical applications, where the usual cotton fabric will not stand up or where asbestos fabrics are undesirable because of their weitht and bulk. Glass cloths are also used for connection between sections of duct work as asound isolator, as curtain or portieres on board ship, and for similar applications requireing fireproof fabrics, as a facing material for thermal and a coustical blankets used in aircraft and naval ships, and as a facing materials on insulation boards made of glass mneral wool where a paintable, wear resistants surface is required without the use of metal of othr hard finishes.

Fabrics also have found some application in dust and fume filteration, as anode bages in electroplatig tanks, and for a growing member of speciallized uses. In 1944 glass fabrics came into use as a reinforcement for certain "Contact Pressure" resin to form plastic laminates and aircrft parts of exceptional strength weitht ratio, impact resistance, and dimensional stability.

Now new finising techniques have made possible production of truely decorative glass fabrics, including marquisette curtains, casement cloths and printed and piece-dyed materials. Fibrous glass is also combined with certain plastic resins to make distinctive lamp shades.

Military applications, broadly parallel industrial uses. The desirability of a fire-resistant, high strength, rot-resistant fabric is considerable in many different military, naval and aircraft applications.

The use of fibreglass is mainly in the making of insulating materials as it is a good heat resisting material. It may be used in making tiles and wallcovering, wash basin and insulators and many other articles. Window foils can also be made from fibre glass which has a very good market. On small scale basis, the finished goods of glass fibre may be manufactured such as

suitcase, contaiers, helmets for aeroplane crew-men and other decorative articles. In future many items like body of Šrefrigerator, cars, etc will be fabricated with glassfibre.

PROCESS OF MANUFACTURE

Two distinct type of fibrous materials are produced. One called the continuous filament process, forms filaments indefinite length, measurable in miles, and distinguishable by their brilliance and continuity. The other called the staple fiber process and makes fibers of "Discontinuous", length, i.e. in relatively short lengths resumbling cotton or flax fibers. The length averages about 9 inch and can be made longer or shorter within limits.

In both processes, glass is formulated by precision batch micing using selected silica sand, lime stone, and other glass making mineral ingrediants to produce the type of glass required. This glass is then formed into marble approximately 3/4 in. in diameter, and these are carefully inspected to eliminate those containing "Stones", or other defects that might interrup subsequent production operation, or impair the quality of the fibers drawn from them.

PLANT ECONOMICS OF FIBER GLASS

RATED PLANT CAPACITY		2 Tons/Day
LAND & BUILDING (Land Area 800 sq.mt.)	Rs.	17,80,000.00

PLANT & MACHINERY

1. Elevators with all accessories
2. Storage batch bin
3. Weighing hopper
4. Boiler
5. Batch melting & glass refining
6. Heater
7. Electric furnace
8. Bushing with steam sets
9. Gathering & Lubricating strand of filament
10. High speed winder
11. Other misc. equipment and accessories like piping. fitting & office furniture

FIXED CAPITAL

1. LAND & BUILDING	Rs.	17,80,000.00
2. PLANT & MACHINERY	Rs.	13,25,000.00
3. OTHER FIXED ASSETS	Rs.	1,50,000.00
TOTAL	Rs.	32,55,000.00

RAW MATERIALS

1. Glass
2. Binder
3. Packing materials

TOTAL WORKING CAPITAL/MONTH

1. RAW MATERIAL	Rs.	3,80,000.00
2. SALARY & WAGES	Rs.	60,250.00
3. UTILITIES & OVERHEADS	Rs.	93,000.00
TOTAL	Rs.	5,33,250.00

TOTAL CAPITAL INVESTMENT

TOTAL FIXED CAPITAL	Rs.	32,55,000.00
TOTAL WORKING CAPITAL FOR 3 MONTHS	Rs.	15,99,750.00
TOTAL	Rs.	48,54,750.00

TURN OVER/ANNUM

By sale of 600 tonnes of glass fibre	Rs.	1,08,00,000.00

PROFIT SALES RATIO = Profit / Sales x 100 = 27%

RATE OF RETURN = Operating profit / T.C.I x 100 = 60%

BREAK EVEN POINT (B.E.P) = 43%

19

Fibre Glass Wire

Fibre Glass Wire is gaining immense eminence is modern times, by virtue of its manifoed applications in the field of textile and the engineering fields.

Fibre Glass Wire is one of the signiicant product of Fibre Glass. Textiles of glass have been the dream of man for many centuries, their actual achievement as fabrics that could be folded, or yarns that could be knotted without breaking, dates much earlier from 1936. In the few years that have intervened, a new industry has been envolved and has achieved a significant position in the textile world. The practical utility of glass as an electrical insulation material and the need for fabrics that are fireproof and resistant to not mildew,and moisture made the development of this industry a most are fortunate circustance. Glass textile now plays an important part in military, naval and aircraft material.

Through-out many centuries man developed glass making to an advanced art and necessarily drew fibers for many purposes, such as "Spun glass" decoration on stemware and enchanting.Several attempts to make glass fibers suitable fortextile purpose are recorded, but none attracted much attraction. The fabric used were impracticable, since they could not be folded without breaking the filaments.

It became possible obly in America, through researh and development to draw fine, uniform filaments and devised methods of gathering and arranging them for textile applications. A second textile fiber process followed, and the two became the basis for the production of textile fibers of glass in commercial quantities at costs low enough to find many immediate uses. They also came into use in allover the world and now-constitute the source of practically glass textiles.

PLANT ECONOMICS OF FIBRE GLASS WIRE

Rated Plant Capacity 2 Tons/Day

LAND & BUILDING

(Land 1000 sq.mt.) Rs. 21,00,000.00

PLANT & MACHINERY

1. Elevators with all accesssories
2. Storage batch bin
3. Weighing hopper and automatic recording scales
4. Batch melting & glass refining unit
5. Heater
6. Electric furnace
7. Bushing with steam jets
8. Gathering & Lubricating

FIXED CAPITAL

1. LAND & BUILDING	Rs.	21,00,000.00
2. PLANT & MACHINERY	Rs.	16,35,000.00
3. OTHER FIXED ASSETS	Rs.	3,90,000.00
TOTAL	Rs.	41,25,000.00

RAW MATERIALS

1. Glass
2. Binder
3. Packing Materials

TOTAL WORKING CAPITAL/MONTH

1. RAW MATERIAL	Rs.	1,96,250.00
2. SALARY & WAGES	Rs.	95,760.00
3. UTILITIES & OVERHEADS	Rs.	1,84,000.00
TOTAL	Rs.	4,76,010.00

TOTAL CAPITAL INVESTMENT

TOTAL FIXED CAPITAL	Rs.	41,25,000.00
TOTAL WORKING CAPITAL FOR 3 MONTHS	Rs.	14,28,030.00
TOTAL	Rs.	55,53,030.00

TURN OVER/ANNUM

By sale of 600 tons. Glass Fibers Wire	Rs.	96,00,000.00

PROFIT SALES RATIO = Profit / Sales x 100 = 28%

RATE OF RETURN = Operating profit / T.C.I x 100 = 48%

BREAK EVEN POINT (B.E.P) = 49%

LIST OF THE READY AVAILABLE DETAILED PROJECT REPORTS

AUTOMOBILES, MECHANICAL & METALLURGICAL

1. AGRICULTRAL EQUIPMENTS
2. AGRICULTRAL EQUIPMENTS INCLUDING THRESHERS
3. AIR BRAKE HELICAL COIL
4. AIR COOLER
5. AIR FILTERS(FOR SCOOTER CAR & EXCAVATORS ETC.)
6. ALUMINIUM & ALUMINIUM ALLOYS FROM ALUMINIUM SCRAP TO MAKE UTENSILS (INDUCTION FURNACE MELTED)
7. ALUMINIUM ALLOY WHEELS
8. ALUMINIUM ALLOYS FROM ALUMINIUM SCRAP TO MAKE UTENSILS (INDUCTION FURNACE)
9. ALUMINIUM HOT & COLD ROLLING MILL
10. ALUMINIUM BOTTLE MANUFACTURING (COLD EXTRUSION OF ALUMINIUM)
11. ALUMINIUM/COPPER CABLE LUGS
12. ALUMINIUM CANS FOR BEER PACKAGING
13. ALUMINIUM CANS FOR CAPACITORS
14. ALUMINIUM CAPS FOR INJECTION VIALS
15. ALUMINIUM EXTRUSION
16. ALUMINIUM FURNITURE & HARDWARE
17. ALUMINIUM SHEET ROLLING MILL
18. ALUMINIUM UTENSILS
19. ALUMINIUM UTENSILS & SCHOOL BOXES
20. ALUMINIUM WIRE DRAWING AND SUPER ENAMELLING FOR WINDING
21. ANODISED ALUMINIUM UTENSILS
22. ANODIZING OF ALUMINIUM
23. ANTIMONY OXIDE FROM LEAD SCRAP
24. ARC WELDING FILTER GLASS
25. ALUMINIUM FOIL CUTTING & ROLL MAKING
26. AUTO FLAPS FOR TRUCKS & BUSES
27. AUTOMOBILE WORKSHOP (GARAGE & SERVICE CENTRE)
28. AUTO GEARS
29. AUTO HORNS
30. AUTO LEAF SPRING
31. AUTO TUBES
32. AUTO PISTON RING
33. AUTO PISTON
34. BAKERY AND BISCUITS EQUIPMENTS FABRICATION
35. BALL POINT PEN REFILLS
36. BALL ROLLER & TAPER BEARING
37. BAND SAW BLADES
38. BARBED WIRE
39. BICYCLE SPOKES
40. BRAKE LINING ASBESTOES/ RESIN BASED & ASBESTOES FREE
41. BRASS ARTWARE/HOLLOW WARE CASTING (WITH THE HELP OF PHENOLIC RESIN)
42. BRASS CASTING
43. BRASS PIPES FROM BRASS SHEET WITH LONGITUDINALLY WELDING
44. BRASS WARE BY CASTING METHOD (BRASS ARTICLES VIZ. BRASS POOJA LAMPS AND OTHER CASTED)
45. BRIGHT BARS
46. BUFFING AND POLISHING INDUSTRY (JOB WORK)
47. BUTT HINGE (BRASS SHEET)
48. CARBON BRUSH HOLDER & SLIP RING
49. CO_2 WELDING WIRE ELECTRODES (COPPER/ COPPER ALLOY COATED M.S.WIRE)
50. CARBON FILM RESISTORS
51. CARBURETTORS
52. CAST STEEL PANES FOR MELTING FURNACE
53. CHEMICAL ETCHING OF STAINLESS STEEL
54. CHEMICAL RESISTANT IRON & STEEL
55. COLD FORM SECTION MILL
56. COLD ROLLED FORMING OF SECTION AND OTHER SECTIONS
57. COLD ROLLING OF MS STRIP
58. COLD TWISTED DE-FORMED RIBBED STEEL
59. COMPRESSOR (HERMETIC) FOR AIR CONDITIONERS
60. COMPRESSED NATURAL GAS (CNG KIT) FOR AUTOVEHICLE
61. CONTINUOUSLY CAST STEEL WIRE RODS (5 mm)
62. CONTINUOUS CASTING COPPER WIRE RODS
63. CONVEYOR BELTINGS
64. CONVEYOR BELT, TRANSM -ISSION BELT & V BELTS
65. COOKING RANGES
66. COPPER/BRASS SHEETS, CIRCLE & UTENSILS
67. COPPER FOIL
68. COPPER INGOTS, RODS MAKING & WIRE DRAWING
69. COPPER PRODUCTS FROM COPPER SCRAP
70. COPPER SMELTING PLANT
71. COPPER WIRE RODS FROM COPPER SCRAP
72. CORRUGATED BOX MAKING MACHINERY AND OTHER THEIR PARTS
73. CYLINDER LINER FOR AUTOMOBILES
74. DOOR LOCKS/PAD LOCKS
75. DRILL BITS & TOOL BITS
76. DRUM CLOSURES
77. ERW STEEL CONDUIT PIPE
78. EARTH MOVING EQPT.
79. ENGINE VALVES FOR AUTOMOBILES
80. FABRICATION OF HEAT EXCHANGER
81. FABRICATION OF STORAGE TANKS AND M.S. DRUM
82. FERROUS ALLOY NI-HARDY I.V CASTING
83. FERROUS Mn ALLOY CASTING BY ALUMINA THERMIC PROCESS
84. FERRO ALLOYS
85. FERRO SILICON & FERRO MANGANESE FROM DOLOMITE (SMS GRADE)
86. FIRE EXTINGUISHERS
87. FLIP-TONE CANS
88. FORGED CONECTING ROD
89. FORGING UNIT
90. FOUNTAIN PEN NIBS
91. FOUNDRY SAND
92. FUEL INJECTION SYSTEM
93. GALVANIZED M.S.STRIPS
94. GALVANIZING PLANT
95. GALVANIZED IRON WIRE
96. GAS WELDING TORCHES AND NOZZLES
97. GASKET SHEET
98. GATE GRILLS & WINDOW FRAMES
99. GENERATING SET (DIESEL)
100. HARD ANODISED ALUMINIUM
101. HOSPITAL WARES
102. HOSPITAL FURNITURES
103. HOT DIP GALVANIZING
104. HOT FORGED FASTENERS
105. HOT MIX PLANT
106. INJECTION MOULDED PLASTIC COMPOUNDS WITH TOOL ROOM
107. INJECTION MOULDED PLASTIC COMPONENTS AND METAL PIPE SPINNING UNIT
108. INVESTMENT CASTING
109. IRON/STEEL WIRE GAUGE
110. IRON TAWA
111. KNIVES (S.S.KNIVES)
112. KITCHEN SINK (S.S.)
113. L.P.G REGULATORS
114. MACHINE SCREWS & SELF TAPPING SCREWS
115. MARUTI WORKSHOP CUM SERVICE STATION
116. MAGNESIUM INGOTS & BULLETS CASTING

Above all the "Detailed Project Reports" are available at *"ENGINEERS INDIA RESEARCH INSTITUTE"*. 4449, Nai Sarak (D), Main Road Delhi - 110 006 (India) ● Ph : 91-11-23918117, 2391 6431, 2384 0361 ● Fax : 91-11- 2391 6431 ●E-Mail : eirisidi@bol.net.in ● WebSite : www.eiriindia.org

117. MANUFACTURE OF TIN CONTAINERS
118. MANUFACTURE OF STORAGE TANKS, PRESSURE VESSELS, HEAT EXCHANGERS
119. MARK II HAND PUMPS
120. MARUTI WORKSHOP CUM - SERVICE STATION
121. MECHANICAL JACKS
122. METAL CUTTING DIE DESIGN
123. METAL CUTTING OF AND GRINDING WHEELS (ABBRASIVE CUTTING WHEELS)
124. METAL HOOKS & CLIPS
125. METAL SEPARATION (COPPER , TIN, LEAD) FROM SPENT WASH ACID
126. METALLIC RING JOINTS
127. METALLIC GASKET (SPIRAL WOUND)
128. MICROVÉE & ABSOLUTE FILTER
129. MICROWAVE OVEN
130. MILD STEEL INGOTS
131. MINI STEEL PLANT
132. MODERN VEHICLE WORKSHOP
133. MOPED
134. M.S.HINGES
135. M.S.INGOT AND HR. STEEL STRUCTURALS
136. M.S.INGOT BY INDUCTION FURNACES
137. M.S.PIPES
138. M.S. WELDING ELECTRODE
139. MUFFLERS & SILENCERS FOR THREE WHEELERS
140. NAIL CUTTER WITH FILER & MANICURE
141. NICHROME WIRE
142. NICKEL LINED SCREENS
143. NON-FERROUS ALLOY ROLLING
144. NON-FERROUS FORGING
145. NON-FERROUS FOUNDRY
146. NON PRESSURE
147. INCANDESCENT LAMP
148. NUMBER COMBINATION LOCKS FOR LUGGAGES
149. NUTS & BOLTS
150. PAPER COATED ALUMINIUM AND COPPER WIRE
151. PETROMAX CONTAINER
152. PHOTO ETCHING OF STAINLESS STEEL PLATES
153. PIPE GALVANIZING PLANT
154. PISTON RING-AUTOMOBILE
155. PLANT PROTECTION EQUIPMENTS
156. PLATINUM LABORATORY APPARATUS
157. PRESSURE COOKER & ALUMINIUM UTENSILS
158. PRESSURE COOKER (ALUMINIUM)
159. PRESSURE DIE CASTING
160. PRINTED ALUMINIUM COLLAPSIBLE TUBES
161. PRINTED TIN CONTAINERS
162. PRINTING PRESS (CYLINDER MACHINE)
163. PUMPS FOR CHEMICAL INDUSTRY (SPECIAL)
164. RAILWAY SLEEPERS (M.S.)
165. RAZOR TWIN BLADE
166. R.C.C SPUN PIPES
167. RECONDITIONING OF M.S. DRUMS/BARRELS
168. RE-ROLLING COPPER AND BRASS SHEET AND RODS
169. RE-ROLLING MILLS
170. RESIN COATED SAND
171. RESIN CORED SOFT SOLDER WIRES
172. ROLLING MILL (BY INDUCTION FURNACE) & MANUFACTURE OF BARS, ANGLES, SQUARES, TUBES AND OTHERS
173. ROLLER BEARING & FORGING
174. ROLLING OF STAINLESS STEEL PATTA
175. RUBBER INSULATED PLIERS (HAND TOOLS)
176. RUBBING COMPOUND FOR AUTOMOBILES
177. SCIENTIFIC LABORATORY EQUIPMENTS
178. SCOOTER ASSEMBLING
179. SECONDARY LEAD EXTRAC-TION BY SCRAP BATTERY PLATES,PIPES & SHEET
180. SEAMLESS M.S. TUBES & PIPES
181. SELF TAPPING STEEL SCREW
182. SEWING NEEDLES
183. S.G. IRON & ALLOY STEEL
184. SHEET METAL PRODUCTS, (FERROUS/NON-FERROUS)
185. SHIP/MARINE CONTAINER
186. SHOCK ABSORBERS
187. SHOE EYELETS
188. SHOT AND GRITS BY AUTOMIZATION PROCESS
189. SHOVELS
190. SILICO MANGANESE ALLOYS
191. SILENCERS (MUFFLERS) EXHAUST & TAIL PIPE FOR ALL TYPES OF VEHICLES
192. SINTERED BEARING
193. SINTERED BUSHES
194. SINTERED METAL PRODUCTS
195. SOFT AND HARD FERRITES
196. SPANNERS
197. SPARK PLUGS
198. STEEL PLANT (ELECTRIC ARC FURNACE BASED- EAF)
199. SPHERIODAL GRAPHITE CAST IRON
200. SPRAY DRYER
201. STAINLESS STEEL HINGES
202. STAINLESS STEEL SHEET ROLLING TO PRODUCE STAINLESS STEEL UTENSILS
203. STAINLESS STEEL UTENSILS
204. STAPLE PINS,PAPER PIN , GEM CLIPS ETC.
205. STEEL CASTINGS
206. STEEL CHAIN
207. STEEL FOUNDRY
208. STEEL FURNITURES AND ELECTRICAL APPLIANCES
209. STEEL PLANT (MINI)
210. STEEL RODS AND COILS FROM SCRAPS
211. STEEL ROLLING MILL
212. STEEL STRIPS (COLD ROLLED) SILICON WITH GRAIN RIENTED FOR ELECTRIC USE
213. STEEL TRANSMISSION LINE TOWERS & ROLLING MILL TO PRODUCE STEEL SECTION
214. STEEL FURNITURES AND ELECTRICAL APPLIANCES
215. STEEL WIRE DRAWING AND GALVANIZING
216. STEEL WOOL
217. SUBMERGED ARC WELDED PIPES
218. SUBMERSIBLE PUMP MANUFACTURING
219. SUPER ENAMELLED COPPER WIRE
220. THREE WHEELERS
221. TIE-ROD ENDS
222. TIN CONTAINERS
223. TOOLROOM AND SHEET METAL PRODUCTS
224. TRACTOR TRAILERS
225. TRANSMISSION POWER FITTING
226. TUBULAR POLES
227. SUPER ENAMELLED COPPER WIRES
228. TUBULAR POLES FOR ELECTRICAL TRANSMISSION (BY FABRICATION PROCESS)
229. TUBULAR POLES OF M.S. & HIGH TENSILE STEEL
230. VACUUM CLEANERS
231. VACUUM FLASK (STAINLESS STEEL)
232. VALVES FOR REFRIGERA TION AND AIR-CONDITION
233. VEHICLE WELDING & PAINTING
234. VENETION BLIND
235. WASHING MACHINES (AUTOMATIC & COMPUTERISED)
236. WATER CONTROLLER (AUTOMATIC)
237. WATCH STRAPS/CHAINS/ BRACELETS/BELT BRASS & STAINLESS STEEL
238. WATER COOLERS
239. WELDED WIRE MESH
240. WELDING ELECTRODES
241. WICK STOVES
242. WIND MILL WINDOW FRAME (FERROUS & NON-FERROUS)
243. WRIST WATCH

359. DI ETHYL OXALATE
360. DI METHYL ORTHOPHTHALATE
361. DI-METHYL PHTHALATE
362. DICLOFENAC GEL
363. DIOCTYL PHTHALATE (DOP)
364. DI PHENYL GLYCERINE
365. DI PHENYL OXIDE
366. DINITRO-CHLORO BENZENE
367. DISTILLED WATER
368. DODECYL BENZENE SULPHONATE
369. DUSTLESS CHALK
370. EDTA & ITS SALTS
371. ELECTROLESS NICKEL PLATING ON PLASTICS
372. ENDOSULFAN
373. EPOXY RESIN BASED COMPOUND
374. ETHYL ACETATE
375. EHTYL ETHER
376. ETHYL ALCOHOL (POTABLE LIQUOR)
377. ETHYL HEXANOL
378. EXTRACTION OF ESSENTIAL OILS BY SUGAR CRITICAL FLUID (CARBON DIOXIDE) METHOD FROM FLOWERS, HERBAL & SPICES
379. FERRIC ALUM
380. FERRO CHROME LIGNO SULPHONATE
381. FERRO MANGANESE
382. FERRO SILICONE
383. FERRO VANADIUM FROM VANADIUM SLUDGE
384. FERROUS SILICATE
385. FERROUS SULPHATE
386. FERTILIZER FROM ANIMAL BLOOD & LEATHER WASTE
387. FLUORESCENT TUBE LIGHT POWDER
388. FOAMED PVC COMPOUNDING & ITS PRODUCTS
389. FORMALDEHYDE
390. FRACTIONAL DISTILLATION OF D.M.O (DEMENTHOLIZED OIL)
391. FRACTIONAL DISTILLATION OF ESSENTIAL OIL & MEDICINAL PLANT EXTRACT
392. FRICTION DUST (LIQUID & POWDER) FROM CNSL
393. FRUIT FLAVOURS
394. FURFURAL FROM RICE HUSK
395. GARLIC ACID
396. GASKET SHELLAC COMPOUND
397. GEAR OIL
398. GIBBERELLIC ACID
399. GLASS PUTTY
400. GLYCERINE
401. GOSSYPOL (POLY PHENOL) FROM COTTON SEED OIL
402. GUAR GUM POWDER
403. HAIR FIXER (HAIR GEL TYPE)
404. H - ACID
405. HENNA PASTE MAKING
406. HEPTAL DEHYDE
407. HIGH CARBON FERRO CHROME
408. HYDRATED CALCIUM SILICATE BRICK
409. HYDRATED LIME FROM SEA SHELL
410. HYDROCHLORIC ACID
411. HYDRO FLUORIC ACID
412. HYDROGEN PEROXIDE (BY AUTO-OXIDATION PROCESS)
413. ICE PACKS (SOLUTIONS TYPE, WHITE GEL TYPE, VIOLET SEMI SOLID POLYMER TYPE)
414. IMPROVING DROP POINT PARAFFIN WAX FROM 45-50°C TO 75-80°C
415. INDUSTRIAL ALCOHOL
416. INTEGERATED COMPLEX OF EASTER & ALLIED PRODUCTS (D.O.P, D.B.P, ETHYL ACETATE WIRE ENAMEL & CABLE JELLY)
417. IMFL (WHISKY) & COUNTRY LIQUOR
418. IRON OXIDE FOR MAKING FERITTE
419. IRON SULPHIDE
420. JUTE BATCHING OIL
421. KESH KALA TEL (HAIR DYE LOTION) (VASMOL 33, BLACK NITE TYPE)
422. L-LYSINE MONOHYDROCHLORIDE
423. LACTIC ACID FROM WHITE SUGAR BY FERMENTATION PROCESS
424. LDPE GRANULES FROM VIRGIN (LDPE RESIN)
425. LEAD EXTRACTION FROM BATTERY SCRAP
426. LEAD OXIDE (A) LEAD MONOXIDE (B) LEAD TETRA OXIDE (C) GREYLEAD OXIDE
427. LIQUID GLUCOSE & ITS BY PRODUCTS
428. LIQUID OXYGEN BOTTLING PLANT
429. LIQUID SHOE POLISH
430. LIQUID FLOOR POLISH
431. LUBE OIL VISCOSITY IMPROVED FOR P.P.G/P.E.G.
432. LUBRICANTS ASHLESS 100% COMBUSTION
433. MAGNESIUM CARBONATE AND MAGNESIUM BICARMONATE
434. MAGNESIUM HYDROXIDE POWDER
435. MAGNESIUM SILICATE
436. MAGNESIUM SULPHATE
437. MALACHITE GREEN
438. MALEIC ANHYDRIDE
439. MANGANESE SULPHATE
440. MANUFACTURING OF CARBON MONO-OXIDE WATER GAS
441. MENTHOL BOLD CRYSTALS FROM FLAKES
442. MENTHOL CRYSTAL & MENTHA OIL
443. MERCURIC OXIDE
444. METAL PRE-TREATMENT CHEMICALS
445. METHANE GAS BY SODIUM ACETATE & SODA LIME
446. METHYL ACETYL RICINOLATE
447. METOL
448. METOL FROM HYDROQUINONE & METHYLAMINE
449. MICANITE
450. MICRO NUTRIENT MIXTURE
451. MINERAL WATER
452. MINERAL WATER AND PET BOTTILNG PLANT
453. MINERAL WATER IN BOTTLES, GLASS AND POUCHES
454. MINI CEMENT PLANT (BY ROTARY KILN PROCESS)
455. MIXED FERTILIZER
456. MOSQUITO & FLIES REPELLENT AGARBATTI (INCENSE STICKS)
457. MONO CHLORO ACETIC ACID
458. MONOCROTOPHOS (TECHNICAL)
459. MOSQUITO COIL
460. MOSQUITO COIL & MAT
461. MOSQUITO MAT
462. MOTHER TINCTURE & BIO CHEMIC MEDICINES
463. NAPHTHALENE & PHENYL (INTEGRATED UNIT)
464. NATURAL MINERAL WATER BY REVERSE OSMOSIS PROCESS
465. NICKEL PLATING BRIGHTNER (PRIMARY OR CARRIER BRIGHTNER & SECONDARY BRIGHTNER)
466. NICKEL SULPHATE
467. NICOTINE FROM TOBACCO WASTE
468. NICOTINE SULPHATE FROM TOBACCO WASTE
469. NITRO BENZENE
470. NITRO CELLULOSE SANDING SEALER/LACQUER
471. NITRO MUSK
472. NITROGEN & OXYGEN GAS PLANT
473. NON-IONIC SURFACTANT (WETTING AGENT)
474. NO-CARB PASTE
475. OCTANOL
476. ORTHO NITRO PHENOL
477. OXALIC ACID FROM MOLASSES
478. OXALIC ACID FROMRICE HUSK
479. OXALIC ACID FROM TREE BARK
470. OXALIC ACID FROM WASTE VEGETABLES
471. OXYGEN GAS PLANT
472. OXYGEN GAS PLANT (AIR SEPERATION METHOD)
473. PARA-AMINO BENZOIC ACID
474. PARA-AMINO PHENOL
475. PARA TOLUENE SULPHONIC ACID
476. PECTIN FROM RAW PAPAYA
477. PERFUME (LEMON & OTHERS)

CRUDE NAPHTHA
570. TRIMETHYL AMMONIUM CHLORIDE
571. TRIPHENYL PHOSPHITE (T.P.P)
572. ULTRAMARINE BLUE (LIQUID)
573. UREA FORMALDEHYDE & MELAMINE FORMALDEHYDE POWDER
574. UNDECYLINIC ACID
575. VINYL ACETATE MONOMER
576. VITAMIN C
577. VITAMIN E
578. WASTE WATER TREATMENT PLANT FOR INDUSTRIAL SECTOR IN INDIA (ONLY MARKER SURVEY)
579. WIRE DRAWING LUBRICANT
580. WIRE ENAMEL
581. XANTHATES
582. YELLOW DEXTRIN
583. ZINC CHLORIDE
584. ZINC OXIDE
585. ZINC PHOSPHATING BY COLD PROCESS
586. ZINC SILICATE
587. ZINC STEARATE
588. ZINC SULPHATE
589. ZINC SULPHATE MONOHYDRATE
590. ACID BLACK
591. AURAMINE'O'
592. AZO DYES STUFF
593. DYE & DYE INTERMEDIATE
594. DYE INTERMEDIATES
595. MALACHITE GREEN
596. METHYLENE BLUE
597. PHTHALOCYANINE BLUE
598. PHTHALOCYANINE BLUE & GREEN
599. REACTIVE DYES
600. SULPHUR BLACK DYE
601. VAT DYES
602. WATER CHILLING PLANT
603. WADDING OIL (100%) FOR WADDING OF COTTON HOSIERY CLOTH IN THE DYEING PROCESS
604. WHITE OIL
605. WAX FLOOR POLISH

ELECTRICAL, ELECTONICS, COMPUTERS AND INFOTECH/IT PROJECTS

606. AIR CONDITIONING
607. ALUMINIUM ALLOY CONDUCTOR
608. ALUMINIUM CABLE
609. ALUMINIUM ELECTROYTIC CAPACITORS
610. AUDIO CASSETTE ASSEMBLING & RECORDING
611. AUDIO CASSETTES DUPLICATING RECORDING
612. AUDIO CASSETTES & AUDIO STUDIO
613. AUDIO CASSETTES PLANE & RECORDED
614. AUDIO MAGNETIC HEADS
615. AUDIO MAGNETIC TAPE
616. AUDIO/VIDEO CASSETTES
617. AUTO BULB/LAMPS
618. AUTOMATIC VOLTAGE STABILIZER
619. BATTERY PLATES
620. BACK OFFICE (Rs. 5000/-)
621. B/W TV & COMPUTER MONITOR PICTURE TUBE
622. BREAD BOARDS
623. CALL CENTRE
624. CAMERA (35 MM)
625. CAPACITORS
626. CARBON ELECTRODE USED FOR BATTERY CELL
627. CARBON POTETIOMETERS
628. CEILING FAN
629. CERAMIC INSULATOR
630. CHILDREN INFOTECH TRAINING INSTITUTE (Rs. 5000/-)
631. CHOKE AND PATTI
632. CHOKE AND STARTER
633. CHOKE USED FOR FLUORESCENT LAMPS
634. COLOUR TELEVISION
635. COLOUR AND BLACK & WHITE TELEVISION
636. COMPACT DISC
637. COMPACT DISC PLAYER (AUDIO/VIDEO)
638. COMPUTER EDUCATION INSTITUTE
639. COMPUTER ASSEMBLY
640. COMPUTER HARDWARE
641. COMPUTER KEYBOARD
642. COMPUTER PERIPHERALS
643. COMPUTER PRINTERS
644. COMPUTER RIBBON
645. COMPUTER RIBBON REINKING OR REFILLING
646. COMPUTER STATIONERY
647. COMPUTER STATIONERY & IMPORTED HARDWARE PARTS

648. COMPUTER TERMINALS
649. COMPUTERISED WASHING MACHINE (AUTOMATIC)
650. COMPUTER SOFTWARE
651. CONDENSER FOR MOTOR USING MPP FILM
652. CONTENT DEVELOPMENT CENTRE (EOU) (Rs. 5000/-)
653. CONTROL PANEL BOARD
654. COOLING COIL FOR AIR CONDITIONERS
655. COPPER STRIP COIL FROM SCRAP
656. CORDLESS TELEPHONES
657. CYBER CAFE
658. CYBERKIOSK (Rs. 5000/-)
659. DATA PROCESSING CENTRE (Rs. 5000/-)
660. D.C. MICRO MOTORS
661. D.G.SETS
662. DISH ANTENNA AND CABLE T.V. NETWORK EQUIPMENT
663. DISTRIBUTION TRANSFORMERS & REPAIRS
664. DOMESTIC ELECTRICAL APPLIANCES- ROOM COOLER, WASHING MACHINE, WATER HEATER, ELECTRIC ROOM HEATER
665. E-SCHOOL
666. E-COMMERCE/BUSINESS
667. ELECTRIC ENERGY METER
668. ELECTRIC FANS
669. ELECTRIC HORN FOR AUTOMOBILE
670. ELECTRIC LAMP/GLS (INCANDESCENT LAMP)
671. ELECTRIC MIXER
672. ELECTRIC MOTORS UP TO 10 HP. REWINDING OF ALL TYPES OF MOTORS WATER PUMPS
673. ELECTRIC MOTOR WINDING (FOR FAN, MIXIES, ETC.)
674. ELECTRIC STEAM IRON
675. ELECTRICAL APPLIANCES
676. ELECTRICAL FIXTURES
677. ELECTRICAL STAMPING
678. ELECTROLYTIC CAPACITORS
679. ELECTROMAGNETIC RELAY
680. ELECTRONIC BALAST/CHOK
681. ELECTRICAL CHOKE
682. ELECTRONIC DIGITAL WATCHES
683. ELECTRONIC DIGITAL WEIGHING MACHINE
684. ELECTRONIC FIRE ALARM
685. ELECTRONIC GAS STOVE LIGHTERS
686. ELECTRONIC PRESSURE INDICATORS, ELECTRICALS, ELECTRONIC LIQUID LEVEL INDICATORS, ELECTRONIC TEMPERATURE INDICATOR, DIGITAL TACHOMETER
687. ELECTRONIC TELEPHONE INSTRUMENTS
688. ELECTRONIC TOYS
689. ELECTRONIC WATCHES & CLOCKS
690. FAX MACHINES
691. F.H.P MOTORS
692. FLOPPY DISKETTES
693. FLUORESCENT LAMP STARTER
694. FLUORESCENT TUBULAR

Above all the "Detailed Project Reports" are available at *"ENGINEERS INDIA RESEARCH INSTITUTE"*. 4449, Nai Sarak (D), Main Road Delhi - 110 006 (India) ● Ph : 91-11-23918117, 2391 6431, 2384 0361 ● Fax : 91-11- 2391 6431 ●E-Mail : eirisidi@bol.net.in ● WebSite : www.eiriindia.org

LAMPS WITH INTRODUCTION TO MERCURY VAPOUR LAMP

695. FRANCHISEE COMPUTER EDUCATION CENTRE (Rs. 5000)
696. GAS DETECTOR (L.P.G)
697. GENERATOR SET & PUMP SETS
698. GENERATOR (BATTERY OPERATED)
699. GIS SERVICE CENTRE (GEOGRAPHICAL INFORMATION SYSTEMS)
700. HARDWARE FITTING FOR TRANSMISSION LINE OVERHEAD LINE MATERIAL
701. HEADERS FOR TRANSISTOR ICS SEMI CONDUCTOR
702. H.T & L.T INSULATORS
703. H.T & M.V INDUSTRIAL CUBICAL SWITCH BOARD
704. INFORMATION MOVING DISPLAY (L.E.D TYPE)
705. INSURANCE CLAIM PROCESSING CENTRE (EOU) (Rs. 5000/-)
706. INTEGRATED CIRCUITS
707. INTERNET BASED STOCK TRADING (Rs. 5000/-)
708. INTERNET SERVICE PROVIDER (I.S.P.)
709. JELLY FILLED TELEPHONE CABLES
710. LAP TOP COMPUTERS
711. LEAD ACID BATTERIES
712. LEAD ACID BATTERY PLATES AND ASSEMBLING OF BATTERY
713. LEGAL TRANSCRIPTION & SECRETARIAL SERVICES CENTER (EOU)(Rs. 5000/-)
714. LIGHT EMITTING DIODES (L.E.D)
715. LINEAR ICS TRAINER KIT
716. LOUD SPEAKER
717. L.T TRANSFORMER REPAIRING
718. MEDICAL TRANSCRIPTION CENTRE
719. METAL FILM RESISTORS
720. METALLISED POLYPROPYLENE, POLYESTER FILM CAPACITOR
721. MICA BASE ELECTRONIC COMPONENTS
722. MICA PAPER WASTE PAPER FROM MICA WASTE
723. MICRO PROCESSORS TRAINER KITS BASED ON MICRO PROCESSORS
724. MINI COMPUTER (PERSONAL COMPUTER)
725. MINIATURE CIRCUIT BREAKER (M.C.B)
726. MINIATURE WATCH BATTERIES (BUTTON CELL)
727. MIXER/GRINDER (MIXI)
728. MONO CHROME COMPUTER MONITOR
729. MOTOR START ELECTROLYTIC CAPACITOR
730. MULTI LAYER P.C.B
731. MULTIPLE RELAY FOR LOW VOLTAGE
732. NEON INDICATOR
733. NEON SIGN MANUFACTURE
734. OPTICAL FIBRE CABLES
735. ON LINE SHOPPING MALL (Rs. 5000/-)
736. OPTO MECHANICAL & ELECTRICAL EQUIPMENTS
737. PHOTO COLOUR LAB
738. PICTURE TUBE (B/W)
739. PLAIN PAPER COPIER
740. PLASTIC FILM CAPACITORS
741. POLYESTER CAPACITORS
742. PORTABLE GENERATOR SET
743. PORTAL
744. PORTABLE TELEVISION(TV)
745. POWER CAPACITORS
746. POWER INVERTERS
747. POWER PLANT
748. POWER TRANSFORMERS UP TO 600 KVA
749. PRINTED CIRCUIT BOARD
750. PVC WIRES & CABLES
751. RE-CONDITIONING OF PICTURE TUBE
752. RESIN CAST CT & PT (1 KV)
753. SEMI CONDUCTOR DEVICE
754. SEMI CONDUCTORS FOR TRANSISTORS & DIODES
755. SETTING UP OF A VIDEO STUDIO
756. SMOKE DETECTORS
757. SOLAR CELLS
758. SOLAR MODULES
759. SOLAR PHOTO VOLTAIC SYSTEM
760. SOLDER FLUXES
761. SOLAR WATER HEATING PANELS
762. STEEL FURNITURE & ELECTRICAL APPLIANCES
763. STEREO AMPLIFIERS
764. STEREO CASSETTE RECORDERS/PLAYERS
765. STREET LIGHT FITTINGS SURGE SUPPRESSOR
766. TANTALUM CAPACITORS
767. TEFLON COATED ELECTRIC CABLE
768. TELEMEDICINE (DISTANCE HEALTH CARE) (Rs. 5000/-)
769. TELEPHONE CORD/CABLE
770. TELEPHONE (PUSH BUTTON TYPE)
771. TELEPHONE (PUSH BUTTON & CORDLESS)
772. TELEVISION (CTV & B/W)
773. TELEVISION (3-D)
774. TELEVISION DEFLECTION COMPONENTS
775. TELEVISION SIGNAL BOOSTERS
776. TELEVISION TUNERS
777. TRACTION BATTERIES
778. TRAINING INSTITUTE OF MEDICAL TRANSCRIPTION
779. TRANSFORMER FOR B/W TV
780. TRANSFORMER FOR VOLTAGE STABILIZER & E.H.T
781. TRANSMISSION POWER LINE FITTING
782. TRANSMISSION TOWER FITTING
783. TV AUDIO EQUIPMENT CABINETS & THEIR ASSEMBLING UNIT
784. UN-INTERRUPTED POWER SUPPLY (U.P.S)
785. VARIABLE FREQUENCY
786. VARIABLE VOLTAGE A.C. DRIVE
787. VIDEO CASSETTES (COMPLETE MANUFACTURING & ASSEMBLING)
788. VIDEO CASSETTES RECORDER (V.C.R)
789. VIDEO FILM STUDIO
790. VOLTAGE REGULATOR FOR AUTOMOBILES
791. VOLTAGE STABILIZERS
792. VOLTAGE STABLIZER & T.V. GAIN BOOSTER
793. WAX AND CHEMICAL COATED, BRAIDED TINSEL WIRE
794. WEBSITE DESIGN & E-MAIL REGISTERING
795. WELDING ELECTRODES
796. WIND ENERGY POWER PROJECT (10 MW) WIRE WOUND POTENTIOMETERS

FOOD, AGRO FOOD, PROCESSED FOOD, AGRO PLANTATION, CULTIVATION, FARMING, DAIRY/MILK, TOBACCO/PAN MASALA, BREWERY & DISTILLERY, EDIBLE OILS, EOU FOOD PRODUCTS AND ALLIED PRODUCTS

797. ALCOHOLIC BEVERAGES & VENEGAR FROM COCONUT WATER
798. ALCOHOL DRINKS FROM ETHYL ALCOHOL BY MIXING OF VARIOUS FLAVOURS
799. ANTI SCALE COMPOUND FOR ADDING INTO SUGAR JUICE BOILING
800. APPLE JUICE CONCENTRATED & DEHYDRATED FRUIT & VEGETABLES
801. ARTIFICIAL FISH MEAL FOR POULTRY FEED
802. AUTOMATIC BISCUIT PLANT
803. BABY CEREAL FOOD AND MILK POWDER
804. BACTERIA FOR CANE JUICE
805. BAKER'S YEAST
806. BAKERY INDUSTRY
807. BANANA PUREE
808. BEER & WINE
809. BEER PLANT (BREWERY)
810. BIDI
811. BIDI & CIGARETTE
812. BISCUIT PLANT

813. BREAD (AUTOMATIC PLANT)
814. BLACK PEPPER (SPICES)
815. BREAD AND BISCUITS
816. BREEDING FARM
817. BROILER CHICKEN
819. BUTTON MUSHROOM CULTIVATION & PROCESSING
820. CANNING OF RASAGULLAS IN METAL CANS
821. CAFFEIN FROM TEA WASTE
822. CANNING OF FRUITS & VEGETABLES
823. CASEIN AND BY-PRODUCTS
824. CASHEW FRUIT JUICE FROM CASHEW FRUIT APPLE
825. CASHEWNUT KERNEL EXTRACTION FROM CASHEWNUT FRUIT
826. CASHEWNUT SHELL LIQUID & KERNEL PROCESSING
827. CASHEW FENI
828. CATECHEU (BY CHEMICAL PROCESS)
829. CATTLE FEED FROM TAPIOCA
830. CHEWING & BUBBLE GUM
831. CHICKEN/SHEEP MEAT PROCESSING
832. CHOCOLATE (MILK)
833. CIGARETTE AND BEEDIES
834. COCOA BUTTER FROM COCOA MASS
835. COCONUT PRODUCTS & BY PRODUCTS PROCESS COMPLEX
836. COLD/SOFT DRINKS
837. COLLECTION OF MILK AND MILK MAKING POWDER
838. COLLECTION OF MILK AND PACKING IN POLYTHENE POUCH (1/2 KG. 1 KG. & 2 KG.)
839. CONDENSED MILK (SWEETNED)
840. CONFECTIONERY INDUSTRY (TOFFEE & CANDY, SEMI-AUTOMATIC PLANT)
841. COUNTRY LIQUOR FROM MOLASSES
842. CIGARETTE
843. DAIRY FARM AND DAIRY (MILK) PRODUCTS (PASTEURISED MILK, BUTTER, GHEE, PANEER)
844. DAIRY FARM TO PRODUCE MILK & PACKING IN POUCHES (50%) & CAN(50%)
845. DAIRY FOR MILK PROCESSING
846. DAIRY FARM (BUFALO)
847. DAL (PULSE) MILL UNIT
848. DEHYDRATION OF CARROT & GARLIC
849. DEHYDRATION & CANNING OF FRUITS & VEGETABLES
850. DEHYDRATION OF FIGS
851. DEHYDRATION OF FRUITS AND VEGETABLES
852. DEHYDRATED ONIONS AND ONION POWDER
853. DRY ICE BY BREAKING OF AIR
854. DRYING OF RED CHILLIES, HALDI, DHANIA, AND GREEN PEAS
855. EGG POWDER (40,000 EGGS PROCESSING PER DAY)
856. EXPORT OF PROCESSED FOODS AND MARINE PRODUCTS
857. FISH CANNING & POUCHING
859. FISH FARMING (PRAWN & OTHER MARINE PRODUCTS)
860. FISH MEAL
861. FLOUR MILL AND MUSTARD OIL
862. FOOD COLOUR & ORASTED GROUNDNUT GRAM PEAS, ETC IN POUCHES
863. FROG LEGS PROCESSING
864. FROZEN MEATS PROCESSING
865. FOOD FLAVOURS (WHISKY) VODKA, GRAPE, BUTTER SCOTCH)
866. FOOD PRODUCTS COMPLEX (DEHYDRATED ONIONS, GARLIC POWDER & FLAKES, CATTLE FEED, TOMATO POWDER, TOMATO PRODUCTS, CANNED FRUITS & VEGETABLES, TOMATO PURE, GROUN NUT OIL, REFIND OIL, DEHYDRATED GRAPES, BANANA POWDER & WAFFERS)
867. FRUIT JUICE, JAM, JELLIES & ALLIED PRODUCTS
868. FRUIT JUICE, PICKLES PROCESSING AND CANNING
869. FRUIT JUICE MAKING & PACKING IN PLASTIC CONTAINER/POUCHES
870. FRUIT PROCESSING (JAM & JELLIES)
871. FRUIT PULP & JUICE CONCENTRATES
872. FRUIT & VEGETABLE DRYING (FREEZE DRYING METHOD)
873. GOAT & SHEEP FARMING
874. GRAM DALL/PULSE MILL
875. GRAPE DEHYDRATION
876. HARD BOILED CANDY (TOFFEE & CANDY)
877. HERBAL CIGARETTES
878. HONEY PROCESSING & PACKAGING
879. ICE CREAM OF DIFFERENT FLAVOURS
880. ICE CREAM STABILIZER
881. ICE MAKING PLANT
882. INDIAN MADE FOREIGN LIQUOR (I.M.F.L)
883. INSTANT FOOD (IDLI MIX, DOSA MIX, GULAB JAMUN MIX)
884. INSTANT FOOD (INSTANT FOOD & FAST FOOD PARLOUR)
885. INSTANT NOODLES
886. INSTANT TEA
887. INSTANT TEA FROM BLACK TEA
888. INTEGERATED STARCH BAKING POWDER/YEAST INDUSTRY
889. IODIZED SALT
890. IODIZED SALT (ORDINARY MOISTURE-LESS/FREE FLOWING IN PLASTIC BAGS AND CONTAINERS)
891. JAM, JELLIES, FRUIT JUICE & ALLIED PRODUCTS
892. KATHA AND CUTCH
893. KHANDSARI SUGAR
894. KHANDSARI SUGAR & IMFL
895. LACTIC ACID FROM WHITE SUGAR BY FERMENTATION PROCESS
896. LACTOSE & BY PRODUCTS PROCESSING FROM MILK
897. LIQUID GLUCOSE AND ITS BYE PRODUCTS
898. MACRONI AND VERMICILLI
899. MALT EXTRACTION FROM BARLEY
900. MANGO PROCESSING (MANGO PULF, JUICE & SLICES)
901. MAYUR BRAND TYPE CHEWING TOBACCO
902. MINERAL WATER
903. MILK PRESERVATION & MARKETING TO WHOLE SELLERS (INPOUCH PACKING BY UHT TECHNOLOGY)
904. MILK PROCESSING AND PACKAGING OF MILK PRODUCTS
905. MILK PRODUCTS (CASEIN, LACTOSE, GHEE & WHEY POWDER)
906. MILK TOFFEE
907. MINI FLOUR MILL
908. MINI SUGAR PLANT
909. MISRI (PEARL SUGAR CANDIES)
910. MODERN RICE MILL
911. MURABBA
912. MUSTARD OIL EXTRACTION & REFINING
913. MUTTON TALLOW
914. NAMKEEN INDUSTRY (BHUJIA, CHANA CHUR ETC.)
915. NAMKEEN & SWEETS
916. NON-BASMATI RICE FROM PADDY
917. OLEORESIN, ESSENTIAL OIL, DYES & POWDER OF SPICES
918. OLEORESIN EXTRACTION FROM DIPTERO-CARPUT TURMINATUS AND PINUS KHASYANA
919. OLEORESIN EXTRACTION FROM CHILLI
920. PAN MASALA AND POUCH

1059. BUFFALO HORN TIP, HOOF
1060. BANQUET HALL
1061. BUTTON
1062. CALCINED PETROLEUM (C.P) COKE
1063. CANVAS SHOES
1064. CANVAS SHOES, JUNGLE BOOTS
1065. CARBON BRUSH, BRUSH HOLDER & SLIP RING
1066. CEMENT SHEETS WITH COIR FIBRE & OTHER SEGMENTS
1067. CERAMIC TILES (GLAZED) BY DOUBLE FIRING/HEATING
1068. CHILDREN RECREATION CENTRE
1069. COAL BRIQUETTES
1070. COLD STORAGE & ICE
1071. COLD STORAGE FOR FRUITS AND VEGETABLES
1072. COMPRESSOR (HERMETIC) FOR AIR CONDITIONER
1073. COSTUME JEWELLERY/ IMITATION JEWELLERY
1074. DECORATIVE LAMINATED SHEET (SUNMICA)
1075. DIAMOND CUTTING & EXPORTS
1076. DRINKING STRAW FROM PROPYLENE
1077. ENGINEERING COLLEGE
1078. ENTERTAINMENT CLUB
1079. FASHION TECHNOLOGY INSTITUTE
1080. FAST FOOD PARLOUR
1081. FAST FOOD (INSTANT FOOD & FAST FOOD PARLOUR)
1082. FIRE EXTINGUISHERS (SODA ACID TYPE)
1083. FISH NET
1084. FLORICULTURE (CUT FLOWER ROSE) WITH GREEN HOUSE
1085. FLOOR COVERING SHEET
1086. FILM STUDIO (VIDEO)
1087. FLUSH DOOR, CHIP BOARD, WOOD WOOL & OTHER INSULATING BOARDS
1088. GAS DETECTORS OF L.P.G
1089. GEMS MANUFACTURING
1090. GLASS BOTTLE BY SCRAP
1092. GOAT & SHEEP FARMING
1093. GOLD ELECTROPLATING
1094. GOLD JEWELLERY (E.O.U)
1095. GOLD PLATED SILVER JEWELLERY & CUTLERY
1096. GRANITE SLAB AND TILES
1097. GREEN HOUSE
1098. HARD CHROMIUM PLATING
1099. HEALTH CLUB AND BEAUTY PARLOUR CUM HAIR SALOON WITH SONA BATH
1100. HEALTH CLUB CUM BEAUTY PARLOUR TRAININGINSTITUTE
1101. HORN TIP,HOOVE BUTTON
1102. HOSPITAL
1103. HOSPITAL (100 BEDS)
1104. HOSPITAL (200 BEDS)
1105. ICE MAKING PLANT
1106. IMITATION AND COSTUME
1107. JEWELLERY (NECKLACE, EARRINGS EAR TOP ETC.)
1108. INITMATE SCENT CHEMICALS FROM ALL TYPES OF FLAVOUR
1109. INVESTMENT CASTING
1110. JUTE, COIR, GLASS ROPE/ SUTLI
1111. JUTE TWINE
1112. L.P.G BOTTLING PLANT
1113. L.P.G REGULATOR (DOMESTIC PURPOSE)
1114. LAMINATED PARTICLE BOARD & HARD BOARD
1115. LAMINATED SAFETY AND TOUGHENED GLASS
1116. LEASING & HIRE PURCHASE
1117. LICHEN (CHARILA)
1118. MANILA ROPES
1119. MEDICAL COLLEGE
1120. MATCH UNIT FROM WAXED PAPER
1121. MEDIUM DENSITY FIBRE BOARD
1122. MELAMINE CROCKERY
1123. MINERAL WATER
1124. MINI CEMENT PLANT
1125. MIRROR SILVER, GOLDEN, PINK, BLACK & SMOKES
1126. MODERN ADVERTISING AGENCY WITH DTP & FILM STUDIO
1127. MOTEL/SMALL HOTEL
1128. MULTI COLOUR PRINTING
1129. MULTI STOREY COMMERCIAL COMPLEX ALONGWITH RESIDENTIALAND DELUX FLATS FOR FOREIGN TOURISTS & REVOLVING RESTAURENT AT THE TOP
1130. MULTIPLE LAMINATION INDUSTRY
1131. MUSHROOM GROWING AND PROCESSING (BY DEEP FREEZING METHOD)
1132. NEWS PAPER PRINTING
1133. NICKEL LINED INDUSTRIAL SCREEN
1134. OFFSET COLOUR PRINTING PRESS (SIX COLOUR)
1135. OFFSET PRINTING PRESS
1136. P.C.C ELECTRIC POLES
1137. PHOTOGRAPHIC DEVELOPER & FIXER
1138. PVC EXTRUSION PROFILE (DOOR & WINDOWS)
1139. POP-CORN
1140. PHOTO ETCHING OF S.S.
1141. PRE STRESSED CEMENT CONCRETE PIPES
1142. PILFER PROOF CAPS
1143. PILFER PROOF CAPS AND CROWN CAP
1144. POUCH MAKING & GRAVURE PRINTING (ROTO PRINTING)
1145. POULTRY & FISH FARMING (INTEGERATED UNIT)
1146. PRINTING OF TIN SHEETS
1147. READYMADE GARMENTS
1148. RESTAURANT
1149. ROSE PLANTATION AND ROSE OIL EXTRACTION
1150. ROTOGRAVURE PRINTING
1151. SAFETY BELTS
1152. SAFETY MATCHES
1153. SHOE LACES
1154. SILK COCOON CULTIVATION (GROWING OF SILK COCOON WARM)
1155. SILK SCREEN PRINTING FORMULATIONS FOR PLASTIC, PAPER & CLOTH
1156. SPIKENARD (JATAMANSI)
1157. STENCIL COATING SOLUTION
1158. SUGAR CANDY (MISRI)
1159. SUGAR CANE PLANTATION
1160. SUGAR CANE JUICE PRESERVATION
1161. SURAT ZARI
1162. SYNTHETIC SHOES & SOLES
1163. TEA PACKAGING INDUSTRY
1164. TENNIS BALLS
1165. THREE STAR HOTEL
1166. TRAVELLING AGENCY
1167. TRAYS, TROLLEYS FOR HOSPITAL WITH SCRATCHLESS COATING
1168. WAX EXTRACTS (TANNING POWDER)
1169. WIRE ROPE SLINGS
1170. WOOD WOOL SLAB
1171. WOODEN CANE FURNITURE WITH EXPORT POTENTIAL
1172. WOODEN FURNITURE
1173. WOODEN PANEL INCLUDING KILN SEASONING
1174. WOODEN FURNITURE
1175. WATCH CASE BUFFING
1176. WATCH DIAL
1177. WRIST WATCHES
1178. WATCHES (ELECTRONIC)
1179. ZEDOARY (KACHUR)

EDIBLE OILS, ESSENTIAL OILS LURICATIING OILS, GREASES, VEGETABLE OILS, WAXES, CAMPHOR, PERFUMES & PERFUMERY COMPOUNDS AND REFINED OILS ETC.

1180. AROMATIC PERFUMERY COMPOUND
1181. AEROSOL
1182. AGARBATTI PERFUMERY COMPOUND
1183. BEES WAX MANUFACTURE
1184. CAMPHOR
1185. CARDANOL FROM CASHEW NUT SHELL LIQUID
1186. CASTOR OIL
1187. CASTOR OIL DERIVATIVE OLEORESINS
1188. CHILLI OIL
1189. CITRONELLA OILS
1190. CLOVE OIL
1191. CONCENTRATE OF ROSE JASMINE & LILY ETC.
1192. COLOURED FLAME CANDLE

1193. CANDLES (SEMI-AUTOMATIC)
1194. CORN OIL (MAIZE OIL)
1195. DEHYDRATED CASTOR OIL
1196. EUGENOL FROM CINNAMON LEAF OIL
1197. EXTRACTION OF ESSENTIAL OIL (CARDAMON, JEERA, AJOWAN, GINGER OILS ETC. & PACKAGING OF GROUND SPICES)
1198. EXTRACTION OF JASMINE ESSENCE
1199. EXTRACTION OF ESSENTIAL OILS BY SUPER CRITICAL FLUID METHOD FROM FLOWERS, HERBS & SPICES
1200. EUCALYPTUS OIL
1201. EXTRACTION OF OIL FROM OIL SEED EXPANDEREXTRUSION TECHNOLOGY)
1202. FAT LIQUOR SULPHATED OIL
1203. FLAVOURS FOR FOOD
1204. GARLIC OIL & POWDER
1205. GINGER OIL, SANDALWOOD OIL AND NAGARMOTHA OIL
1206. GINGER OIL
1207. GINGER OIL & GINGER DUST
1208. INTEGERATED WAX COMPLEX
1209. IONONE FROM LEMON GRASS OIL
1210. JASMINE & LILLY FLOWER OIL
1211. LEMON GRASS OIL
1212. LIQUID PARAFFIN
1213. LUBE OIL & GREASE
1214. LUBRICATING OIL
1215. MENTHOL CRYSTALS
1216. MENTHOL OIL & CRYSTAL
1217. MICRO CRYSTALLINE WAX
1218. MUSTARD OIL (EDIBLE OIL)
1219. OIL FROM ARTEMISIA HERBS
1220. PALM OIL CRUSHING UNIT
1221. PAN MASALA
1222. PARAFFIN WAX
1223. PARAFFIN WAX FROM SLACK WAX
1224. REFINED OIL-SUN FLOWER OIL, GROUNDNUT OIL, STAFF FLOWER OIL & COTTON SEED OIL
1225. REFINED VEGETABLE OIL
1226. RECLAMATION OF USED ENGINE OIL
1227. RICE BRAN OIL (R.B.O)
1228. ROSE OIL EXTRACTION
1229. SMOKE LESS CANDLE
1230. SPICE OIL & OLEORESINS
1231. SOLVENT EXTRACTION PLANT (OIL CAKE BASED)
1232. SYNTHETIC ALMOND OIL
1233. SYNTHETIC TALLOW
1234. SYNTHETIC GHEE
1235. VEGETABLE OIL EXTRACTION & REFINING
1236. WADDING OIL (100%) FOR WADDING OF COTTON HOSIERY CLOTH IN DYEING PROCESS
1237. WAX EMULSION FOR TEXTILE
1238. WAX FLOOR POLISH

PAINT, ENAMEL, SOLVENTS, THINNERS, INKS & VARNISH

1239. ACRYLIC EMULSION PAINTS
1240. ALUMINIUM PAINT
1241. AUTOMOBILE PAINTS
1242. BALL POINT PEN REFILL INK
1243. BITUMINIOUS ROAD EMULSION
1244. BITUMEN
1245. BITUMINIOUS FELTS FOR WATER & DAMP PROOFING
1246. BITUMINIOUS ROAD EMULSION RAPID MEDIUM & SLOW SETTING
1247. BUFFING & POLISHING
1248. CEMENT PAINT FOR WHITE & GREY CEMENT

1249. DISPERSANT
1250. DRY DISTEMPER
1251. DRY DISTEMPER & CEMENT PAINT
1252. DUPLICATING INK BLACK FOR GESTNER DUPLICATOR
1255. EMULSION PAINTS (WATER BASED)
1256. HAMMERTONE PAINT
1257. INSULATING VARNISH & WIRE ENAMEL
1258. IRON OXIDE PIGMENTS
1259. INSULATING VARNISH (POLY VINYL BUTYRAL BASED, FFC GRADE)
1260. LIME COLOUR (CEMENT COLOUR)
1261. SYNTHETIC RED OXIDE FOR FLOORINGS
1262. SOLVENT & THINNERS
1263. MARKING INKS (WATER PROOF)
1264. METAL NAPHTHANATE (AS DRIER FOR PAINTS)
1265. N.C.PUTTY
1266. OFFSET PRINTING INK
1267. OIL BOUND DISTEMPER PAINT
1268. PAINT BRUSHES
1269. PAINT REMOVERS
1270. PAINT INDUSTRY
1271. PAINT & VARNISH
1272. PICTURE VARNISH
1273. POWDER COATING PAINT
1274. PRINTING INKS (OFFSET, FLEXO & ROTO GRAVURE)
1275. PRIMER PAINT & ENAMEL PAINT
1276. PUTTY & WATER PROOFING PAINT
1277. PRINTING INKS (FLEXO-GRAPHIC INK)
1278. PUTTY (METAL CASEMENT)
1279. RED OXIDE PRIMER (ANTI CORROSIVE)
1280 REFRECTORY PAINT (GRAPHITE BASED)
1281. SCREEN PRINTING INKS
1282. SILK SCREEN PRINTING INK FORMULATION FOR PLASTIC, PAPER, CLOTH
1283. STAMP & PAD INK
1284. STOVING PAINT
1285. SPIRIT SOLUBLE MALEIC RESIN
1286. TEXTURE PAINT
1287. THINNERS AND ITS ALLIED PRODUCTS
1288. TONER INK
1289. VARNISH THINNER (SOLVENT)
1290. VACUUM METALLIZING LACQUERS
1291. WOOD PRIMER

PHARMACEUTICAL, DRUGS, AYURVEDIC/HERBAL COSMETICS & MEDICINES, HOMOEOPATHIC MEDICINES, DISPOSABLE SYRINGE, DENTAL COLLEGE & FINE CHEMICALS ETC.

1292. AROMATIC PILLS
1293. ASPIRIN
1294. AYURVEDIC PAIN BALM OINTMENTS
1295. AYURVEDIC CHURAN AND TABLETS
1296. AYURVEDIC TABLETS (HAJMOLA TYPE)
1297. AYURVEDIC/HERBAL PHARMACY
1298. AYURVEDIC SHERBATS
1299. AYURVEDIC PRODUCTS
1300. BULK DRUGS (E.O.U)
1301. BLOOD BAGS
1302. CALCIUM GLUCONATE
1303. CAPSULE, TABLET & INJECTION WITH MODERN INSTRUMENTS
1304. CASHEW FENI
1305. CHLOROQUINONE PHOSPHATE (BULK DRUGS)
1306. CLINICAL THERMOMETER
1307. DENTAL CLINIC

1308. DENTAL COLLEGE
1309. DENTAL GRADE EUGENOL
1310. DEXTROSE MONOHYDRATE, LIQUID GLUCOSE
1311. DEHYDRATED ONION & ONION POWDER
1312. DEXTROSE POWDER (ANHYDROUS FROM STARCH)
1314. DEXTROSE SALINE SOLUTION
1315. DISTILLERY (I.M.F.L)
1316. DISPOSABLE NEEDLES FOR SYRINGES
1317. DISPRIN
1318. DISTILLED WATER
1319. EMPTY HARD GELATINE CAPSULES
1320. FILLING & PACKING OF CAPSULES
1321. GLUCOSE - D - POWDER
1322. GLYCERINE
1323. HERBAL COSMETICS
1324. HERBAL SHAMPOO
1325. HERBAL HAIR OILS (AYURVEDIC)
1326. HOMOE & BIO-MEDICINES WITH MOTHER TINCTURE
1327. HOMOEPATHIC MEDICINES
1328. HYPODERMIC NEEDLES
1329. I.V. FLUIDS
1330. IBUPROFEN
1331. INFUSION & TRANSFUSION SETS (I.V. SET)
1332. INJECTABLE FOR PHARMACEUTICALS
1333. INJECTION AMPOULES PACKAGING BOX
1334. INTEGERATED SURGICAL COTTON
1335. ICE MAKING PLANT
1336. ICE & COLD STORAGE
1337. LACTOSE & BY PRODUCTS PROCESSING FROM MILK
1338. LICHEN (JATAMANSI CHARILA)
1339. LIQUID GLUCOSE AND ITS BY-PRODUCTS
1340. L-LYSINE MONOHYDRO CHLORIDE
1341. LIQUID GLUCOSE FROM POTATOES
1342. MEDICAL COLLEGE
1343. NICOTINE FROM TOBACCO WASTE
1344. OINTMENT-AYURVEDIC (YELLOW & WHITE)
1345. PHARMACEUTICAL AND FOOD GRADE GELATINE
1346. PHARMACEUTICAL INDUSTRY (TABLETS, CAPSULES, LIQUID, GEL, OINTMENT POWDER INJECTABLE)
1347. PHARMACEUTICAL UNIT (EOU) WITH FORMULA TIONS, INJECTABLES, ETC. PYRIDINE & DERIVATIVES
1348. SALT (IODIZED SALT)
1349. SALINE & INJECTION WATER
1350. SALINE WATER & DEXTROSE SOLUTION (I.V.FLUID IN PLASTIC BOTTLES)
1351. SORBITOL
1352. STARCH (MAIZE)
1353. SURGICAL ADHESIVE PLASTER
1354. SURGICAL BANDAGES
1355. SURGICAL GLOVES
1357. SURGICAL COTTON
1358. SURGICAL COTTON AND BANDAGE
1359. SYNTHETIC CAMPHOR POWDER
1360. TABLETS & CAPSULES
1361. TISSUE CULTURE
1362. TINCTURE FROM RECTIFIED SPIRIT
1363. TRIMETHOPIME
1364. VETERENARY MEDICINES (ONLY FORMULATIONS)
1365. VITAMIN 'C', SORBITOL' ANHYDROUS DEXTROSE, STARCH

PULP, PAPER, STRAW/GREY BOARD, KRAFT PAPER, PACKAGING, PAPER CARRY BAGE, PAPER FROM AGRO WASTE & STATIONERY ETC.

1366. AMMONIA PAPER
1367. AUTOMATIC BOOK BINDING
1368. ADHESIVE (FEVICOL TYPE)
1369. ALL PIN & GEM CLIPS
1370. CARBON PAPER
1371. CARD BOARD
1372. CARBON LESS PAPER
1373. CELLPHANE PAPER
1374. COMPUTER FORMS & SECURITY PRINTING PRESS
1375. CORRUGATED BOARD & BOX (PRINTED & LAMINATED)
1376. CORRUGATED BOARD AND BOXES FROM FROM CARD BOARDS
1377. CORRUGATED CARTONS FROM PLAIN PAPERS
1378. CORRUGATRED PACKING & MATERIAL (BULB & TUBES PACKING)
1379. DESK TOP PUBLISHING
1380. DEFOAMING AGENT FOR PAPER PLANT
1381. DRINKING STRAW PAPER
1382. D.T.P CUM OFFSET PRESS
1383. EGG TRAYS
1384. EXERCISE NOTE BOOK, REGISTER AND PAD
1385. FLEXOGRAPHIC INK
1386. GREETING CARD BY OFFSET PRESS
1387. HAND MADE PAPER FILTER PAPER
1388. HARD BOARD
1389. INJECTION AMPOULES PACKAGING BOXES
1390. INSULATIING PAPER
1391. KRAFT PAPER
1392. KRAFT PAPER FROM BAGASSE
1393. LAMINATED PACKAGING PAPER WITH PRINTING
1394. LAMINATION & COATING ON PAPER
1395. M.G. PAPER FROM WASTE PAPER
1396. MILL PAPER FROM WASTE PAPER
1397. MILL BOARD FROM RICE & WHEAT STRAWS
1398. MILL BOARD FROM WASTE PAPER
1399. MINI PAPER PLANT FROM SISAL
1400. MINI PAPER PLANT
1401. MULTI WALL PAPER SACKS
1402. NEWS PAPER FOR CHILDREN
1403. NEWS PRINT PAPER FROM RICE STRAW BAGASSE
1404. NEWS PAPER CHILDRENS
1405. NEWS PRINT PAPER
1406. OFFSET AND TREADLE TYPE PRINTING PRESS
1407. MILL BOARD BASED ON RICE STRAW
1408. PAPER AND BOARD FROM STRAW
1409. PAPER & PAPER PRODUCTS
1410. PAPER ENVELOPES
1411. PAPER CARRY BAGS
1412. PAPER BOARD CARTON
1413. PAPER CONES FOR LOUD SPEAKERS
1414. PAPER FROM AKRA
1415. PAPER FROM BAGASSE WITH CORRUGATED BOARD & BOXES
1416. PAPER FROM BAMBOO
1417. PAPER GLASSES FOR BEVERAGES
1418. PAPER FROM RICE HUSK & WHEAT HUSK
1419. PAPER FROM TREE BARK, EUCALYPRUS WOOD
1420. PAPER PRODUCTS
1421. PAPER PLANT (WHITE WRITING & NEWS PAPER FOR PULP & WASTE PAPER)
1422. PAPER PLATES, PAPER GLASS
1423. PAPER CONES & TUBES
1425. PAPER PLANT WITH DTP & PRINTING & PUBLISHING UNIT
1426. PAPER BASED PHENOLIC SHEET
1427. PAPER CUP FOR ICE CREAM
1428. PAPER TUBES SPIRAL WINDING COMPOSIT CONTAINER
1429. PAPER LABLE FOR BEER BOTTLES
1430. PARTICLE BOARD & BLACK BOARD WITH SANDING & LAMINATION OF PARTICLE BOARD
1431. PARTICLE BOARD FROM RICE HUSK
1432. POUCH FILLING & MAKING FOR TOMATO SAUCE
1433. POUCH MAKING &

GRAVURE PRINTING
1434. PROCESSING OF PAPER FOR FEEDING IN COMPUTER
1435. PULP FROM BAMBOO & WOOD
1436. PAPER FILES
1437. PLAYING CARDS
1438. ROSIN SIZING AGENT (FOR PAPER PLANT)
1439. SAND PAPER
1440. SANITRY NAPKINS
1441. SILICON COATED PAPER
1442. STENCIL PAPER
1443. STRAW BOARD AND GREY BOARD
1444. STRAW BOARD & MILL BOARD
1445. STRAW BOARD AND PAPER BOARD
1446. TISSUE PAPER FACIAL
1447. TISSUE MOIST TOILETERY CLEANSING TISSUE AND RELATED PRODUCTS
1448. TISSUE PAPER ROLLS
1449. TETRA PACK FOR MILK PACKAGING, GHEE & OTHER LIQUIDS
1450. TOILET PAPER ROLLS
1451. TOILET PAPER & NAPKINS
1452. WAX COATED PRINTED PAPER
1453. WET FACE FRESHNER TISSUE
1454. WHITE WRITING & PRINTING PAPER
1455. WRITING & PRINTING PAPER (PAPER MILLS)

PLASTIC, B.O.P.P, ACRYLIC, DISPOSABLE PLASTIC PRODUCTS, PET PRODUCTS, P.V.C, H.D.P.E, P.P, L.D.P.E., P.U, A.B.S, THERMOFOARMING, MASTER BATCHES, & POLYMER AND RUBBER PRODUCTS, TYRE, TUBE, ADHESIVE, SHEET, COIR & MANY OTHERS

1456. ABS GRANULES FROM ABS SCRAPS FROM OLD T.V. CABINETS, WHITE GOODS ETC.
1457. ACRYLIC BEADS
1458. ACRYLIC COPOLYMER EMULSION
1459. ACRYLIC LATEX
1460. ACRYLIC SHEET
1461. ACRYLIC SHEET & MOULDED PRODUCTS
1462. ACRYLIC TEETH
1463. AUTO TUBES
1464. AUTO FLAPS FOR TRUCKS & BUSES
1465. AUTO TYRES & TUBES
1466. BABY BOTTLES (PLASTIC) WITH WHITESILICON RUBBER NIPPLES
1467. B.O.P.P. FILM
1468. B.O.P.P. PRESSURE SENSITIVE SELF ADHESIVE TAPE
1469. BABY NIPPLE (SILICON)
1470. BABY NIPPLE (BIG SIZE)
1471. BALLOON PLASTIC ADVERTISING
1472. BLISTER FILM PVC
1473. BLISTER PACKAGING & POUCH PAKAGING
1474. BLOW MOULDING PLASTIC CONTAINER
1475. COATING ON METALIZED POLYESTER FILM/METALISED PAPER/ ALIMINIUM FOIL
1476. COATING ON PLASTIC (ELECTROLYSIS) & GLASS
1477. COIR FOAM (RUBBERISED)
1478. COLOUR COATING ON PLASTICS
1479. COLOUR MASTER BATCHES FOR VARIOUS PLASTICS
1480. CYCLE TYRES AND TUBES
1481. DISPOSABLE PLASTIC CUPS GLASSES, ETC.
1482. DISPOSABLE PLASTIC SYRINGES & NEEDLES
1483. DISPOSABLE PLASTIC SYRINGES
1484. DOUGH MOULDING COMPOUND (D.M.C)
1485. EPOXY RESIN
1486. EXPANDED POLYESTRENE MOULDING (THERMOCOLE)
1487. F.R.P AUTO,SCOOTER ROOFS & CEILINGS
1488. F.R.P PRODUCTS (HELMET, WASHBASIN SHEETS, ROOFING SHEETS)
1489. FIBRE REINFORCED PLASTIC (HIGH PRESSURE MOULDING WITH SMC BMC AND DMC)
1490. FIELD RUBBER CONVERTED TO THE 60% LATEX RUBBER
1491. FLEXIBLE P.U. FOAM
1492. FORMALDEHYDE CROCKERY & OTHER ITEMS
1493. FORMALDEHYDE RESIN (UREA, PHENOL,MELEMINE)
1494. GASKET SHEET
1495. GUM BOTTLE (PVC)
1496. GLASS BEADS
1497. HDPE COATED PAPER SACK
1498. H.D.P.E. BAGS
1499. H.D.P.E. CONTAINERS (BLOW MOULDING)
1500. H.D.P.E. CONTAINER, POLY JARS BY INJECTION MOULDING (FOOD GRADE)
1501. H.D.P.E. JERRY CANS
1502. HDPE MANUFACTURING FROM ETHYLALCOHOL
1503. H.D.P.E PIPE AND FITTINGS
1504. H.D.P.E. PIPES
1505. H.D.P.E PRINTED BAGS
1506. H.D.P.E TWINES AND ROPES
1507. H.D.P.E. & L.D.P.E PIPES AND FITTINGS
1508. H.D.P.E/PP BOX STRAPPING
1509. H.D.P.E/PP WOVEN SACKS USING PLAIN LOOMS
1510. HOLOGRAM STICKERS-3D
1511. H.M BAG PLANT WITH PRINTING UNIT
1512. HAWAI CHAPPALS (RUBBER)
1513. I.V PLASTIC BOTTLE
1514. ICE CREAM CUP (PLASTIC)
1515. INJECTION MOULDED AUTO COMPONENTS
1516. INJECTION & BLOW MOULDED PLASTIC PRODUCTS
1517. INJECTION MOULDED PLASTIC PRODUCTS
1518. INTEGERATED COMPLEX ESTER'S & ALLIED PRODUCTS (D.O.P,D.B.P, & ETHYL ACETATE, BUYTL ACETATE, WIRE ENAMELS, JELLY CABLE COMPOUND)
1519. L.D.P.E. (LOW DENSITY POLY ETHYLENE) GRANULES FROM VIRGIN (L.D.P.E. RESIN)
1520. INTEGERATED SURGICAL RUBBER GOODS INDUSTRY
1521. INJECTION MOULDED PLASTIC BALLS
1522. L.D.P.E FROM ETHYL ALCOHOL
1523. LDPE MOULDED PRODUCTS
1524. LAMINATION OF COEXTRUSION MULTILAYER FILM IN ROLL FORM
1525. LATEX RUBBER
1526. LATEX RUBBER CONDOM
1527. MASTER BATCHES (COLOURED, P.V.C, L.D.P.E, H.D.P.E, ETC.)
1528. MELAMINE FORMALHYDE RESIN
1529. MOULDED LUGGAGE
1530. MULTI-LAYER (3 LAYER BAGS)
1531. MULTI-LAYER (3 LAYER) FILM WITH LAMINATION & PRINTING
1532. OIL SEAL
1533. PET BOTTLE/CONTAINERS
1534. PET BOTTLES FROM PRE FORM
1535. PET BOTTLE & MINERAL WATER
1536. PET PRE-FORM FROM PET RESIN
1537. PET PRE-FORM CUM PET BOTTLES
1538. PET PRE-FORM PET BOTTLES CUM MINERAL WATERS
1539. POLY CARBONATE RESIN
1540. PTFE COMPONENTS
1541. PU/PVC SOLE FOR SPORT SHOE BY IMPORTED M/C.
1542. PVC BATTERY SEPARATOR
1543. P.V.C COMPOUNDS (FRESH)
1544. P.V.C COMPOUNDS (SCRAP)
1545. P.V.C ELECTRICAL INSULATING TAPE
1546. P.V.C. EXTRUSION PROFILES
1547. P.V.C FITTINGS
1548. P.V.C FLEXIBLE FUSIBLE POWDER HEAT FUSIBLE POWDER
1549. P.V.C GRANULES (FOR

INSULATION & SHEETS GRADES)

1550. P.V.C GRANULES FROM PVC SCRAPS (WITH POLLUTION CONTROL)
1551. P.V.C HOSES
1552. P.V.C LEATHER CLOTH
1553. P.V.C FLEXIBLE PIPES
1554. P.V.C PIPES AND FITTINGS
1555. POLYTHENE BAGS (PRINTED)
1556. PVC PLASTICS FILM SHEET SOFT/RIGID
1557. PVC RESIN AND COMPOUND
1558. PVC RULAR
1559. PVC STABLIZERS (SINGLE PACK SYSTEM)
1560. PVC WIRE AND CABLES
1561. PAPER BASED PHENOLIC SHEET FOR ELECTRICAL
1562. PHENOL FORMALDEHYDE RESIN
1563. PHENOLIC RESIN
1564. PLASTIC BEADS FROM PLASTIC SCRAPS
1565. PLASTIC BUTTONS
1566. PLASTIC CANS
1567. PLASTIC COLLAPSIBLE TUBE
1568. PLASTIC CORRUGATED SHEET & BOXES
1569. PLASTIC FILM AND SHEETS WITH PRINTING FLEXO & ROTO/LDPE/HDPE/PP/HM/PVC
1570. PLASTIC FILTER MASTER BATCH & OTHER MASTER BATCHES FOR VARIOUS PLASTICS
1571. PLASTIC JERRY CANS
1572. PLASTIC GRANULES OR POWDER FROM PLASTIC SCRAP
1573. PLASTIC INJECTION MOULDED T.V. CABINETS
1574. PLASTIC ITEMS MANUFAC TURE FROM POWDER MELAMINE
1575. PLASTIC GOODS
1576. PLASTIC PIPES & TARPAULINES
1577. PLASTIC SHEET FROM SCRAP
1578. PLASTIC PLANT (BLOW MOULDING & INJECTION MOULDING)
1579. PLASTIC PRODUCTS (GOLD, SILVER, NICKEL)
1580. PLASTIC TOYS
1581. POLYESTER BEADING
1582. POLYESTER FILM
1583. POLYTHENE BAGS & AUTOMATIC PRINTING
1584. POLYTHENE PRINTED BAGS
1585. POLYURETHANE FOAM AND ITS PRODUCTS
1586. PROPYLENE FILM (PRINTED) & BAG MANUFACTURING
1587. PLASTIC MATS
1588. RAINBOW COLOUR ON PVC FILM & SHEET
1589. RED MUD PVC PIPES AND FITTINGS
1590. RE-RUBBERISED OF SOLID TYPE
1591. RESIN COATED SAND REXINE
1592. REXINE CLOTH & ALLIED PRODUCTS
1593. RUBBER ADHESIVE
1594. RUBBER AUTO PARTS
1595. RUBBER BELTING
1596. RUBBER MOULDING UNIT INCLUDING LINING RUBBER SHEETING
1597. RUBBER RECLAIMING
1598. RUBBER ROLLERS FOR TEXTILE MILLS & PAPER INDUSTRIES
1599. RUBBER & PLASTIC SHEETS, MATS & FLAPS
1600. RUBBER SHEET AND ALLIED HOSPITAL RUBBER GOODS
1601. RUBBERIZED PVC GASKET
1602. RUBBERISED COIR
1603. RUBBER COMPOUND FOR AUTOMOBILES
1604. SAFETY BELTS
1605. SILVER AND GOLD PLATING ON PVC AND NYLON-6
1606. SILICONE RUBBER NIPPLES/ TEATS
1607. SPECTACLE FRAMES (PLASTIC)
1608. SPUNGE RUBBER
1609. SURGICAL EXAMINATION GLOVES
1610. SYNTHETIC PEARL COATING ON POLYSTYRENE BEADS
1611. SYNTHETIC RUBBER ADHESIVE
1612. TEFLON MANUFACTURING
1613. TEFLON TAPE
1614. TEFLON TAPES & CABLES
1615. THERMOCOLE SHEET AND MOULDED PRODUCTS EXPANDED POLYESTERENE EXTRUSION PROFILES
1616. THERMOFORMED PACKAGING (BLISTER PACKAGING & POUCH PACKAGING)
1617. THERMOPLASTIC POLYURETHANE
1618. THERMOFORMED CUPS, PLATES & GLASS WITH HIPS SHEET
1619. THERMOCOLE
1620. THERMOCOLE BASED DISPOSABLE GLASS, CUPS & PLATES
1621. TOOTH BRUSHES
1622. TOY BALLOON, DECORA TIVE & INDUSTRIAL BALLOONS
1623. TREAD RUBBER
1624. TYRE RETREADING (HOT)
1625. TYRE RETREADING BY COLD PROCESS
1626. TYRE TUBES & FLAPS
1627. TYRE & TUBES
1628. UNSATURATED POLYESTER FOR REXINE
1629. V-BELT AND FAN BELT
1630. VINYL ASBESTOS AND PVC WALL PAPER
1631. VITON (FLUORO ELASTOMER)

SOAP, COSMETICS & PERFUMS

1632. ACID SLURRY, SYNTHETIC DETERGENT POWDER
1632. ACID SLURRY
1633. AGARBATTI SYNTHETIC, PERFUMERY COMPOUND
1634. AFTER SHAVE LOTION
1635. ANTISEPTIC CREAM
1636. BETA IONONE
1637. BLEACHING POWDER
1638. BLUE DETERGENT POWDER
1639. CLEANING POWDER (VIMTYPE)
1640. COLD CREAM
1641. COLOURED FLAME & PERFUMED CANDLES (RED, BLUE, GREEN FLAME)
1642. COSMETIC INDUSTRY (MODERN)
1643. COSMETIC INDUSTRY (SHAMPOO, SPRAY PERFUME, TALCUM POWDER
1644. DETERGENT POWDER (ARIEL TYPE)
1645. DETERGENT POWDER (NIRMA TYPE) FULLY AUTOMATIC PLANT
1646. DETERGENT WASHING POWDER
1647. FISH OIL SOAP
1648. GLYCERINE TRANSPARENT SOAP
1649. HAIR REMOVING CREAM
1650. HERBAL COSMETICS
1651. HERBAL SHAMPO & CREAM
1652. HERBAL/AYURVEDIC COSMETICS
1653. INCENSE POWDER, INCENSE STICKS & INCENSE CAKE
1654. OPTICAL WHITENERS
1655. ROSE OIL EXTRACTION
1656. SHAMPOOS (COCONUT OIL BASED COLD PROCESS)
1657. SHAVING CREAM
1658. SINDUR (KUMKUM)
1659. SOAP COATED PAPER
1660. SPRAY DRIED DETERGENT POWDER
1661. STAIN REMOVER
1662. TALCUM POWDER (FACE & TOILET POWDER)
1663. TOILET AND HERBAL SOAP
1664. TOOTH PASTE & POWDER
1665. WASHING DETERGENT POWDER AND WASHING SOAP
1666. WASHING POWDER LIQUID DETERGENTS, LOTION & SHAMPOO

TEXTILE INDUSTRIES, READYMADE GARMENTS, COTTON, DYEING, BLEACHING, CLOTH, HOSIERY, POWER LOOM, HAND LOOM, WOOLLEN, SILK, SOCKS, SURGICAL COTTON & MANY OTHERS

1667. ANGORA RABBIT WOOL
1668. BUCKRAM
1669. CANVAS SHOES, JUNGLE BOOT, BOOT RUBBER KNEES & BOOT COMBAT
1670. CARPET FROM COTTON WASTE
1671. CERAMIC THREAD GUIDE
1672. COTTON BUDS/SWABS
1673. COTTON FROM WASTE YARN
1674. COTTON ROLLS
1675. COTTON SPIDERS FOR LOUD SPEAKERS
1676. DENIM CLOTH
1677. DENIM CLOTH (INTEGERATED UNIT WITH BLEACHING, DYEING AND PRINTING)
1678. DISPERSENT FOR TEXTILE
1679. DYEING & BLEACHING
1680. DYEING OF HANK YARN
1681. EMULSIFIER FOR WOOL BATCHING OIL
1682. EMBROIDERY ON FABRICS
1683. GARMENT DYEING, WASHING & STITCHING (JEANS, JACKETS, SKIRTS & SHIRTS)
1684. GOVES KNITTING
1685. GUNNY BAGS
1687. HDPE WOVEN SACKS
1688. HDPE TARPAULINS USING PLAIN LOOM WITH LAMINATION
1689. HDPE/PP WOVEN SACKS USING CIRCULAR LOOMS
1690. HOSIERY CLOTH (COTTON) PROCESSING (BLEACHING, DYEING, FINISHING OF CLOTH)
1691. HOSIERY INDUSTRY
1692. HOSIERY MERCERISING
1693. HOSIERY PRODUCTS LIKE VEST, BRIEF, T-SHIRTS & SOCKS
1694. JACQUARD FABRICS
1695. JUTE COIR, GRASS ROPE/ SUTLI MAKING
1696. JUTE FELT
1697. JUTE TWINES
1698. KNITTED FABRICS
1699. LAMINATED JUTE BAGS
1700. LAMINATION OF HDPE WOVEN CLOTH (JUTE,COTTON, PAPER)
1701. NYLON YARN CRIMPING, DOUBLING AND BLEACHING
1702. PIGMENT BINDER FOR TEXTILE PRINTING
1704. POLYESTER RESIN FOR WIRE ENAMEL
1705. POLYESTER RESIN
1706. POLYESTER YARN FROM WASTE POLYESTER ZIP FASTENERS
1707. POWER LOOM
1708. READYMADE GARMENTS & HOSIERY
1709. READYMADE GARMENTS MERCHANDISE
1710. READYMADE GARMENTS & COVERS
1711. READYMADE GARMENTS & EMBROIDERY OF GOWNS, SHIRTS, BLOUSES, T-SHIRTS ETC. (ONLY LADIES)
1712. READYMADE SALWAR SUIT
1713. RECOVERY OF NYLON FROM NYLON WASTE
1714. ROTARY PRINTING AND DYEING ON COTTON, SYNTHETIC TEXTILE
1715. SANITARY NAPKINS
1716. SCREEN PRINTING ON COTTON CLOTH
1717. SEWING THREAD REELS & BALLS MAKING INDUSTRIES
1718. SCREEN PRINTING ON COTTON, POLYESTER & ACRYLIC
1719. SHAWLS (WOOLLEN)
1720. SHOE LACES
1721. SILK FABRICS ON HANDLOOM
1722. SOCKS KNITTING
1723. SPINNING, DOUBLING DYEING MERCERISING & BLEACHING OF COTTON YARN
1724. SPINNING & CARDING OF WOOL INTO YARNS
1725. STARCH BOOK BINDING CLOTH
1726. SURAT JARI
1727. SURGICAL COTTON & BANDAGE
1728. SYNTHETIC TEXTILE INDUSTRY(SUITING, SHIRTING, SAREES) TERRY CLOTH
1729. T-SHIRTS
1730. TOWELS, BED SHEET COVERS
1731. TERRY TOWEL
1732. TERRY FABRICS WEAVING UNIT
1733. TEXTILE AUXILLIARIES & CHEMICALS
1734. TEXTILE BLEACHING, DYEING & FINISHING & PRINTING OF COTTON FABRICS
1735. TEXTILE (HOSIERY)
1736. TEXTILE MILL
1737. TEXTILE DYEING & PRINTING
1738. TEXTILE PRINTING (JOB WORK)
1739. TEXTILE PIGMENT PRINTING BINDER
1740. TOWEL (TERRY)
1741. VELVET CLOTH BY FLOCKING PROCESS
1742. VISCOSE STAPLE FIBRE
1743. WADDING OIL (100%) FOR WADDING OF COTTON HOSIERY CLOTH IN THE DYEING PROCESS
1744. WEAVING OF DASUTI CLOTH WITH PRINTING, DYEING, EMBROIDERY & FINISHING
1745. WASHING OF JEANS & OTHER GARMENTS
1746. WORSTED WOOLLEN YARN CLOTH
1747. ZARI GLITTER SALMA SITARA OF PLASTIC FILM

INFOTECH/IT, HOSPITALITY, HOSPITAL, COLLEGE, SCHOOL, MEDICAL, ENTERTAINMENT CLUB, WARE HOUSING & REAL ESTATE, PROJECTS

1748. AMUSEMENT PARK
1749. AMUSEMENT PARK CUM WATER PARK
1750. BANQUET HALL
1751. CALL CENTER (DOMESTIC)
1752. CALL CENTER (INTERNATIONAL)
1753. CHILDREN RECREATION CENTRE
1754. COLD STORAGE
1755. COMMUNITY HALL
1756. COMPUTER EDUCATION INSTITUTE
1757. COMPUTER SOFTWARE
1758. COLLEGE
1759. CYBER CAFE
1760. DENTAL CLINIC
1761. DENTAL COLLEGE
1762. DIAGONOSTIC CENTRE
1763. E-COMMERCE/BUSINESS
1764. E-SCHOOL (Rs. 5000/-)
1765. ENGINEERING COLLEGE
1766. ENTERTAINMENT CLUB
1767. ENTERTAINMENT CLUB, HOLIDAY RESORT, 4 STAR HOTEL, AMUSEMENT PARK CUM WATER PARK, MUSHROOM & ITS PRODUCTS, FISH FARMING, LAKE FOR BOATING, DEER PARK
1768. FASHION TECHNOLOGY INSTITUTE
1769. FAST FOOD PARLOUR
1770. FIVE STAR HOTEL
1771. FOOD PARLOUR
1772. FRANCHISE TRAINING PROGRAMME FOR IIT & ENGINEERING ENTRANCE EXAMS.
1773. GOLF COURSE
1774. HEALTH CLUB, BEAUTY PARLOUR
1775. HEALTH CLUB AND FITNESS CENTER
1776. HEALTH RESORTS
1777. HOLIDAY RESORTS
1778. HOLIDAY RESORT CUM

ENTERTAINMENT CLUB WITH 4 STAR HOTEL
1779. HOSPITALS
1780. ICE CREAM PARLOUR
1781. INTERNET SERVICE PROVIDER (I.S.P.)
1782. MEDICAL COLLEGE
1783. MEDICAL COLLEGE, HOSPITAL & RESEARCH INSTITUTE
1784. MEDICAL TRANSCRIPTION CENTRE
1785. MENTAL RETARDATION HOSPITAL & CEREBRAL PALSY
1786. MOTEL/SMALL HOTEL
1787. MULTISTOREY COMMERCIAL COMPLEX
1788. MULTISTOREY RESIDENTIAL COMPLEX
1789. NURSERY SCHOOL
1790. NATURE CARE CENTRE
1791. NURSING HOME
1792. ONLINE SHOPPING MALL (RS. 5000/- REPORT)
1793. PORTAL
1794. REHABILITATION CENTRE FOR AGED & NEEDY PERSONS
1795. RESIDENTIAL CUM COMMERCIAL COMPLEX
1796. RESTAURANT
1797. RESTAURANT WITH PUB
1798. SCHOOL (PRIMARY)
1799. SCHOOL (HIGHER SECONDARY)
1800. THREE STAR HOTEL
1801. TOURIST CLUB
1802. TRAINING INSTITUTE FOR MEDICAL TRANSCRIPTION
1803. VIDEO FILM STUDIO
1804. WARE HOUSE
1805. WEBSITE DESIGN & E-MAIL REGISTERING

AGRO BASED INDUSTRIES

1806. COAL BRIQUETTES FROM AGROWASTE
1807. FURFURALFROM RICEHULL
1808. MUSHROOM CULTIVATION & PROCESSING (BUTTON)
1809. MUSHROOM GROWING & PROCESSING WITH AIR CONDITIONING
1810. MUSHROOM CULTIVATION & PROCESSING UNIT DEHYDRATION & PACKAGING OF OYSTER & PADDY STRAW MUSHROOMS
1811. ORGANIC MANURE
1812. PAPAYA CULTIVATION
1813. PAPAYA & TOMATO CULTIVATION
1814. PROCESSING & UTILISATION OF COCONUT
1815. PROCESSING OF SHEEP HAIR TO PRODUCE WOOL

BAKERY, CONFECTIONERY & FOOD PRODUCTS

1816. AGROLACTOR SOYA MILK
1817. APPLE FRUIT JUICE WITH CANNING BOTTLING
1818. AYURVEDIC SHARBAT
1819. BAKERY UNIT (PASTRIES, BREAD, BUNS, CAKE, TOFFEE ETC.)
1820. BAKING POWDER
1821. BANANA & ITS BY PRODUCTS
1822. BANANA POWDER
1823. BANANA WAFERS
1824. BANANA CULTIVATION
1825. BEER INDUSTRY
1826. DEHULLING OF JAUN FOR BEER
1827. BEER & WINE
1828. BEER, ALCOHOL, IMFL
1829. BESEN PLANT
1830. BISCUIT PLANT
1831. BREAD & BISCUIT PLANT
1832. BOTTLING PLANT COUNTRY LIQUOR FROM RECTIFIED SPIRIT
1833. BRANDY
1834. BREAD RUSKS
1835. CANNED FRUITS & VEGETABLES
1836. CANNING & PRESERVATION OF MEAT
1837. CANNING & PRESERVATION OF VEGETABLES
1838. CANNING OF MANGO PULP & MANGO SLICES
1839. CARBONATED BEVERAGS
1840. CASHEW FENI
1841. CASHEW NUT (DRIED & FRIED)
1842. CATTLE BREEDING
1843. CATTLE BREEDING & DAIRY FARM TO PRODUCE MILK
1844. CATTLE FEED FROM TAPIOCA
1845. CHEWING GINGER & AMLOKI
1846. CHEWING GUM
1847. CHILLI SAUCE
1848. CHILLI POWDER
1849. CHOCOLATE
1850. CIDER PLANT
1851. COCOA POWDER
1852. COCOA BUTTER & COCOA POWDER
1853. COCONUT SHELL POWDER
1854. COCONUT WATER
1855. COCONUT SWEET (WATERY)
1856. COCONUT MILK POWDER (DEHYDRATED)
1857. COCONUT PRODUCTS & BY PRODUCTS (INTEGRATED PLANT)
1858. COLD DRINK
1859. CURRY POWDER
1860. DAIRY FOR MILK PROCESSING (GHEE, BUTTER & PANEER)
1861. DAIRY PRODUCTS
1862. DAIRY PRODUCTS MILK PACKAGING IN POUCH (GHEE, BUTTER, ETC.
1863. DAIRY FARM TO PRDUCE MILK WITH PACKAGING (COW)
1864. DAIRY FARM TO PRDUCE MILK WITH PACKAGING (BUFALLOE)
1865. DAIRY FARM & MILK PRODUCTS
1866. DAL MOTH, CHANACHUR & BHUJIYA
1867. DEHYDRATION OF FRUITS & VEGETABLE
1868. DESICCATED COCONUT POWDER FROM COCONUTS
1869. DEHYDRATION & CANNING OF FRUITS & VEGETABLES
1870. DRY FRUIT ROASTING & PACKAGING
1871. DRYING OF RED CHILLIES, HALDI, DHANIYA, PEAS & GROUND NUT
1872. EGG POWDER
1873. FISH CANNING IN TIN & POUCHES
1874. FISH DEHYRATION (DRYING OF FISH)
1875. FISH MEAL
1876. FISH PROCESSING (BEAST FREEZING PROCESSES)
1877. FLAVOURS FOR FOOD INDUSTRIES
1878. FLOUR MILL (ROLLER)
1879. FROZEN MEAT
1880. FOOD DEHYDRATION (FRUITS & VEGETABLES)
1881. FRIED & ROASTED GROUND NUT, GRAMS, PEAR ETC.
1882. FRUIT JUICE MAKING & PACKAGING IN PLASTIC CONTAINER
1883. FRUIT JUICE IN TETRA PACK (DRINKS)
1884. FRUIT JUICE, SQUASHES, SAUCE & KETCHUP, JAM, JELLY, VINEGAR ETC.
1885. GARLIC FLAKES
1886. GARLIC POWDER
1887. GHEE & BUTTER
1888. GINGER (PULVERISED)
1889. GINGER GLAZING & PRESERVATION
1890. GINGER STORAGE
1891. GINGER PROCESSING
1892. GINGER OIL & GINGER DUST
1893. GINGER POWDER (DRY) & OLEORESIN
1894. GRAPE DEHYDRATION
1895. GRAPE CULTIVATION
1896. GRAPE JUICE
1897. HONEY PROCESSING & PACKAGING
1898. ICE CREAM & ICE CANDY
1899. ICE CUBE
1900. INVERT SUGAR
1901. IDLI MIX, DOSA MIX SAMBHAR MIX, VADA MIX, GULAB JAMUN MIX
1902. INSTANT COFFEE & INSTANT TEA